IMPLEMENTING
QUALITY
IN THE
PUBLIC
SECTOR

IMPLEMENTING
QUALITY
IN THE
PUBLIC
SECTOR

TONY BENDELL,
LOUISE BOULTER &
JOHN KELLY

FT
PITMAN
PUBLISHING

PITMAN PUBLISHING
128 Long Acre, London WC2E 9AN

A Division of Longman Group Limited

First published in Great Britain 1994

British Library Cataloguing in Publication Data
A CIP catalogue record for this book can be obtained from the British Library.

ISBN 0 273 60523 2

1 3 5 7 9 10 8 6 4 2

Typeset by Northern Phototypesetting Co. Ltd, Bolton
Printed and bound in Great Britain by
Bell & Bain Ltd, Glasgow

*The Publishers' policy is to use paper manufactured
from sustainable forests.*

CONTENTS

ACKNOWLEDGEMENTS

The authors would like to express their gratitude to all of the people and organisations that have contributed to this book.

In particular we would like to acknowledge the time and effort contributed by the following individuals and organisations: The Federal Quality Institute (FQI) for the provision of some interesting material and for permitting us to use the Presidential Award for Quality criteria and the Quality Improvement Prototype Award criteria in Chapter 5. John Brockman, Whitehall Library, Co-ordinator for Ministry of Defence Total Quality Management Information Network for providing us with some useful sources of information for Chapter 5. The Charter Unit in the Cabinet Office for permitting us to use the Charter Mark Award criteria in Chapter 6. The Efficiency Unit in the Cabinet Office for checking the draft of Chapter 7 and for permitting us to use Figures 7.1, 7.2 and 7.3. Dr Derek Lees, Head of Market Testing and Contractorisation, Ministry of Defence (MoD) for contributing the case study on MoD in Chapter 7. The Development Division of the Office of Public Service and Science (OPSS) in the Cabinet Office for checking the draft of Chapter 8. BSI Standards for permitting us to use Figures 9.2 and 9.3 extracts from BS 5750: Part 8: 1991 featured in Chapter 9. (Complete copies can be obtained by post from BSI Customer Services, 389 Chiswick High Road, London W4 4AL: tel 0181 996 7000.)

Finally, a very special thanks to Richard Wells and Barry Wragg of South Yorkshire Police, Rob Atkins of Braintree District Council, (author of Braintree District Council case study) Jonathan Denby of Anglia Railways, and Penny Fowler and Fiona Wood of East Gloucestershire NHS Trust for all their help and time, which enabled us to put together the case study material featured in Chapter 6.

1

QUALITY AND THE PUBLIC SECTOR INTRODUCTION

EVERYONE IS TALKING ABOUT QUALITY

In the last few years, more than ever before, everyone in the UK public sector is talking about *Quality*. However one defines the public sector – that in itself is becoming increasingly more difficult – public sector organisations are going through dramatic change. In that change, quality of service to the 'customers' and quality of management have become major preoccupations.

Whilst extreme in the UK, the rest of the world is not immune. It is now a few years since the first author – almost in shock – was transported, with a handful of other encouragers of public sector change from around the globe; to a conference hall of several hundred Greek civil servants waiting to be enlightened. Why is it happening? Is it just a temporary fad? Is a new dawn emerging on the public sector around the world, or will in time-honoured public-sector tradition everything get back to normal sooner or later? Who was it that said that in the public sector, change is finding a new precedent?

Perhaps in the UK more than anywhere else, the answers to these questions are relatively easy. Here it is possible to say with some confidence that things will never be the same again. The Thatcherite years and what has followed – albeit without such a visible firm hand – has implemented, precipitated and delivered the most fundamental change we have seen in the public sector for a long time.

There is no doubt that *Market Testing* and *Compulsory Competitive Tendering* are foremost in the minds of many public sector employees when they focus their attention on quality. Quality is about survival. Service to the customer – albeit sometimes an internal but separated customer – and the best value for public money, have now become the universal goals, in an increasingly cash-driven public sector.

Other pressures too have come from quality needs in pursuing Agency status and from Central Government policies in relation to distributed 'public sector' organisations to which they provide funding. A classic example are the Training and Enterprise Councils (TECs) which from April 1994 need to have in place Supplier Quality Assurance and Quality Management, in line with the Department of Employment's 'Blue Book'.

And then there is the *Charter Initiative*. Charters clearly contain quality requirements, although often of a somewhat arbitrary nature. They provide 'customer' focus and the pursuit of the desirable charter mark leads to serious consideration of quality issues.

But there are pressures too from other stakeholders. Charters typically represent a restatement of the rights of disempowered stakeholders – the public, or customers – and at the bequest of the most powerful of stakeholders, the Government. But there is also a greater expectation of quality of service in the public sector, because of the major developments that have been taking place also in the private sector, and customers are not so ignorant or passive as they used to be. The employees also represent another stakeholder with a big desire for change, often frustrated by the bureaucratic systems and their inability to provide a real service to the customers, due to constraints beyond their control. Rising expectations, in the society as a whole, tied to Government aspirations for dramatic change, all contribute to the *quality revolution* that is sweeping the British public sector at this time.

TOTAL QUALITY MANAGEMENT (TQM) HAS CHANGED

Whilst there have been many accounts of Total Quality Management's (TQM) failures, the last ten years has seen TQM spread across the Atlantic and transform Western management thinking. The failures have been associated with ineffective programmes that did not deliver results, or with the failure of TQM against competition from other management imperatives and objectives, not just pure neglect. Whilst TQM has endured as a management philosophy, and is now going through its ten-year watershed, early TQM models were not always coherent, well thought through, well implemented or effective.

But TQM has now changed. Despite the forecasts of gloom, surveys showing ineffective programmes from either side of the Atlantic, and the disillusionment of the recession, TQM has evolved. Indeed its very flexibility and elasticity are a reason for its survival, possibly *the* reason. It has absorbed process thinking and *Business Process Re-Engineering* has been subsumed naturally into its structure. Of course, people use different titles for different things, and large consultancies need a stream of new products. They may not call it TQM any more, but the fundamental intention of the programme, the structure and the purpose has not really changed that much.

What has changed with the recession is the increase in focus. Like the public sector generally, the private sector is now very much focused on money, whether it be cost, shareholder value, cash flow or profitability. Business purposes more generally also come to the fore when survival is at stake. The main difference today is that the public sector now also shares this. What all this means, is that from a somewhat wishy-washy continuous improvement, empowerment and involvement view of quality management, we have moved to a more focused one.

In many organisations TQM has thus been integrated into the business, that is, into the business objectives and plans. The *Mission* which defines the organisations' reason for being, is followed up by defining *Critical Success Factors* which translate what would otherwise have been a nebulous concept, unrelated to the actuality of what happens at the grass roots in the business, into managed action. A small number of Critical Success Factors provide clear measurable indicators of performance as top level measures, answering the question, 'What do we mean by best?' since best appears so often in mission statements. Targets can then be set on these top level measures on a short-term as well as a long-term basis, so that annual improvement and long-term strategy can be unified. The measures typically include non-financial as well as financial Critical Success Factors. The next step is to ask how are we going to achieve the targets against time, set on these measures. The answer is by focusing on the key business processes; mapping, measuring and improving/re-engineering them.

With this new effective push for TQM programmes in the private sector, and the clear focus on clarity of priority and translation into action, pressure on the public sector has risen. The customers and commentators on the public sector are private sector employees, entrepreneurs and customers who having seen private sector improvement programmes now expect it, and look for it, in the public sector also.

IMPLEMENTING THE ILLUSIVE CONCEPT

The problem is that it is a big cultural change. From a world in which there was no concept of a market, we move to a world in which the market dominates, and in virtually zero time. But that is not the only problem, the public sector is different and many of the concepts of private sector quality do not fit easily into the public sector world. There are a lot of differences. For example, in the public sector, we very often do not know who the customer really is. To give a classic example – when a policeman arrests someone, is the customer the criminal? the victim? the society? the law courts? the Home Office to which he has to provide statistics? the witnesses? etc.

The process of cultural change is never simple and it can never, in reality, be instantaneous. Many public sector employees today are going through this change to a world with an all encompassing focus on the market. They are uneasy. Whilst the great majority now recognise both the inevitability and the virtues of the change, they also see the downside. More than this however, they feel uncomfortable and, unsure of themselves, recognising a need to take action, but not being confident in the action that they must take. It is for this very reason that the authors – who are all involved in the developments in public sector quality – chose to bring the book forward at this time.

THIS BOOK AND THE MEANING OF QUALITY IN THE PUBLIC SECTOR

This book then is about quality in the public sector, but what do we mean by that? Today, for the people in the system and the customers, the term is ambiguous and somewhat of a mystery. Public sector organisations, employees and practices vary dramatically in terms of their implementation of, concern for, or awareness of quality. Some look aggressively at the private sector, hoping to transfer best practice from manufacturing or retail or other service organisations. Others look inwards, identify internal customers and believe that the serving of internal customers is what quality is all about. This is an error which has been made too, in the private sector on occasion in the past. Many employed consultants perhaps come in with their own solutions, which may or may not be suitable for the public sector organisations to which they apply them.

Not surprisingly, the lack of clarity about the meaning of quality in the public sector has provided a field day for consultants who claim they can solve it all. The buyer must beware ('Caveat Emptor') of the consultant with all the answers who has been in the private sector for a long time, peddling TQM solutions.

Consultants are useful, they can provide a breadth of experience, depth of technical knowledge, an advisory voice for the hand at the tiller, an objective overview of the current situation, a precautionary word at the right moment, expert training and facilitation and much more. To make any real progress in the pursuit of quality management within any organisation, top management commitment is crucial. Here is also an area where consultants can be of assistance since people seldom heed the prophet in their own land. Top management must be convinced, and a champion or champions must be found in order for an organisation to take this subject seriously. In the process of convincing top management, of strategically building quality into the business plan and the future as well as in the introduction of skills, spreading of experiences from the mistakes of others, and in the facilitation role, consultants can be a great help. *But they should not do it for you. Quality of customer service should be a matter for your organisation, implemented by your organisation and in order to ensure the survival and contribution of your organisation. The responsibility is yours.*

TOTAL QUALITY MANAGEMENT ISO 9000 AND OTHER STRANGE ABERRATIONS

As we shall see in Chapter 3, quality means different things to different people, and often different things to the same people. Essentially TQM is about the quest for the self-improving organisation. That is, the organisation that if nothing else was ever done to it again, would carry on improving – since this is a natural part of the culture of the organisation, the way things are done there and part of everybody's work. A quality organisation is one in which quality is really embedded.

So what about **ISO 9000** or **BS 5750** or **EN 29000** or **BS EN ISO 9000?** These too are making a major impact upon the public sector, partly as a genuine desire to tidy up systems, partly in response to public scrutiny and partly a safeguard in the dangerous days of market testing, and compulsory competitive tendering. The international standard, which originated in defence procurement, has spread from manufacturing to private sector service and now into the public sector.

The spread of BS 5750 within the UK, its adoption as a European standard (EN 29000) and as an international standard (ISO 9000) may truly be said to be unprecedented. ISO 9000 is the international standard for *quality systems* which provides a basis for assessing your organisation, or part thereof, against objective requirements of organisational discipline and control, traceability and the like. The standard requires that management show, define and document its policy and objectives for, and its commitment to, quality.

In addition, management is responsible for ensuring that the policies are understood, implemented and maintained at all levels of the organisation. Responsibility and authority throughout the organisation also must be defined, as well as the inter-relationship of all personnel involved who manage, perform and verify work affecting quality. In-house verification requirements must be identified, and adequate resources and trained personnel must be assigned for verification activities. A management representative for quality must be assigned, who irrespective of other duties, has defined authority and responsibility to ensure that requirements of the international standard are implemented and maintained.

The organisation must establish and maintain a documented quality system. This must include the preparation, implementation and maintenance of procedures, and work instructions must be periodically reviewed by management. Another clause specifically requires that the organisation establishes and maintains procedures for contract review. Procedures must be established and maintained to control and verify the design of the service or product in order to ensure that it meets the specified requirements. Document control is required.

Purchased product has to conform to specified requirements and the organisation must ensure that this takes place. Adequate purchasing data must be included on purchasing documents. Where appropriate, the organisation needs to establish and maintain procedures for identifying products from applicable specifications or drawings or other documents throughout all stages of service or production, delivery and installation.

Other clauses deal, for example, with process control; inspection and testing, inspection, measuring and test equipment; the control of non-conforming product or service; corrective action; and handling, storage, packaging and delivery. Yet more are concerned with the keeping of quality records, the conduct of internal quality audits, identification of training needs and the provision of training. Where appropriate, servicing, and the use of statistical techniques are also covered. ISO 9000 then, provides a basic requirement in terms of a degree of belief in the organisational integrity of the organisation. But how does this view of quality fit with TQM and quality of service to the customer?

The answer is not easy. To be sure of getting it right for the customer one does need to have well-disciplined and structured systems as well as the desire to improve, and the desire of the people empowered in the system to make it happen. Integrating the two concepts is not impossible; many private sector organisations having started from BS 5750 and then progressed to TQM, or vice versa.

There are other strange terminologies in use. *Investors In People (IIP)* is concerned essentially with developing the people of the organisation in order to develop the organisation. Administered by the Training and Enterprise Councils (TECs), many public sector organisations as well as private sector organisations are now pursuing this standard.

Then there is the *European Quality Award* model and the more recent *UK Quality Award*. Many public sector organisations are taking these very seriously, including for example, British Railways, the Royal Mail and the South Yorkshire Constabulary.

But more of all this later. The fundamental question is 'How to start?'.

HOW TO START

Many authors seem to have very preconceived notions of the purpose of their book, or why the reader may wish to read it, if indeed as all authors hope, they really do. We hope that the reader's interest is a broad one in order to obtain a deep understanding of the nature of quality in the public sector as it currently exists, including what is currently being done, whether it is relevant and what should change. Nonetheless we realise that many of you readers will be rather impatient. You will flick through the book looking for the key messages, reading parts of plausible chapters in the course of a few minutes that have taken many months of research and writing to present to you. Whilst we know that you may only gain a limited first comprehension of the subject from this approach, nonetheless in a world in which we all learn by doing, we would not wish to discourage you from learning enough to get started in this way.

If you must do it this way, then we wish you luck, but ask you to be careful. Depending on where you are coming from, do not ignore the chapter dealing with Special Factors in the Public Sector (Chapter 4). Do pay attention to the case studies and in particular to the key guide that is given in Chapter 10, and do pay attention to Chapter 11, on How to Get Started. Do build an action plan, do not rush ahead and get started and plan afterwards. Through researching this book we have found many examples of organisations in the public sector who have done it that way naïvely. The better ones learnt from their disappointing experiences, but many gave up. **Please do not make the same mistake, it might just be your last!**

WHY THIS BOOK IS ALREADY OUT OF DATE!

There is one other thing that you must remember. With accelerating reform, the restructuring of the Civil Service including the flattening of the management pyramid as in the private sector, and the developing new role of the new Civil Service, a book like this must of necessity always be a little out of date. Coping with constant change is what the future is about.

2

TOTAL QUALITY MANAGEMENT STARTED IN THE PUBLIC SECTOR

A DISTORTED VIEW OF HISTORY

In Chapter 3, we shall discuss the meaning of quality. However, it is clear that Total Quality Management (TQM) is about a management philosophy and approach and not just a narrow concept of product or service quality.

The origins of quality as we know it today can be traced back almost to antiquity, although much of the concept was developed in Japan following the Second World War. The definition of TQM as an all embracing organisational management philosophy came later and is linked to the public sector.

In many senses public administration is the most natural place for the introduction of TQM. Historically, *bureaucratic administrative structures* were likely to exist here rather than in the commercial world where financial and competitive pressures mitigated against the growth of bureaucracy and assisted employees in recalling quite clearly the purposes for the existence of the business and the importance of the customer. Historically in public administration such clarity of purpose has not been always apparent and the importance of the 'customer need' has not always been paramount.

In public administration it has often been the case that the provision of the service to the public has not been that of a supplier to a customer but rather that of an *authority to a subject*. Public administration may not be deliberately belligerent or malevolent but nonetheless public employees have often found themselves primarily as *agents of the State* carrying out an official State purpose, rather than service personnel involved in the provision of a defined service to a customer. Public administration was after all a *monopoly*; there was little concept of realistic pricing of service against market alternatives and the punitive power was in the hands of the public administrator rather than the customer; it was not that the customer could withdraw his custom but the public administrator could refuse to facilitate it.

Against this background, the need for the TQM revolution was clearly greater in the public rather than the private sector. It is no surprise therefore that apparently the first usage of the phrase 'Total Quality Management' was in the context of the American Department of Defense programme based upon the development of ideas due to Dr W. Edwards Deming and many others. Earlier origins of the terminology can be found in the work of Armand Feigenbaum who in the early 1950s was one of the American experts sent by the government to Japan to lecture on quality control.

The further development of TQM has not neglected the areas of public administration or public service. In the UK, the United States of America and the world, Government Departments, Government Agencies, Public Utilities and uniformed and non-uniformed public services have been amongst the forefront in TQM. This very much reflects the increase in ideas such as the Citizen's Charter and general pressure of market testing, compulsory competitive tendering and other Government policies.

Indeed, the first author's special relationship with East Midlands Electricity is typical of the importance of TQM and Quality Assurance in the transfer of public service organisations from public administration to private sector public utilities. This interest can currently be seen across UK public utilities and in the preparation for the pursuit of Agency status by branches within British Government public administration. Active interest can be seen too in Government Departments and elsewhere; from the Department of Employment to the Ministry of Defence, from the Inland Revenue to the Defence Research Agency, from the Health Service to the police force, from the fire service to education and training, from forensic science to British Railways.

IN THE BEGINNING

In the beginning there were quality standards for *products*. The establishment and adoption of measures and standards indicates a conscious effort to achieve conformity, to reduce variation, to control a certain quality feature, perhaps with the aim of replicating a desirable outcome or to make improvements on current performance. Measures and standards were also developed to compare one product with another and to ascertain 'value for money'.

The story starts about 2000 BC. The early Egyptians devised measures of length (the cubit) and also area (squared cubit). The 'royal cubit' was accepted and used as the master standard for linear measurements. They were also able to calculate the area of a circle and used a more accurate value for pi than any of the other ancient civilisations. They were the first to establish the 365¼-day year and divide it into 12 months with 24 hours per day. Using these measures and their flair for arithmetic and geometry they were able to develop basic geographical maps and star charts and also to predict the timing and extent of the periodic Nile flooding.

The earliest evidence of the strict control of quality, though, is often cited as the Code of Law of Hammurabi, King of Babylon, circa 1800 BC. The uniformity of the Babylonian weights and measures was well established as also was the quality of the Babylonian weapons of war.

The ancient Greeks have also left us many examples of the quality of design, architecture and art that their civilisations were able to produce. In the fields of philosophy, science and mathematics, Pythagoras, Plato and Archimedes readily spring to mind. Later, the Romans continued this development and are perhaps particularly remembered for their engineering skills and their ability to construct bridges, aqueducts, roads and buildings to standardised designs.

IN BRITAIN

Standards of weights were first introduced into England during the early part of the Middle Ages, in Saxon times. It was some three centuries later that statutes defining length and area were formulated, during the reign of Edward I (1239–1307).

It was also during the Middle Ages that the various trades' and craftsmen's guilds were established by master craftsmen, both in England the throughout the rest of Europe. These associations set *standards* for quality, working conditions and wages in an effort to protect and enhance the livelihoods of their members; The Guild Act in England stated that the wardens of the crafts were appointed 'to see the work to be good and right'. The same period saw the rise of the merchant classes and a move towards living in towns.

Manufacturing, however, was still carried out mainly by individuals or perhaps small groups of people. Quality could be said to be operator-controlled; the person supplying the goods or services dealt directly with the end user, establishing his needs and receiving feedback on satisfaction – a type of bespoke operation.

The Industrial Revolution, which began in Britain sometime after the middle of the eighteenth century, was to make a radical change in this respect. Based on ample deposits of iron and coal, and starting mainly in the textile industry – following inventions by people like Hargreaves, Arkwright and Crompton – mechanisation meant that manufacturing began to be increasingly centred in large factories. People moved from the land to work in the new industrial regions located around mining areas such as Manchester, Newcastle, Glasgow and Birmingham. In many areas of manufacturing, the skills of the craftsman were no longer needed and poorly educated workers were recruited to operate the machines that satisfied the demand for exports. The owners of the businesses frequently delegated the running of the factory to *managers*, and the workforce became mere machine operators.

Adam Smith (1723–90), a professor at Glasgow University, wrote that:

> The directors of such companies, being the managers rather of other people's money than of their own, it cannot well be expected that they should watch over it with the same anxious vigilance with which the partners in a private co-partnery frequently watch over their own. Negligence and profusion . . . must always prevail more or less, in the management of the affairs of such a company . . . The only trades which it seems possible for a joint stock company to carry on successfully . . . are those of which all the operations are capable of being reduced to what is called a routine, or such a uniformity of method as admits of little or no variation.

It is a logical consequence of the Industrial Revolution that manufacturing should become increasingly concerned with uniformity, variance reduction and control. This is the origin of the need for quality measurement in modern manufacturing.

A friend of Smith, the inventor James Watt (1769–1848), and his colleague Matthew Boulton (1770–1842), obviously agreed with this point of view at their Soho foundry where they manufactured the famous steam engines. They drew up detailed specifications, controlled materials and components, developed standard operating procedures and planned production flows. Records were kept on all aspects of the process and the profit accruing from the sale of each machine was calculated.

ACROSS THE OCEAN

Although Britain was the birthplace of the Industrial Revolution and for a time was the world's wealthiest nation, the rest of Europe and the United States of America were not far behind. In America, Eli Whitney (1765–1825), the inventor of the cotton gin (for mechanically extracting cotton fibre from its seed pods), applied mass production techniques to the manufacture of 10,000 muskets for the US army. He speeded up the assembly operation by creating jigs – templates or moulds – that ensured that the manufactured parts were identical and therefore interchangeable. During this period, responsibility for quality control was in the hands of the *supervisors* and Whitney analysed work loads to determine how many operators a supervisor could manage effectively.

Another American, Frederick Winslow Taylor (1856–1917), developed work analysis much further and created what he called *Scientific Management* – also known as Taylorism. Stop watches were given to foremen (whose duties were now redefined), jobs were broken down into their component elements and times to achieve an optimum performance were recorded and became work standards. *Technical standards* were also created, by engineers and other specialists. Differential piece rates were introduced. In *Principles of Scientific Management* (1911), Taylor explained that, '*What we hoped to ultimately determine was . . . how many foot-pounds of work a man could do in a day.*'

Taylor's objective seems to have been to dehumanise the workforce and create a group of 'robots' who blindly followed the laid-down instructions. Although many of the principles advocated by Taylor were taken up by several companies in the US, in Britain there was great resistance from the stronger labour movements resulting in the impact being much weaker. Interestingly, Taylor's works were translated into Japanese.

One of the consequences of Taylorism was that supervisors now had more people reporting to them. They also had extra duties brought about by the increasing complexity and size of many manufacturing organisations as the use of mass-production methods spread. By the end of the nineteenth century, in order that supervisors could concentrate more on production issues, it was common for the quality to be checked by *inspectors* who had no direct involvement with, or responsibility for, the production process. *Inspection as an approach to monitoring quality had become a separate function.*

QUALITY BECOMES STATISTICAL

The advent of the First World War stimulated the need for more mass production and more inspection. The Technical Inspection Association was formed in Britain soon after the war and was incorporated as the Institute of Engineering Inspection in 1922. It later became the Institute of Quality Assurance in 1972.

However, 100 per cent inspection as a method of assuring quality to customers is not 100 per cent reliable, even if the inspection criteria are clearly defined and understood. It is also very time consuming and expensive and adds another link in the chain between manufacturer and customer.

In America in the 1920s, the telecommunications giant, Western Electric, was looking for a more rigorous quality control method, to increase customer confidence in, and support for, their instruments and appliances. In 1924 they set up the Inspection Engineering Department at their Bell Laboratories in New York and it was there, in the same year, that Dr Walter A. Shewhart and his co-workers designed the first *control charts* and started work on other techniques which applied statistical methods to the measurement and control of quality. Shewhart is generally regarded as the inventor of the control chart and the founder of what is now known as *Statistical Process Control*, or *SPC* for short.

One important feature of Shewhart's control chart is that it again necessitates quality measurement and quality control being applied during manufacture or creation of service rather than purely at the end of the line. With SPC, instead of inspecting work at the end of the line, critical steps in a process are sampled regularly and the measurements taken are recorded chronologically on control charts.

Various chart interpretation rules that have been developed allow the process operators to determine whether the process is still in (statistical) control or not. If the latter is the case, then the cause of the out-of-control condition can be investigated and remedied before poor product is produced. Excessive incidence of nonconforming product is prevented during the process instead of being appraised at the end of the process. The opportunities for reducing nonconformities and for making cost savings, when compared with end-of-the-line inspection, are obvious.

The methodology can also bring about further quality improvements. Shewhart stressed the difference between *common causes* of variation and *special* or *assignable* causes. The former are part of the system and beyond the operator's control; the latter can be assigned to a specific circumstance. The initial work in SPC prior to setting up the control charts necessitates the removal of as many of the special causes as possible so that the process runs in statistical control, demonstrating only common causes of variation. Similarly, during use, additional special causes may present themselves for removal and management can also take steps to remove some of the common causes and thus improve the overall variability of the process.

In 1925, one of Shewhart's colleagues, Harold E. Dodge, developed statistically-based methods of *acceptance sampling*; methods which allow the user to get an accurate appreciation of the quality of a consignment or batch by inspecting and measuring only a part of it.

Investigations into the use of statistical methods to analyse variation had been carried out on both sides of the Atlantic since the end of the nineteenth century and it was in Britain, also in 1925, that R. A. Fisher (later Sir Ronald) published a work detailing the design of experiments concerning potato yields at Rothamstead Agricultural Research Station.

Shewhart's, *Economic Control of Quality of Manufactured Product* was published in America in 1931, and it was following his invited lectures at the University of London in 1932 that the Industrial and Agricultural Section of the Royal Statistical Society was formed. 1935 saw the publication of Fisher's, *The Design of Experiments* and also the first British Standard on quality control. Developed by E. S. Pearson, BS 6000 was entitled, *Application of Statistical Methods to Industrial Standardisation and Quality Control.*

The Second World War led to the rapid deployment of statistical techniques for measuring, evaluating and controlling quality – both in the UK and in the USA. Indirectly, it also paved the way for the revolution in the emphasis on quality management as the driving force for manufacturing excellence that has made Japan the world power that it is today.

In some industries, the last fifty years have seen the level of product defects being no longer routinely measured in percentages (parts per hundred), but in parts per *million* and even parts per *billion*. Again, in some areas, product quality is simply taken for granted; the market differentiator is seen as *quality of service* and therefore *customer satisfaction levels* become the key area to measure. As the world shrinks, business survival depends on quality. According to Armand Feigenbaum, *quality is now the single most important force in organisational success and growth.*

In the next sections of this chapter, we examine the messages of some of the quality experts, or gurus, who have, since the Second World War, contributed to the meaning of quality, quality achievement and quality measurement as we know them today.

DR W. EDWARDS DEMING

Dr W. Edwards Deming died in December 1993 at the age of 93. He was born in Iowa in 1900 and was awarded his PhD in Mathematical Physics from Yale in 1928. He joined the United States Department of Agriculture and in 1936 he came to England to study for a time under R. A. Fisher.

Deming had met Dr Walter A. Shewhart in 1927 and worked closely with him thereafter. Whereas Shewhart had concentrated on manufacturing processes, Deming believed that the same concepts could be applied in other areas. In 1939, when Deming moved to the National Bureau of the Census he applied Shewhart's statistical techniques to routine clerical operations. This resulted in some processes showing a *sixfold productivity improvement*, massive savings and the census report being published earlier than usual.

Attempts to meet the increased demand for materials for the American war effort meant that many unskilled personnel were recruited by the manufacturing industries. Quality levels fell as a result and, in 1942, courses to teach various *statistical approaches for the measurement and control of quality* were quickly organised throughout the USA, with some 31,000 personnel undergoing training. Both Deming and Shewhart were active in this effort and Deming himself led 23 courses. His training, in his own and Shewhart's methods, of designers, inspectors and engineers, resulted in substantial reductions in scrap and rework together with productivity improvements. Several people involved in this training programme banded together in 1946 to establish the American Society for Quality Control.

The gains in the use of statistical techniques for quality control made during the war were short-lived, both in the UK and USA. In the boom market that developed, everything would sell, regardless of quality. Furthermore, many of the managers running the factories were not fully committed to the approach. To quote Deming from Nancy R. Mann's, *The Keys to Excellence*, published in 1985:

> 'The courses were well-received by engineers, but management paid no attention to them. Management did not understand that they had to get behind improvement of quality and carry out their obligations from the top down. Any instabilities can help to point out specific times or locations of local problems. Once these local problems are removed there is a process that will continue until someone changes it. Changing the process is management's responsibility. And we failed to teach them that.

Shortly after the war, Deming went twice to Japan to assist Japanese statisticians in studies of housing and nutrition, and for preparation of the census of 1951. It was during these visits that he met members of JUSE, the Union of Japanese Scientists and Engineers, which had been founded in 1946 to aid the rebuilding of Japan. A delegation from Bell Telephone Laboratories also visited Japan at about this time to demonstrate how the statistical methods, as developed and taught by Shewhart and Deming, could be used for controlling and improving quality in the Japanese telecommunications industry. Deming was invited to Japan again, this time by JUSE.

The Japanese were aware of British Standard BS 6000 and also the Z-I American Standards developed during the war but, because the statistical approach was difficult to understand, it was not accepted widely. Ishikawa, in *What is Total Quality Control? The Japanese Way*, wrote:

> In management, Japan also lagged behind, using the so-called Taylor method in certain quarters. . . . Quality control was totally dependent on inspection, and not every product was sufficiently inspected. In those days Japan was still competing with cost and price but not with quality. It was literally still the age of "cheap and poor" products.

Deming returned to Japan in June 1950 and taught over 500 managers and engineers about the importance of understanding and controlling variation and the use of control charts, in a series of eight-day courses. He also introduced a systematic approach to problem solving and improvement, known variously as the *Shewhart cycle* (by Deming himself), the *Deming cycle* and the *Plan, Do, Check, Action cycle*.

This Plan, Do, Check, Action cycle, shown in Figure 2.1, is an improvement methodology involving a feedback loop. The normal tendency, without the discipline imposed by the cycle, is to skimp on the planning and checking phases (target setting and monitoring), and perhaps to concentrate on the doing element. This leads to reacting or fire-fighting instead of a controlled assessment of the situation and then further action based on fact. It has been suggested that this may be because of the results-oriented society we live in, where doing is seen as being productive (and is easily measurable) and planning may be seen as procrastination.

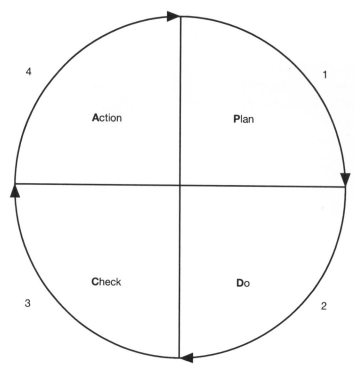

Figure 2.1 The Shewhart Cycle

Deming was determined to avoid a repetition of the situation that he had seen develop in America after the war. He made arrangements through JUSE to address senior managers to make them aware of the *roles and responsibilities* that they must take on board if Japanese industry was to turn itself around by making improvements in its quality performance so that they could compete internationally. He stressed the need for working closely with suppliers to improve the uniformity and quality of incoming materials and also the need for maintenance of equipment.

He also emphasised the *importance of the consumer* and, in subsequent visits in 1951 and 1952, when he addressed many more engineers and top managers, he supplemented his usual courses with lessons on *consumer research* and *modern methods of sampling*. He taught that '. . . *the consumer is the most important part of the production line*', and his courses committed his students to carrying out door-to-door surveys in order to measure consumer requirements.

In the West, it was not until the 1970s that Deming started to make an impact. In 1980 when NBC, the American broadcasting company, made a documentary entitled, *If Japan Can, Why Can't We?*, many more became aware of his concepts. However, until his death at the end of 1993, Deming was constantly reviewing and refining his ideas and his later work was more management-based than statistically-based. His famous *14 Points for Management* were produced to help people to understand and implement '. . . *the total transformation of Western style of management*' that he believed to be necessary. The 14 points, and more of Deming's later thinking was captured in his 1986 book, *Out of the Crisis*.

Deming was awarded the Shewhart Medal by the American Society for Quality Control in 1956 and, in 1960, he became the first to be awarded the Second Order of the Sacred Treasure, the highest decoration that can be conferred on a non-Japanese. He was awarded the National Medal of Technology in America in 1987.

DR JOSEPH M. JURAN

Another recipient of the Second Order of the Sacred Treasure, although not until 1980, is Joseph Juran. Juran was born in Rumania in 1904 and moved to America at an early age. He trained as an engineer but his career has been varied; industrial executive, government administrator, university professor, labour arbitrator, corporate director and management consultant. He went to Japan in 1954, also at the invitation of JUSE.

With his broad experience in management, coupled with his expertise in quality methods, he was able to discuss the wider issues of quality and to appeal to senior Japanese managers. His lectures focused on *planning and organisational issues, management's responsibility for quality*, and *the need to set goals and targets for improvement*. He emphasised that quality control should be conducted as an integral part of management control. His lectures were followed up at more junior management levels by JUSE and the Japanese Standards Association. Large companies started internal training, courses for foremen were offered on national radio and booklets were made available at newspaper kiosks.

In the first edition of the *Quality Control Handbook*, published in 1951, edited (and mainly written) by Juran, he coined the phrase, '*There is gold in the mine*'. This was a reference to the huge cost saving that can be made by measuring and resolving quality problems. However, it is not at the surface; you have to dig for it. Juran knew that making quality improvements is not easy; there are many barriers and obstacles to be overcome. He used the measurement of costs attributable to quality problems within organisations to capture the attention of senior management in the West.

Quality costs can also be used to prioritise and monitor improvement activity. Juran believes that *at least 80 per cent of quality problems result from the systems and procedures laid down by management and therefore exhortations to the workforce to try harder will only serve to alienate them*. Instead, he advocates the use of cross-functional management teams for achieving quality improvement. He teaches a project-by-project approach to solving quality problems and was probably the first to recommend the use of the *Pareto principle* for prioritising actions; *identifying and tackling the 'vital few' problems* and not the 'useful many'.

Juran also stresses the need for *planning for quality*. He sees quality planning as part of the quality *trilogy* of quality planning, quality control and quality improvement.

Quality control is the responsibility of the operating personnel, maintaining the status quo by following procedures, monitoring outputs and fire-fighting if necessary. *Quality improvement* concerns the measurement and reduction of what Juran calls chronic quality problems.

Quality planning uses the lessons learned whilst making improvements to ensure that similar problems are avoided in the future. In *Juran on Planning for Quality*, published in 1988, the key elements in implementing *company-wide strategic quality planning* are seen as identifying customers and their needs; establishing optimal quality goals; creating measurements of quality; planning processes capable of meeting quality goals under operating conditions and producing continuing results in improved market share, premium prices, and a reduction of error rates in the office and factory.

Each stage of the planning process has inputs and outputs. Throughout the process there are a series of suppliers (of the inputs) and customers (for the outputs). Juran sees these internal *supplier-customer relationships* extending beyond the planning phase and on through all the steps involved in actually *supplying the goods or service to the end user or consumer*. The *public* in general may be regarded as a customer if the product or service (or the provision of it) impacts sufficiently on it.

Measurement must be introduced throughout this supplier-customer chain to evaluate, control and improve what the customer (internal or external) receives. The type, frequency and method of measurement will depend on the stage of the process and the people who will use it.

Juran, like Deming, has been critical of senior management in the West but he *sees the 1990s as the time when the improvement efforts made by western organisations over the last decade will finally bear fruit.*

DR ARMAND V. FEIGENBAUM

Armand Feigenbaum was the third major American quality expert to visit Japan in the 1950s. As Head of Quality at the General Electric Company, he had extensive contacts with Japanese companies such as Toshiba and Hitachi and his 1951 book was translated into Japanese.

Feigenbaum argued for the involvement of all functions within the quality process, not just the manufacturing area. The idea is to *build in quality at an early stage instead of relying on process control and inspection further down the line.* His concept of *Total Quality Control* extends the administrative function to include the measurement and control of quality at every stage, from customer specification and sales, through design, engineering, assembly and shipment. In *Total Quality Control*, published in 1983, Total Quality Control is seen as providing the structure and tools for managing quality so that there is a continuous emphasis throughout the organisation on quality leadership. The need for *quality-mindedness* throughout all levels is emphasised and quality control within the organisation is seen as both:

- a channel for communication for product quality information; and
- a means of participation in the overall plant quality programme.

A Total Quality System is defined by him as:

> The agreed company-wide and plant-wide operating work structure, documented in effective, integrated technical and managerial procedures, for guiding the co-ordinated actions of the people, the machines, and the information of the company and plant in the best and most practical ways to assure customer quality satisfaction and economical costs of quality.

Operating quality costs can be divided into:

- prevention costs – including quality planning;
- appraisal costs – including inspection;
- internal failure costs – including scrap and rework; and
- external failure costs – including warranty costs, product recall.

Feigenbaum argues that reductions in operating quality costs result from establishing a Total Quality System for two reasons:

1 Lack of existing effective customer-oriented standards may mean that current product quality is not optimal and, given use,
2 expenditure on prevention can lead to a several fold reduction in internal and external failure costs.

Dr Feigenbaum founded the International Academy for Quality and is a past president of the American Society for Quality Control, which presented him with the Edwards Medal and the Lancaster Award for his international contributions to quality and productivity. In 1988, he was appointed to the board which oversees the Malcolm Baldrige National Quality Award Programme and, in 1991, the fortieth anniversary edition of *Total Quality Control* was published.

DR KAORU ISHIKAWA

Dr Ishikawa was born in 1915 and graduated from Tokyo University in 1939 with a degree in applied chemistry. His name will perhaps be best known to many people from the *Ishikawa Diagram*, otherwise known as the *Cause & Effect Diagram* or the *Fishbone Diagram*. Ishikawa invented the diagram (in 1952) to supplement the other tools and techniques that he advocated for the measurement, control and improvement of processes in (mainly) Japanese companies for many years, until his death in 1989.

After the war, Ishikawa returned to Tokyo University and in 1948 began to study statistical methods. By 1949, he had joined JUSE's Quality Control Research Group and, following Deming's visit in 1950, began teaching the application of statistical methods for quality control, making it compulsory for his engineering students at the university.

Ishikawa's contribution to the turn-round of Japan's industry since the war can hardly be overstated. As well as teaching the techniques of quality control directly to *all levels* within diverse organisations, he was a pioneer of the Quality Circle movement in Japan, initiated quality conferences, contributed regularly to quality journals and worked closely with the Japanese Industrial Standards Committee which led to him becoming chairman of the Japanese Chapter of the International Standards Organisation in 1977.

Ishikawa had the rare ability to adapt technical methods and make them accessible and palatable to all levels within an organisation. In particular, he championed the use of what are commonly called the

Seven Tools of Quality Control:

1 Pareto charts – to prioritise action.
2 Cause & Effect diagrams – to identify causes of variation.
3 Stratification – to divide data into subsets.
4 Check-sheets – for data collection.
5 Histograms – to display variation graphically.
6 Scatter diagrams – to confirm or deny relationships between two factors.
7 Shewhart's control charts and graphs – to monitor and control variation.

An aspect of Ishikawa's approach is that *the same set of tools should be used on a team basis at all levels and by all functions within the organisation* for the measurement, evaluation, control and improvement of all business activities, not just for quality control of the product. Furthermore, because the output from the use of the tools is graphical, the information displayed can be understood by all, helping to reduce misunderstandings and communication problems.

Ishikawa's book, *Guide to Quality Control*, based on articles written for the *Quality Control for the Foreman* journal, is a classic text describing the use of these tools. One of Ishikawa's pet themes, highlighted in the book, is the accurate collection and use of data. He argued that *all data should be treated with suspicion and historical databases should be ignored. Plus, all data should be collected as and where it is needed.*

Company-wide quality

Ishikawa was a key player in the company-wide quality control movement which started in Japan around 1955, following the visits of Deming and Juran. Company-wide quality control necessitates measurements by all. Everyone studies statistical methods. Every function and all levels participate in the improvement process; research, design, engineering, manufacturing, sales, clerical, personnel, etc. Quality control concepts and methods are used to measure, monitor and improve incoming raw materials, manufacturing processes, personnel issues and sales problems. In Ishikawa's concept, *quality does not only mean the quality of the product but also after-sales service, quality of management, the company itself and the human being.* As a result he argued that:

• product quality improves and becomes uniform and defects are reduced;
• product reliability is improved;
• cost is reduced;

- productivity increases and it becomes possible to make rational production schedules;
- wasteful work and rework are reduced;
- technique is established and improved;
- expenses for inspection and testing are reduced;
- contracts between vendor and vendee are rationalised;
- the sales market is enlarged;
- better relationships are established between departments;
- false data and reports are reduced;
- discussions are carried out more freely and democratically;
- meetings are operated more smoothly;
- repairs and installations of equipment and facilities are done more rationally; and
- human relations are improved.

Quality control circles

Quality Control (QC) Circles are a major feature of company-wide quality control and illustrate Ishikawa's commitment to *education for all and measurement by all*. In 1962 Ishikawa became chairman of the editorial board of a low-price journal entitled, *Quality Control for the Foreman*. This was published by JUSE and built on the success of another regular JUSE publication, *Statistical Quality Control*, which originated in 1950. The purpose of the new magazine was to get the message and techniques of quality measurement to the operators in the front line. QC circles began in Japan as study groups – workers and their foremen being encouraged to read and discuss the concepts and methods advocated in *Quality Control for the Foreman* and then to try the approaches in their own work areas.

The nature and role of Quality Circles in Japan varies between companies, but the following is a general guide: Small groups of five to ten people from the same work area meet voluntarily on a regular basis to discuss, investigate, measure and analyse work-related problems. The Circle is led by a foreman or one of the workers and the seven tools of quality control are used. Depending on the organisation, solutions to problems identified by the Circle are either presented to management for authorisation before implementation, or the team has authority to implement directly. Typically, Circle members receive no direct financial reward for their improvements.

The aims of the QC Circle activities are to:

- contribute to the improvement and development of the enterprise;

- respect human relations and build a happy workshop offering job satisfaction; and
- deploy human capabilities fully and draw out infinite potential.

The QC Circle concept spread rapidly, within both manufacturing companies and service organisations. Encouraged by books, seminars, lectures, annual conferences and visits to other organisations, the number of individuals involved in Circles activity in Japan is now calculated as in excess of ten million. Ishikawa was central to masterminding much of this growth and in laying down the ground rules for Circle activities.

Ishikawa is often regarded as '*the father of Japanese quality*'. He was awarded the Deming Prize, the Nihon Keizai Press Prize, the Industrial Standardisation Prize and the Grant Award. The latter was presented by the American Society for Quality Control in 1971 in recognition for his education programme on quality control.

DR GENICHI TAGUCHI

Genichi Taguchi and Shigeo Shingo are two further Japanese quality gurus whose ideas contributed tremendously to Japan's post-war turn-round. Both primarily evolved methods for the prevention of quality problems in manufacture, but also for the design of efficient processes. Their methods are now finding increasing use in the West.

Genichi Taguchi was born in Japan in 1924. When the Nippon Telephone and Telegraph Company established its Electrical Communications Laboratory (ECL) in 1949, he was recruited to improve the efficiency of their research and development activities. His first book was published in 1951 and earned him the Deming Award for Literature on Quality. The book introduced statistical methods for minimising the number of trials or tests that need to be carried out in order to arrive at a satisfactory design. In 1954–5, Taguchi visited the Indian Statistical Institute where he conducted several experiments and also met Shewhart and Fisher. Part of Taguchi's methodology is based on the work begun by Fisher in England in the 1920s, but expanded and adapted for industrial applications.

During the 12 years that Taguchi spent with ECL, he consulted widely amongst many Japanese companies, including Toyota. Like Ishikawa, he has been able to simplify complex statistical methods and make them comprehensible to non-academics. Taguchi's methods, which in essence *build quality into processes and products at the design stage*, were therefore available to many Japanese companies from the 1950s. The diagram shown in Figure 2.2 illustrates the relative contributions of the different approaches to quality control used in Japan since the Second World War.

Taguchi methods can be used for trouble-shooting in production but their main application is in the design of new processes and products. Within a process, the number of factors that contribute to the quality and consistency of the output can be many. Which are the important ones, and how important are they? Are they always important or only under certain conditions? To test out and measure the effect of all of the possible combinations – of variables and at different levels – would be an impossible task. How long can you wait to get a new product or service to market?

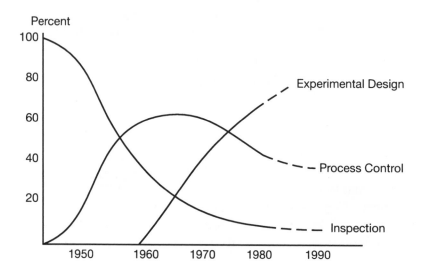

Figure 2.2 Approaches to Quality Control used in Japan

Conventionally, the need to get new products or services to market quickly, can mean that processes are set up based on previous experience, a few trials that nearly worked, and with 'fingers crossed' as production starts, in the hope of meeting the agreed deadline. As problems occur, they are dealt with as far as possible by problem-solving and at great cost in terms of defectives produced, time wasted, customer dissatisfaction, etc. The process variables are subsequently 'twiddled' in an effort to improve consistency of output and minimise poor output.

Instead, Taguchi's approach uses a standard set of tables to optimise the number of experimental trials that need to be carried out initially. These '*orthogonal arrays*' reduce the number of tests dramatically by giving an experimental design pattern which does not measure the effect of every possible combination or level of factors but gives sufficient data on each for decisions to be made. Further trials to home-in more precisely on the optimum levels can be made if required. As an example of the power of the method: seven different factors each at two levels would require 128 experiments if tackled conventionally; Taguchi uses just eight. For six factors at five levels, equivalent to 15,625 combinations, Taguchi would carry out 25 experiments.

By carrying out the designed experiments, the optimum level and relative importance of each variable is established having regard to the sensitivity of the process to environmental and other uncontrollable factors. Efficient and robust processes can then be set up using this data, and Statistical Process Control (SPC) can be used to monitor and control quality characteristics in the critical areas identified.

The *Quality Loss Function*, developed by Taguchi in the early 1970s, may be used to measure and evaluate design decisions on a financial basis. The cost element is defined as 'loss imparted by the product to society from the time the product is shipped'. The loss includes not only the normal company costs of scrap, rework, downtime, warranty, etc., but also costs to the customer in terms of poor product performance and reliability, which themselves may result in the manufacturer or supplier losing future business. To minimise this loss to society, the variation from the target, for any particular quality characteristic, must be minimised. By using the quality loss function – a mathematical formula – decisions can be made to determine or verify whether additional costs in production will actually prove to be worthwhile in the market place.

Since 1980, more and more American companies have implemented Taguchi methodology – including Xerox, Ford and ITT. In Europe, with one or two exceptions such as Lucas, Taguchi's approach found little application until, in 1987, the Institute of Statisticians organised a conference in London to publicise the methods. The UK Taguchi Club (now part of the Quality Methods Association) was formed later that year.

SHIGEO SHINGO

Shingo was born in Japan in 1909. Shigeo Shingo is perhaps not as well known in the West as the two previous Japanese quality gurus although the impact of his work, especially in Japan, has been immense. After graduating in Mechanical Engineering at Yamanashi Technical College in 1930, he joined the Taipei Railway Factory in Taiwan where he introduced the methods of scientific management. In 1945 he became a professional consultant with the Japan Management Association where, as Education Department Chairman in 1951, he first became aware of statistical quality control techniques.

From 1955 he was responsible for industrial engineering and factory improvement training at the Toyota Motor Company. In the period between 1956 and 1958, while working at Mitsubishi Heavy Industries in Nagasaki, Shingo was responsible for halving the time for hull assembly of a 65,000 ton supertanker from four months to two months. His methods quickly spread to other Japanese shipyards. In 1959 he left the Japan Management Association and established the Institute of Management Improvement.

From 1961 Shingo started to develop *Poka-Yoke* systems. *Poka-Yoke* literally means mistake-proofing and was the name he adopted for the technique after he received complaints for calling the method fool-proofing (*baka-yoke*). Most people will be aware of the basic idea. In the West, we often see this approach where safety is an issue but in Japan it is also used extensively where quality is the main concern. Essentially, *Poka-Yoke systems, use devices or work methods which prevent defects from occurring*. The approach was developed for man-ufacturing systems, but also has clear application in administrative and other non-manufacturing systems. *Poka-Yoke* systems in general involve two phases: the detection aspect and the regulatory aspect. In manufacturing, detection can be accomplished by various means: phys-ical contact, limit switches, photoelectric cells, pressure-sensitive switches, thermostats, etc. Regulation can be by either giving a warn-ing (eg flashing light, alarm buzzer) or by taking control (prevention, automatically shutting a machine down) – or both.

Shingo distinguished between 'errors' and 'defects', the latter being caused by the former. He recognised that people do make mistakes, for a variety of reasons, but the errors need not result in defects. His method is to stop the process whenever an error occurs and to establish the source of the error by inspection, and then to prevent its recurrence. *Poka-Yoke devices, in effect, give 100 per cent inspection, but during the process when prevention is possible and not after the event when it is too late.* Using Shingo's concept of *Zero Quality Control*, zero defects can be achieved.

Shingo had been a firm believer in the application of statistical pro-cess control since he first learned about it. Gradually, as he did more and more work with *Poka-Yoke* systems, his enthusiasm for SPC waned. Improvement from statistical methods partly comes from the detection and measurement of defects and a reaction to them; his methods prevent defects. Furthermore, statistical methods use sampling techniques; his *Poka-Yoke* methods allow for 100 per cent inspection and yet make non-automated measurement unnecessary.

By 1977, he was 'finally released from the spell of statistical methods' when a plant in Matsushita's Washing Machine Division had seven months of defect-free operation in their drainpipe assembly line involving 23 workers producing 30,000 units per month. Since then, many more companies have run for several months without producing defects by using Shingo's Zero Quality Control methods.

Poka-Yoke systems improve process efficiency, save waste and reduce costs; critical factors for improvement in any organisation. In 1969 while working for Toyota, Shingo developed a system known as Single-Minute Exchange of Die, or SMED. This improvement methodology similarly reduces waste. The purpose of SMED is to *minimise the amount of time taken when making changeovers.* It reduces downtime and increases production flexibility, obviating the need for long production runs and large batches. Inventory can be reduced dramatically as there is less need to maintain stock to cover for hold-ups.

At Toyota, the set-up time for a 1,000 ton press was four hours, twice as long as it took Volkswagen in West Germany. Within six months, Shingo had reduced Toyota's set-up time for the operation to one and a half hours. Following this initial success, a new target was given – three minutes! Shingo achieved this within a further three months! Other examples show set-up times being reduced from six hours to six minutes and work-in-progress inventory being slashed by 90 per cent.

Set-up time is made up of two elements which can be measured separately: internal set-up time, when the machine must be stopped, and external set-up time, when the machine need not be stopped. The optimisation process involves converting as much internal set-up time to external set-up time – and then relentlessly improving both aspects. The improvements are made by a variety of *simplification* and *deskilling* methods: jigs, clamps, quick-release fastenings, standardisation of fittings, etc.

When production hold-ups are reduced dramatically by the application of SMED techniques and when output can be virtually guaranteed by zero defect production, Just-In-Time (JIT) operating methods, Kanban and non-stock production become possible. Shingo was a key player in the introduction of these approaches within several companies and Toyota's production system in particular.

Shingo was awarded the Yellow Ribbon Decoration in 1970 for his services in improving production. He wrote more than 14 major books, several of which have now been translated into English and other European languages. Shigeo Shingo died in 1990.

WHAT HAPPENED THEN – FROM THE QUALITY GURUS TO TOTAL QUALITY IN THE PUBLIC SECTOR

The American and Japanese quality gurus set the scene for TQM, as the natural consequence of the desire to integrate their related but sometimes conflicting philosophies and tools. Much of this development was, at a crucial stage – public-sector-led – with the American Department of Defense taking a crucial part in early quality initiatives and around 1985 in the defining of this new panacea.

Most attention then, however, moved to the private sector, as manufacturing and service industries focused on the imperatives of customer satisfaction and system efficiency. For a while the private, rather than the public sector, led the way in preoccupation with TQM and quality of service.

Evidence of the recent growth of TQM in the public sector is illustrated by the situation in the US where over the last decade TQM has become a prominent feature of public administration. Both NASA and the Department of Defense, during the Reagan and Bush administrations have made sustained efforts in relation to the implementation of TQM, as did other federal departments and agencies. Indeed, TQM has been implemented in nineteen of the largest federal departments and agencies.

It is the Federal Quality Institute (FQI), which has largely been instrumental in the promotion of TQM in public administration within the US Government. (See Chapter 5). In the UK also, the public sector has now become active (See Chapters 6 to 8).

The change in the public sector towards preoccupation with quality of service is irreversible. It has a long prehistory and an exciting future that is only just taking off.

3

WHAT DO WE MEAN BY QUALITY

There is little doubt that quality has become a buzz-word in the 1990s. Advertisements, high-street stores, and even vans and lorries broadcast that a particular organisation or business, and its services and products, are quality orientated. Even the most cursory glance at press, or television advertisements demonstrates that quality has become a much over used word. Here the word 'quality' is probably used as part of a marketing ploy – alongside 'new' and 'improved'. Quality has also become a strategic issue, with many annual reports of major organisations making strong references to the initiatives they have undertaken and the concern they have demonstrated in achieving it.

Leaving aside any marketing hype, the common meaning and importance of the word 'quality' has changed significantly over the past 50 years. Indeed, according to Armand Feigenbaum, one of the American quality gurus who introduced modern concepts of quality to Japanese industry in the early 1950s, *quality in the West has now become the single, most important force leading to organisational success, and company growth in national and international markets.*

What, then, is 'quality'? What does it mean, how has it evolved into Total Quality Management (TQM), that all-embracing improvement culture, and why have so many organisations floundered on the route to its achievement?

The meaning of the word quality is very much dependent upon the context in which it is used, and the perception of the various people who will transmit and receive the message. Indeed, it may often be quite deliberately used ambiguously. It is crucial, therefore, that any organisation and the people within it reach a clear consensus and understanding of what quality means for them, otherwise exhortations to 'improve the quality of service' will be interpreted in different ways by different people, with the ensuing actions leading to confusion. The word quality can also be applied in a general sense, describing for example the way in which the entire organisation is managed, or be used more specifically to the performance of a particular service.

The modern use of the word quality and its high profile originated after Japan's defeat at the end of the Second World War. As described in Chapter 2, it was the Americans who exported the basic concepts of quality control to Japan, and the work of Dr Edwards Deming and Dr Joseph Juran laid the foundations for the subsequent revolution in quality in Japan. It is indeed sad, and with hindsight most regrettable, that these two Americans had to travel abroad in order to have their message heard and understood. However, in Europe and the US the post-war boom was at a height and had created a situation in which the consumer, who had long been starved of essential basic commodities, never mind luxuries, would buy most items offered for sale. It was a supplier-led market, and created an illusion within service and manufacturing organisations that they were efficient.

Inevitably, the post-war boom years, when companies could 'make it and ship it out', came to an end. The markets became saturated and service or product differentiation became less marked. Meanwhile, the Japanese were learning all they could about Western industrialised processes including aspects of marketing, finance, and, of course, quality. It has been said that at that time young Japanese managers came over to the West and saw that we wrote books about quality, made films about quality and gave talks about quality. What they failed to grasp, of course, was that we never actually did any of it! Those of more mature years will remember that during the 1950s and early 1960s the Japanese were taken to task for copying many Western products. Consumer items from the Far East were, in many cases, indistinguishable from 'the real thing'. In the midst of our indignation at this turn of events, Western organisations failed to notice that the Japanese were now setting about improving the products, which they had started by copying. More importantly, by this means, they had not only learned how to improve a product but also a process which was repeatable for the improvement of quality.

Historically, quality has often been used to denote *excellence, goodness, beauty* or *high cost*, for example in a painting, a Sassoon hairstyle, or a Rolls-Royce car. This imprecise concept, however, is of little use within most organisations since, apart from any other considerations, it is extremely difficult, if not impossible, to manage. A useful definition of quality is '*meeting the requirements of the customer*' and a consequent necessary first step is therefore to define those requirements. Frequently the word 'requirements' has been mistakenly equated with 'specification', often ignoring criteria such as price or delivery, so that quality has been defined purely as conformance to specification for the service or product itself.

It is essential to realise then, that meeting the requirements of the customer, should not be restricted only to the functional characteristics of the service or product. There are many examples where satisfaction of ownership are regarded as more important than the properties of the product; this is exemplified by the designer labelling of textile garments, a clear requirement of certain people. Consequently, it becomes evident that the first step is to define those requirements by *asking the customer*. This may be achieved by direct discussion, satisfaction surveys or observations on purchasing behaviour. Using this definition of quality, if the requirements for a car are one which is economical to run, and easy to park in central London, then a Rolls-Royce may *not* be a quality car.

However, this particular approach does have several weaknesses. For example, it can overemphasise checking and inspection which aims to ensure that nothing outside the published requirements is provided to the customer. This can lead to a rather 'hit and miss' type of operation where the only way of protecting the customer from poor service or defective products may be to put a great deal of emphasis on end-point inspection, which is unreliable anyway. An additional difficulty with this approach is that it takes place when the service or product is at its most expensive, this is, when all the work is complete. In addition, it is also the most critical time to ascertain whether the 'end product' is good enough or not, because the next stage is provision to the customer, and failure will usually mean failure to deliver. It is essential to realise that *quality cannot be 'inspected in'*, but must be designed into, the service or product. Increasing the end-of-line checkers tenfold will not improve the quality of the deliverable; it will just reduce the chances of the customer being disappointed over delivery time.

Not only are such checking and inspection processes expensive and time consuming, they can create a climate in which quality for the customer is considered satisfactory because it just meets the stated requirements and therefore does not need to be improved. Furthermore, it does not take into account that the requirements and needs of the customer will inevitably change, and that the marketplace in which the organisation has to operate is continuously evolving.

WHO IS THE CUSTOMER?

It will be crucially important to the success of any organisation embarking upon a TQM initiative to understand what the end customer wants, and to define the needs and expectations of those customers clearly. However, to many people employed within an organisation, meeting the requirements of the customer can seem irrelevant. This is not surprising since perhaps only a very small percentage of all employees ever meet customers, never mind having meaningful face-to-face discussions with them, so how can they hope to understand and interpret their needs? Every person within an organisation, whether a secretary, an accounts clerk or an operator, has a role to play in improving quality for the end customer, but they often fail to realise this because they are distanced from that end customer.

It may be helpful, therefore, if everybody within the organisation is made to appreciate that they are themselves both an internal customer and an internal supplier. The internal customer is the next person or department in line to whom they supply work, information, decisions or resources. Similarly, they will have internal suppliers, that is, all those people who supply what is necessary for them to carry out their work. If, at any stage, there is a breakdown in these continuous customer/supplier relationships within the organisation, then the quality of the end product or service to the external customer will be less than satisfactory, as shown in Figure 3.1.

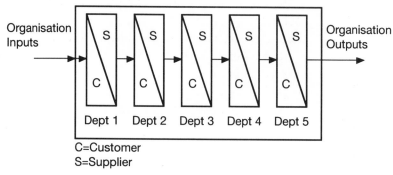

Figure 3.1 The customer/supplier chain

This concept of internal customers and suppliers can be a key to improving the operations within the organisation. We could liken the internal processes within the organisation to a relay race, whereby the inputs (resources, information, materials, etc.,) are converted into the desired outputs. As the process progresses, the resources are passed individual to individual, or department to department, rather like the baton. As in the relay race, it is typically at the handover point that many problems are manifested. Each person is, (or should be), therefore, *the* expert at their own job and will understand better than anyone else the complications which prevent them from doing their job better. This way of thinking forms the basis for introducing improvement departmental teams or Quality Circles.

TOTAL QUALITY MANAGEMENT

Early approaches to quality and, in particular, quality control and Quality Assurance, focused on the outputs, whether service or product. As the markets for products became saturated following the post-war boom years, suppliers began to realise that the customer was looking for a total service, not just the product, and therefore the need became apparent for departments such as marketing, design and accounting equally to identify and focus on the needs of customers. TQM then aims to encompass, in an integrated way, the whole organisation.

It is of course true that some organisations have treated TQM purely as an internal motivational campaign aiming to improve service to external customers. Others have focused on internal training as a way of motivating and giving people tools to undertake improvement activities. Many have identified that beyond training, teamwork and perhaps the use of statistical techniques there is, in TQM, *the quest for the self-improving organisation*. While cultural change, organisational change and the use of simple tools, together with a documented quality system such as ISO 9000, all have a part to play, TQM requires a refocus and redirection of the business. Some of the basic principles of TQM are shown in Figure 3.2.

Some of the organisational problems that are typically present in any organisation are shown in Figure. 3.3. These include subtle deficiencies that go beyond conventional definitions of service or Quality Assurance. Resolving these is what TQM is about. The purpose is to develop

---

- Fundamental cultural shift from Quality Assurance, Quality Control
- Theme of Continuous Improvement
- Customer orientated (internal and external)
- 'Right first time' standard
- Everybody in the company involved
- Led by senior management
- Measure Quality Costs/Critical Success Factors
- Prevention philosophy
- Supported by Quality Management System

Figure 3.2 Basic principles of TQM

a self-improving organisation – that is, one in which the rest position is improvement; one in which if you never did anything else to the organisation again, it would carry on improving (Figure 3.4).

- No clear relationship with customers
- No awareness of cost of quality
- Suspect workforce are underutilised
- No real measurement of staff performance
- Need to understand the real purpose of the group
- No clear picture of total rework
- No description of output quality
- Redundant procedures need updating
- No standard operating model for the department
- Difficulty in identifying internal improvement areas

Figure 3.3 Organisational Issues

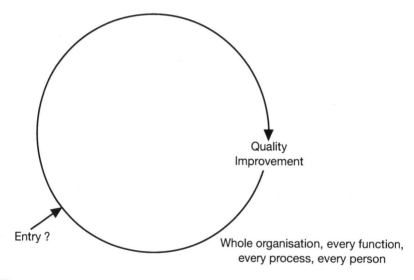

Figure 3.4

TQM is a strategic approach aimed at producing the best that is currently available through innovation and continual improvement. It is recognising that each person within the organisation is – or should aim to be – the expert within their particular role or function, and it is that person who has, quite often, first-hand knowledge of the process and therefore ideas on how to improve it.

In organisations that have treated TQM purely as a motivational campaign, we often see posters around the walls exhorting employees to 'Get it right first time'. While this objective is highly commendable, it can often appear as an insult to someone who has worked for an organisation for, say, ten years and has, as far as he or she is aware been getting it right first time. The problem usually is that they do not know exactly what the 'it' is that they are trying to get right first time, since it has never been explicitly agreed.

IMPLEMENTING TOTAL QUALITY MANAGEMENT

In theory, implementing TQM in any organisation is simple – all we need to do is construct a plan, identify problems and opportunities for improvement, and systematically address them in priority order, reprioritising as the need arises.

In starting to execute this plan, different critical issues will be of different importance in various organisations, partly reflecting their starting point. Those shown in Figure 3.5 correspond to a small manufacturing company – but frequently there is commonality in certain areas, such as the need to clarify vision at top-management level, communication problems and customer focus.

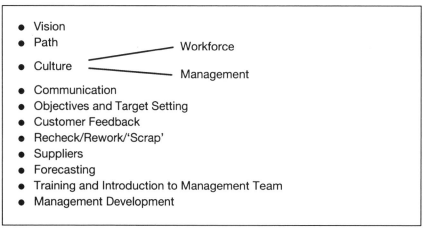

Figure 3.5 Critical Issues

We can conceive of three stages to the path of TQM, as illustrated in Figure 3.6. A crucial stage, often neglected, is to *start by finding out where you are now*. In consequence it is recommended that at the start of TQM implementation the organisation undertakes initial data collection. This should include anonymous questionnaires and independent interviews with all personnel – including heads of function – in order to identify gaps in practices and procedures, inadequate management, poor communication and problems encountered by people in doing their jobs.

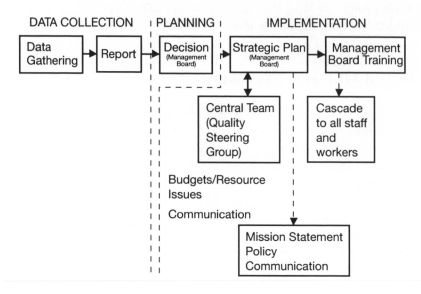

Figure 3.6

A good way forward at the start of the implementation stage is for a small Quality Steering Group, preferably chaired by the senior officer or chief executive, to be established to manage the path of TQM. It will decide resources and monitor, facilitate and remove barriers to progress. This should be followed by basic awareness training and the Management Board or Committee needs to commit itself long term by issuing a *mission statement* to inform the employees, customers, suppliers and any other 'stakeholders' of the decided path forward. Experience suggests that a 'cascade' model of training rather than 'wall-to-wall' training is to be preferred for TQM awareness.

WHERE ARE YOU HEADED?

It can be observed that may mission statements issued by organisations bear a striking resemblance to each other. This is not surprising, since after all there are only so many ways of saying more or less the same thing. Experience shows, however, that an organisation is missing the point if it merely copies another mission statement. It is the journey towards constructing the mission statement which is important; that is, the mental exercise for the Management Board of disagreeing, arguing and coming to a common conclusion about what the organisation is trying to achieve. Typically, the desired vision will be of a secure future, good financial performance, increased growth, greater creativity and innovation, and may well allude to the harnessing of the efforts of every person in the organisation towards their common aims. But how are these to be achieved? The simplistic answer is only by totally satisfying, and indeed delighting, the customer. While this might seem a self-evident truth, it is still not unusual, particularly in the public sector, to see mission statements, policy statements or quality policies which totally ignore the customer.

Also, there is a need to specify what the organisation requires from its sites, departments or individuals; what it wants them to achieve; it is for this reason that the mission statement or quality policy statement is of vital importance.

HOW ARE YOU PROGRESSING?

Agreeing and establishing a mission statement for the organisation can have a salutary effect, particularly on senior managers and directors. Long discussions and arguments, together with several iterations on the statement itself, can lead those involved to *falsely conclude that they have now accomplished their task*. Typically, the organisation will publicise its mission statement, particularly internally to all employees, who will read that the aim is to satisfy customers 'totally' or 'to become the best'. The mission statement, internally at least, will have very little value (and perhaps even a negative impact) unless it is explained to those who will be involved in the improvement process the role they are required to play. The messenger, the uniformed officer and the secretary may well all ask, 'Yes, I understand and agree with the mission statement, but what do you want me to do?'.

Likewise, in say two years' time, how is the organisation to understand whether it has made progress, and whether there are barriers and obstacles still to be overcome? Unless performance is measured, at least internally, there will be no monitor of progress towards the mission. At the very minimum, therefore, it is essential that, at all stages of TQM implementation, clear statements and information is provided to everyone in the organisation about:

1 What the aims are.
2 The current position of the organisation.

SO, WHAT SHOULD YOU MEASURE?

Historically, measurement has typically concentrated upon *outputs* and *inputs*. Examples of this might be the weekly service or production figures, monthly financial performance complaints or costs. This information, while extremely valuable, can often come too late to significantly affect the process to which they relate. This problem has been compounded in many organisations by the fact that measurement has concentrated almost exclusively on financial information. While the language of money is understood by most people, *it does not entirely answer the question of how they should change what they are doing*, in order to achieve better results. Perhaps, even more importantly, *it does not help them prioritise the key factors* which are affecting their output results.

Clearly, some form of measurement is required so that progress can be monitored towards the stated aims of the mission statement. Often in the past, however, measurement has been carried out for its own sake. This has led to a multitude of measurements and measurement methods being employed, particularly at the commencement of TQM initiatives, which are unfocused and therefore extremely confusing to those involved. What is required is a *unified measurement system* which can be utilised for planning, monitoring and driving improvement. Ideally, the measurements used should indicate clearly how the organisation is progressing towards its mission, and should avoid the failures of the past in which most measurement was either financial and/or historic and so unfocused as to be confusing. The key to any successful measurement system is simplicity, both in the nature of individual measures and in the means by which it is unified into a coherent, focused whole.

Moreover, it is extremely important to recognise at the outset that many employees will have an *inherent fear of measurement*. This may possibly be traced back to previous, unhappy experiences at the mercy of badly applied external measurement; that is measurement by those who did not carry out the process itself, but were paid to measure and control the performance of others. To obtain accurate, reliable and meaningful measurement at the point at which control is crucial, it is essential that such fears are removed at the outset.

CRITICAL SUCCESS FACTORS

A unified approach to measurement can be obtained by identifying *Critical Success Factors* (CSFs) for the organisation. These represent a small number of key measurable indicators that are such that, if they are showing satisfactory progress towards targets, the organisation as a whole will be perceived as being successful on its path of quality improvement. The Critical Success Factors identified should be *directly linked to the mission statement* so that as a group they indicate progress, or otherwise, towards the mission of the organisation. This, once again, sets a severe challenge for senior management, since the set of Critical Success Factors needs to be complete in order to convey the total picture. Completeness is essential, since focus on a selected few will inevitably lead to incompatibility with other desired results. However, they must not be so extensive that they confuse the issues involved and the personnel with the organisation. Typically, Critical Success Factors may include measures of financial performance, cost, on-time delivery performance, service levels and so forth. For clarity of vision the organisation should seek to limit the number of Critical Success Factors to about 6 or 8, but certainly no more than 12.

Having established a clear link between the mission statement and organisational performance by means of Critical Success Factors, each department and group of individuals can then begin to identify the measurements that they can contribute to improving in order to help the organisational mission. In order to contribute to improvement in these Critical Success Factors, it will also be beneficial to identify key measurements on particular '*business or organisation processes*', rather than concentrating solely on departmental, or sectorial measurements.

THE COST OF QUALITY

As an alternative to Critical Success Factors the study of the *Cost of Quality* can provide an initial unification to driving quality improvement in an organisation, and offers a basis for identifying and prioritising projects in a language which can be understood by everyone – that of money. However, it must be realised that while opportunities for improvement can be highlighted by a Cost of Quality exercise, the savings may not always be 'real' money. That is, they are not necessarily directly transferable to the bottom line.

For too long, many organisations have believed that improvements in the quality of services and products were not possible, because the cost of effecting the necessary changes was perceived as being too high. Often, cost of quality is seen as being related only, for example, to areas such as public relations, marketing, inspection, or the laboratory facilities. The *cost of failure*, that is the cost of getting it wrong, has often been overlooked, or at best been implicit within complex accounting procedures. Such cost are frequently accepted as a normal, accepted part of life within the service environment, and are not challenged. Very often performance of the organisation in terms of quality has been reported by means of, for example, customer complaints or having to repeat work, but this *has not been translated into financial terms*.

Quality costs may be defined as the cost of assuring and ensuring quality together with the losses incurred through failure, that is, when quality is not achieved. These costs are categorised by British Standard, BS 6143, Part 2, 1990 as follows:

Appraisal cost

The cost of evaluating the achievement of quality requirements including eg cost of verification and control performed at any stage of the quality loop.

Prevention cost

The cost of any action taken to investigate, prevent or reduce the risk of nonconformity or defect.

Internal failure cost

The costs arising within an organisation due to nonconformities or defects at any stage of the quality loop such as costs of scrap, rework, retest, reinspection and redesign.

External failure cost

The cost arising after delivery to a customer/user due to nonconformities or defects which may include the cost of claims against warranty, replacement and consequential losses and evaluation of penalties incurred.

Once an understanding of the elements of cost of quality has been gained, and the potential areas for measuring cost of quality have been identified, the collection of the information can commence. However, experience has shown that prior to collection of the necessary data it is essential that all those who will be involved in its evaluation should be made aware of the purpose of the exercise. For example it is possible that some managers will see it as just another cost-cutting exercise, and construct defensive barriers with their heads well below the parapet! It must be explained that having obtained the information, the organisation will be seeking continuous improvement, and therefore it is important that all hidden costs of quality are 'put on the table' at this stage. In addition, the use of inappropriate comparisons must be avoided. Understanding of the need, and the process to be adopted will remove the element of fear which can so easily disrupt the whole programme.

Another danger which may be faced in the early stages is the involvement of accountants! While their help will almost certainly be required down track, they could possibly provide the main obstacle to progress. The concept of crude cost guestimates is abhorrent to many accountants. However, the initial aim is to prioritise all actions towards improvement and reduction of Quality Costs, and an accuracy of plus or minus 5 per cent, or even 10 per cent, may be good enough initially. Studies carried out have shown that for many service organisations quality-related costs account for 35 to 40 per cent of turnover. This being the case, for a medium-sized department, this may easily amount to £3 or £4 million, and, therefore, attempts to obtain absolute accuracy are unnecessary.

The approach and the system used for reporting will vary with the needs of each organisation. During the early stages, a rough indication will be sufficient to raise awareness, and motivate management to seek improvements. Many years ago, one of the authors of this book was involved in the early stages of an improvement programme and product rejections were in excess of 20 per cent. At that stage someone remarked that they were in fact, 'working one day a week for nothing, merely putting right what they had got wrong last week'. While a cost of quality analysis followed shortly afterwards, this initial statement was sufficient to make everyone more aware of the problem, something that they had come to accept as part of normal working life.

The system required for the measurement and reporting of quality costs, will depend upon the likelihood of them varying within the short term. Very often, they will only change in the medium term because, for example, failure costs are built into costing systems and will not change unless a different approach is used. The problems which lead to these failure costs are unlikely to be easy to solve; if they were, something would already have been done.

It can also be helpful to commence with the collection and analysis of data which already exists within the organisation. This will avoid the necessity for high additional resources during the early stages, and will facilitate the demonstration to senior management of the value of the exercise, and the necessity for its continuation. Some organisations have found it quite useful to express the total quality cost as a percentage of overall turnover or sales, although this has often been the subject of debate. The differences in operating costs between organisations means that this cannot be entirely used as an appropriate comparative measure. In addition, it takes no account of the range of services or products, complexity, market environment, product or service lifecycle or geographical location.

The intention is, of course, *to reduce quality costs over time*, as illustrated in Figure 3.7. To do this, opportunities need to be identified and prioritised. Prioritising the actions necessary following a cost of quality analysis may be usefully undertaken by a *Pareto analysis*. This might also indicate cost of quality elements which require further, more detailed, measurement.

On summary, three basic reasons for carrying out a Cost of Quality

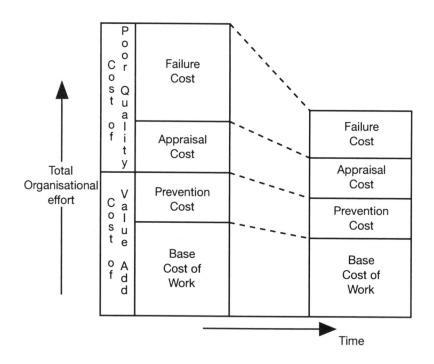

Figure 3.7

Analysis are:

1 It can stimulate senior management's interest in the opportunities offered by a systematic, structured improvement programme.
2 It provides a basis for prioritising projects.
3 It offers an index of internal effectiveness which can be understood by all employees.

It is important to understand that *identification and measurement of Cost of Quality elements, will not, of themselves, effect improvement, but highlight areas for attention.* It will depend on what those areas are, and the causes subsequently identified as to how improvement should be sought. For example, causes of unacceptable Cost of Quality may be inadequate procedures (BS 5750/ISO 9000), poor process design or inadequate control. For this reason, *Cost of Quality is best utilised as a part of an overall improvement strategy, or TQM.* Those involved will then view analysis of costs of quality as a part of the programme, and will be able to put into context the valuable information such an analysis can produce. The organisational culture, or environment, is also an important factor if cost of quality is to be measured and used in a meaningful and effective way, and other initiatives which will be undertaken as part of the TQM initiative will support the positive attitudes and climate necessary.

Removal of such a 'blame' culture is essential if the real potential of a Cost of Quality analysis are to be realised. For example, *it is not unusual for the costs of failure to appear to increase, (at least over the short term), during the commencement of quality improvement programmes.* The reason for this is that as the organisation's understanding increases, further failure costs are identified. Such honesty in recognising the real extent of 'waste' within the organisation is crucial for future progress, and it is crucial to avoid the temptation to hide the reality as unpalatable (particularly for senior management).

KEY ORGANISATIONAL PROCESSES

Having identified the organisation's Critical Success Factors, we need to look at the organisation's key processes in order to ascertain how given targets on the CSFs can be obtained.

But what is a process? Processes can be defined as the mechanism by which inputs are transformed into outputs. Outputs may well include a service, product, paperwork or materials, which differs from the original inputs because we have added value. For example, the generation of a purchase order to a supplier may well involve several different stages or process steps. Each of these stages, typically, will belong to different personnel or different departments and *often no one person within the organisation is responsible for the total process*, other than the senior officer or managing director. Historically, most organisations have been structured on a vertical, departmental or functional model. However, most processes within the organisation flow across the organisation, that is *horizontally*, passing from department to department or person to person. It is not surprising, therefore, that the external customer very often does not receive what was requested. As said earlier, we can liken many business processes to a relay race, with the baton passing from section to section within the organisation. As in a relay race, in real life the problems occur at the changeover points where the baton is dropped.

Identifying key business or organisational processes, the owners of each process and the boundaries of each part of the process are key elements in the full implementation of TQM. There are techniques available to assist with this identification, such as Process Deployment Flow Charting, but these are not the subject of this book. In satisfying this requirement for the clarification and simplification of processes, documented quality management systems such as ISO 9000 may also have a key part to play, but are not in themselves the full answer.

Various types of measurement can be used in relation to processes. *Effectiveness* measures how good is the output from the process. One aspect of this is *accuracy*, ie is it correct or not and how exactly? Others are: *reliability*, ie how many times it is correct? *Timeliness*, it could be correct all the time but always late, and if so by how much? *Volume*, ie it may always be correct and on time, but the customer may perhaps only get half the required volume. Other aspects are *ease of use, completeness, capability* and *efficiency*.

Efficiency tells us how well the resources are utilised. In addition, there is *adaptability*; how well the process can adjust to special requirements or long-term change, for example an environmental condition, ageing or even the ability of staff to change.

While the above aspects of measurement are appropriate at the end of the process, it is more important to use them *at the end of each process stage, internally to the process itself*. This will assist the organisation to ensure early while the process is running that the outcome to the ultimate customer will be satisfactory. Process measurement can also provide *prompt feedback* which gives an individual or department the opportunity to improve or compensate for change while the work is being performed, so that they can immediately correct the parameters within their control. Feeding back information in this way directly into the process also enables savings to be made since, for example, employees (hopefully) do not continue to make errors once detected, and resources are not added to an already effective system.

It is essential that process measurements are taken as close as possible to the source of any potential errors, or shortcomings or control points. Some measurements may be only taken for a short time, for example where a particular parameter or performance level is difficult to measure. This will ensure that disruption to process flow is minimised.

To *identify a process* then, we must look at the provision of service or product to a customer and the steps taken to provide it, we must ask how it is delivered and follow the work flow through the organisation, from first input stage. To *describe a process*, some sort of flow charting is particularly useful or alternatively we can rely on procedure writing such as is usual in quality assurance systems and implementing ISO 9000. To *analyse processes*, we can look at those flow charts, at the exception paths and the boundaries, and all other aspects, in order to identify deficiencies. These may include *'holes' in the process* where certain particular peculiar circumstances can occur, *unnecessary repetitive operations*, clear *organisational inefficiencies*, inherent *lack of customer contact, overcomplicated procedures* of a bureaucratic nature and *lack of ownership*. We can also monitor and measure the processes with a view to an improvement in performance and customer satisfaction.

To put such measurement into place, the crucial thing is that we must have a clear consensus as to why it is necessary and how we are going to do it. Top management must be clearly and visibly behind it, and they must take the trouble to explain to the organisation what it is, why it is being implemented and how.

4

SPECIAL FACTORS IN THE PUBLIC SECTOR

THE PUBLIC SECTOR IS DIFFERENT

While ideas of quality and Total Quality Management (TQM) are as applicable to public administration as to private sector manufacturing and service industry, their application in public administration is typically more problematical. The models of TQM largely evolved and developed in the private sector have focused on customer satisfaction and efficiency in order to ensure profitability. While increasingly we talk in the public sector the language of 'customers', and 'profitability' or at least value for money or financial viability, nevertheless *the private sector models of TQM do not carry across directly into public sector applications*, or indeed into the voluntary sector.

There are many reasons for the difference. For example, typically, the public sector has a fundamentally different style of *culture*. There is a *lack of individual ownership*, or indeed of *responsibility* or *client care*. Allied to this is *a lack of staff empowerment*, with *authority centralised* and perhaps *bureaucratic proceduralisation*.

Bureaucratic and non-responsive systems remain the historical legacy of a different age, reflecting a different need in the public sector. The speed of systems, like speed of life was naturally slower than today's requirement, the acceleration factor which is being applied to private sector systems has not been applied to the same extent yet in the public sector.

Another problem is the lack of clarity about the *multiple customers* and *stakeholders* involved in even single transactions. 'Who is the customer?' remains a major problem in the public sector and confusion abounds. Misuse of the concept of internal customers – so that these are seen as an end in themselves – is probably more common here than even in the private service sector. As well as this, a public administrator may *simultaneously serve various customers* – for example, who is the customer of a school or university – the child, the parent, the future employer etc?

It is also true that the level and extent of service in the public sector is typically not the product of market forces. Political, as opposed to market determined, levels and extent of service, may be seen as service shortfalls by the public, especially for subsidised and zero-priced services.

There are also *problems of scale and complexity* associated with the large centralised organisations – the Ministries and Government Departments. This is particularly true if there is a large-scale technological basis.

The public sector does, however, have a large potential for the development and improvement of its processes and procedures. This chapter explores some of the special factors in the public sector application of TQM and to how these are currently being addressed and to a large extent, overcome.

CHANGE IN THE PUBLIC SECTOR

Change is coming. The process has started and the public sector in the UK at least will never be the same again. As has been said previously, there are many contributory factors to this change process. Foremost perhaps, is the Government policy of market testing and compulsory competitive tendering.

It is the professed policy of Her Majesty's Government to ensure that the services it undertakes are provided and managed so as to give better service to the public and optimum value for money to those who use and pay for them. In recent times, this policy has been implemented by putting certain previously identified functions within a wide range of government activities out to competitive tender. Under this policy, the Government's own departments bid and external bids from the private sector are assessed against the same criteria. This is the policy known as 'market testing'.

On 16 March 1994, the Citizen's Charter Second Report was published. The report detailed the achievements made by departments against their 1992–3 commitments and announced their plans for 1993–4. Between April 1992 and December 1993, the following were among the main achievements:

- £1.1 billion activities have been market tested, or otherwise evaluated to see how best value for money can be achieved.

- Annual savings of £135 million pounds have been generated by under £600 million of the programme – an overall average of 22 per cent. These savings are seen as being repeated each year.
- In over a third of market tests, departments reported that they expected improvements in service quality. In the remainder, quality was maintained usually at a lower cost.
- The private sector had been awarded £855 million work (subject in some cases to continuing negotiations), of which £768 million has been contracted out with no in-house bid.
- In-house teams bid in 229 out of the 389 market tests. In these, they won 68 per cent of the work by value (£189 million).
- The 1993–4 Competing For Quality Programme (October 1993 to September 1994) covers activities valued at £830 million, involving 35,000 staff in addition to the remainder of the 1992–3 programme.

William Waldegrave made the following comments on the report:

> This report is about the Citizen's Charter in Action: About improving services and raising standards over time; whether through the appointment of an independent adjudicator for tax complaints, or through market testing saving the taxpayer money.
>
> Changes are happening where they matter most: in services which people use and rely on every day of their lives and there is more to come; these reforms are now gaining momentum and will bring yet further benefits over time.

The procedure for market testing is reproduced in Chapter 7. The respective Government Departments and Agencies have identified the following activities as services for which they are responsible that could be performed for them by other suppliers. During the market testing year to 30 September 1994, each proposed activity identified is to be exposed to competition, in order that the Government may evaluate whether the private sector is capable of carrying out the undertaking to the same, or indeed an improved standard of quality, while providing better value for money.

Each department's programme for 1993/1994, plus where applicable those activities still to be market tested for their 1992–3 programmes according to the Market Testing Bulletin Magazine are listed below. This list may be added to during the year as departments identify additional activities for market testing:

DEPARTMENTAL MARKET TESTING PROGRAMMES FOR 1993/1994

Department	£m	Staff
Ministry of Defence	216.50	8815
Department of Social Security	130.00	9000
Inland Revenue	103.90	4630
Home Office	70.27	2505
Department of Employment	60.31	1912
Department of Transport	50.00	1512
Department of Health	29.80	350
HM Customs & Excise	39.00	1500
Office of Public Service and Science (inc Central Office of Information, HMSO)	23.70	582
Department of the Environment	20.00	177
Scottish Office	13.60	850
Northern Ireland Civil Service	11.75	740
Ministry of Agriculture, Fisheries and Foods	11.00	80
Department of Trade and Industry	9.60	199
Foreign and Commonwealth Office	8.00	271
Welsh Office	3.40	174
HM Treasury	2.00	37
Department for Education	1.99	93
Overseas Development Administration	1.50	40
Department of National Heritage	0.02	0
Lord Chancellor's Department	0	0
Total	**792.34**	**33467**
Others	**37.90**	**1782**
Grand total	**830.24**	**35249**

There is no doubt that the process of market testing is raising awareness of quality, both in terms of quality of service and of efficiency of systems, to a very high level within the British public sector. So change is happening, but how is total quality being applied in the public sector?

THE APPLICATION OF TQM IN PUBLIC ADMINISTRATION

While the need is great and the origins early, the application of TQM and quality of service in public administration are particularly difficult. There are many reasons for this, one of the foremost is cultural. While increasing public administration is needed to move closer to the 'real world' in terms of financial accountability, management, quality assurance and productivity and effectiveness, nevertheless the history of public administration is one in which staff could be expected to have a job for life, to rise on time served, or perhaps connections, to have little incentive and much disincentive to show ingenuity, new thinking or effective teamwork and above all, not to question the system.

This backdrop is one to which the concept of customer service and TQM, the new imperatives, will seem particularly alien and this could make the process of getting TQM established very difficult. Thus, staff culture, lack of individual ownership of the work of the process of the public administration function, or the customer relationship, together with lack of responsibility and any concept of client-care or staff-empowerment all represent negatives that need to be overcome by the design and implementation of the TQM programme.

The systems themselves in public administration also often tend to be bureaucratic and non-responsive. The lack of the incentive of the marketplace for quick response, flexibility, simplicity and the availability of information on short timescales means that introducing these requirements as needs within a TQM programme is once again a big step. Bureaucracy and non-responsive systems are not just in themselves the opposite of what we are trying to achieve within TQM, they also hinder its introduction and its development and slow its progress.

Even where there is the will to transform public administration towards a TQM culture system and management style, technical problems still remain due to the nature of the TQM models currently in general use. Such models need adaption for the application in the public sector. A major orientation of most TQM models is the predominance of the *customer* in the purpose of the organisation and its infrastructure. In public administration this *single customer focus* is not so clear; it is not just there are multiple types of customers, but rather *there are multiple customers and stakeholders involved in even single transactions.* For example when a police officer arrests a potential criminal, is the officer's customer the criminal, the victim, the witnesses, the courts, the Home Office or the community?

Public service organisations have attempted to solve this technical difficulty of the concept of TQM by the introduction of the *stakeholder* concept. Stakeholder models can now be found in many aspects of public administration and public service worldwide, for example the Royal Mail identify their stakeholder as customers, employees, shareholders and the community, while East Midlands Electricity also add suppliers to the list.

The problem however is that these generic stakeholder groups can tend to be somewhat unfocused in themselves. The community is by its nature a very large and inhomogeneous group, with divergent opinions on divergent issues. Lack of focus is what we are trying to avoid with TQM and market testing and so much has to be done in the attempt to clarify. Even where this is done, down at the operational level in the process of public administration, there may still be a problem. Staff have to have very clear priorities in their relations to the various stakeholder groups so that the organisation can be focused towards their various purposes for existing in the right proportion. This requires clear policy from the top, as well as clear staff understanding and discussion at all levels.

Another problem is that in public administration the market itself does not determine the level and extent of service, at least not in all cases. Decisions may be taken at a political level and broadly there may be no limit to the demand for a zero price, or subsidised service. This then creates shortfalls in the availability in service provision which appear to the consumer/customer as inefficiencies. The consequence is that confusion can remain in the customer's mind – the public – between productivity and quality. This problem is in-built into the nature of public administration and represents a particular challenge for the staff involved.

Yet another problem is that public administration may necessitate large centralised organisations with associated complexity and problems of scale, combined with a bureaucratic management style. This implies that most employees will be a *long way from the customer*. Even frontline employees suffer, since they are a *long way from decision making* and are themselves at the mercy of the internal systems. Such problems may be exacerbated if the organisation has a large scale technological basis (such as perhaps as existed in nationalised power provision), or dependence upon a major computer system (such as perhaps as in tax collection).

STRATEGIES FOR SUCCESS IN THE PUBLIC SECTOR

As indicated previously, the potential problems of implementation of a TQM programme within the organisational structure of public administration are many. The following examines some of the strategies for success, as well as looking at how the public sector as a whole has responded to this challenge.

As in the private sector, TQM should become part of the *'real work'* of a public sector Department or Unit as early as possible. Senior management must realise that TQM cannot be delegated and that it is sensible for a Steering Group of the most senior managers to be set up at Departmental/Agency level to facilitate the transformation in the organisation. Ideally this should be chaired by the most senior officer. For it is only in this way that TQM can become part of the overall job. The Steering Group will be able to identify and focus on the mission of the organisation, the stakeholder groups, the intrinsic values and their purpose for existing. The whole of the workforce should be involved in the quality improvement process, but it should commence 'top-down' before returning 'bottom-up'. While employee training will be necessary two important aspects should be taken into consideration.

First, middle managers should be adequately prepared for the change in behaviour, and indeed of attitudes, which will be expected and required of them for the programme to be successful. Second, as indicated in Chapter 3, cascade training is preferable to 'wall-to-wall indoctrination'.

In cascade training, the members of the Quality Steering Group themselves explain to their own direct reports the new focus and what the TQM programme is about, what they are intending to do in their own area and perhaps come up with suggestions as to what their direct reports may wish to do and to ask for their opinions. At each level down the hierarchy the same process is repeated; each manager explaining to his own direct reports what it is all about and discussing how it may be implemented within their employee's area and what might be tackled first. With this system, each employee can put TQM in the context of his own job, which is typically not the reality with 'wall-to-wall' training. It also dramatically reduces the amount of help that the public administrator would need from outside consultants, though it is conventional for consultants to assist in the preparation of materials for cascade training and in the nature of the programme. Such assistance by experienced consultants is extremely important; and to this end the consultant may temporarily join the Steering Group.

A systematic approach to the quantification of quality improvement within public administration is also highly desirable, since otherwise the programme can be unfocused. As indicated in Chapter 3 this may be initially undertaken by a Cost of Quality approach, or subsequently by the development of Critical Success Factors. Both systems represent a unified approach to measurement whether by looking at all the money that is wasted by doing things wrong and the prevention costs involved, or in the case of Critical Success Factors, identifying the small group of (preferably less than eight) Critical Success Factors on which the progress of the organisation and its mission will be judged. These measures then provide a yardstick for improvement activities lower down in the organisation. Priority activities are those which impact on the measures most heavily.

Typical Critical Success Factors in the public sector include *end-to-end measures* as utilised by the Royal Mail and the Benefits Agency, as well as other *non-financial measures* associated with *customer or stakeholder satisfaction*. These are additional to the conventional financial measures associated perhaps with *return on investment, cost control and cash flow*.

Targets may be set on the Critical Success Factors against time and the improvements in these will be delivered by focusing on the fundamental business or organisational processes which are behind the public administrator's activities. Process mapping may be highly beneficial as well as the application of technique such as Quality Function Deployment (QFD) to help focus the internal business processes to meeting the customers' and other stakeholders' requirements.

5

IMPLEMENTATION IN THE PUBLIC SECTOR – THE US EXPERIENCE

THE US NAVY AND THE ORIGINS OF TQM

It appears that the origins of what is known today as Total Quality Management (TQM) can be traced to the US Navy in the early 1980s when the Navy Personnel Research & Development Center carried out research to ascertain whether a total quality approach could be applied to Navy industrial commands. Quite significantly, it was also at this time that the Naval Air Rework Facilities were experiencing difficulties in competing with private contractors both in terms of quality and cost of aircraft maintenance and rework.

In 1984, a demonstration project commenced at the Naval Air Depot (California) and by 1985 the project developed further to include all Naval Aviation Depots, as well as the Naval Air Systems Command. It was the Naval Air Systems Command working in conjunction with the Navy Personnel Research and Development Center, who are associated with 'coining' the term Total Quality Management to describe their Japanese-based approach to quality improvement. In 1986, the Department of Defense (DOD) published a position paper on the subject, and in 1988 a statement was issued by the Secretary of Defense effectively establishing the Department's commitment to the principles of quality management.

Yet in spite of this 'history', it is surprising to learn that it has only been over the past five years that senior elected officials and top Civil Servants within US Federal Government agencies have begun to develop a TQM focus, whereby an environment exists which not only sustains, but actively encourages TQM, and is seen to be a driving influence throughout Federal Government.

FACTORS INFLUENCING THE GROWTH OF TQM IN US FEDERAL GOVERNMENT

TQM would not exist in any organisation, whether private or public, without commitment from the top, and the facilitation of an environment which actively encourages its implementation. Amongst some of the more important factors which actively contribute to the growth and awareness of TQM in US Federal Government are; legislation, the Federal Quality Institute and recognition for the successful implementation of TQM within Federal agencies through Federal Quality Awards.

Legislation

One factor that, by its very nature cannot be ignored, is the impact that legislation has had upon the implementation of TQM programmes within Federal agencies. Not only does it set down an explicit set of guidelines – it sets down an explicit set of guidelines for the implementation of TQM that have to be adhered to by Federal agencies.

The 'Productivity Improvement Program for the Federal Government', was signed by President Reagan on 27 April 1988. Section 3 of that Order imposes clear guidelines on managers for the introduction of quality programmes within their organisations, whereby managers should:

- inform agency managers and employees that they are expected to be responsible for improvements in the quality, timeliness, and efficiency of services;
- include productivity and quality improvement goals in the performance appraisals of managers and supervisors; and
- encourage employee participation in the productivity program through employee training, employee involvement in work-related decision, incentives, recognition, and rewards and by taking actions to minimise negative impacts that may occur as a result of the productivity program.

It does not stop here, in 1993 further legislation was introduced. The Government Performance and Results Act of 1993 (PL103–62) requires Federal agencies to, 'plan strategically, develop goals that are outcome-focused, consult with their customers when developing their strategic plans, and develop performance plans that look to intended results, and not just inputs and outputs' (Federal Quality

News, Aug–Sept 1993). The main features of this legislation are being piloted, at time of writing, in phases by a few agencies commencing in fiscal year 1994.

The principal areas that the Act will affect are strategic plans, performance plans and reports of all Federal Agencies. Agencies will be required to submit a five-year plan to the Office of Management & Budget (OMB); including a mission statement with outcome related goals and objectives together with a description of how these goals and objectives will be achieved, how performance goals are related, and how evaluations will be carried out.

Federal agencies will also have to submit annual performance plans to OMB. Their plans will have to include measurable performance goals and must describe what is required to meet the goals, performance indicators, and a basis for comparing and measuring results against goals. Finally, agencies will have to submit a report to the President and Congress on programme performance for the previous fiscal year by 31 March 2000.

Certain features of the 1993 Act are being piloted by selected agencies as follows:

1994   Up to ten agencies will test three-year projects in performance measurement and reporting.

1995   Up to five agencies will test managerial accountability with administrative waivers.

1998   Up to five agencies will test performance budgeting, which is not in the Act.

Any amendments to the legislation will be made by the Director of OMB by 1997 based on the first two sets of pilots, and recommend whether or not to adopt performance budgeting after the third set of pilots.

The Federal Quality Institute (FQI)

The Federal Quality Institute (FQI) plays a major role by facilitating a practical working environment within which TQM is able to take a major and strategic position within Federal agencies.

The FQI was established in 1988, by the Reagan administration for the promotion of TQM in the Federal Government. It is staffed by approximately 20 senior individuals who are 'lent' to the FQI by their Departments for one or two years. These individuals come from the top career bands in the US government service, and are chosen for both their knowledge and support of TQM in Federal Government organisations. The FQI is directed by a board of senior federal departmental officials.

Upon its foundation the aims of the FQI were laid down as follows:

1 To introduce senior officials to the concepts of TQM.
2 To establish a vehicle to help agencies contract for TQM implementation services in a timely manner.
3 To provide information on quality management through its Resource Center.

The FQI has developed a variety of channels through which it fulfills the above criteria including:

- **awareness seminars** whereby senior managers are given a working familiarity with managing Total Quality, by demonstrating some of the key concepts and approaches that successful practitioners have adopted;
- **startup services** whereby Federal agencies are helped to implement quality management by bringing it to the point at which informed decisions can be made on the overall direction and key strategies.
- **quality awards**, the FQI administers two awards – The President's Award for Quality and the Quality Improvement Prototype Award (QIP). The awards are instrumental in disseminating information about the implementation of TQM; the winners act as models for the rest of the government by preparing videotapes and case studies. In addition to which they also present workshops about their organisational experiences. (The Federal Quality Awards will be discussed in more detail later in the chapter.)

The Institute also operates in partnership with the National Technical Information Service. This is an information network which includes a centralised data base of documents and information on TQM for Federal Agencies. Even though the information service is wholly dependent upon Federal Agencies themselves providing the documentary input, it remains a useful source of information.

THE FEDERAL QUALITY AWARDS

The Federal Quality Awards represent a recognised standard of excellence for the achievement of TQM by Federal agencies. They also act as a channel for disseminating information to other Federal organisations. Prior to 1995 two awards will be administered by the FQI after this time the awards will be amalgamated. The two awards, The President's Award for Quality and Productivity Improvement and The Quality Improvement Prototype award, are given on an annual basis.

Principles upon which the awards are based

The criteria of both awards illustrate the key concepts of quality management within Federal Agencies. These have been identified by the Federal Quality Institute as follows:

- quality is defined by the customer;
- a focus on continuous improvement is part of all operations and activities;
- prevention of problems and waste is achieved through building quality into products, services, and processes;
- success in meeting quality and performance goals depends on workforce quality and involvement;
- senior management creates a customer orientation, clear and visible quality values, and high expectations;
- reinforcement of values and expectations requires substantial personal commitment and involvement;
- employees are valued and recognised for their involvement and accomplishments;
- management decisions are made based upon reliable information, data and analysis;
- long-term commitments are made to customers, employees, suppliers, and the community;
- public responsibilities are fulfilled; and
- partnerships are built with other agencies and the private sector, to better accomplish overall goals.

PRESIDENTIAL AWARD FOR QUALITY

The Presidents Award for Quality was established in 1988 to;

> . . . recognise organizations that have implemented total quality manage-

ment (TQM) in an exemplary manner, resulting in high quality products and services and the effective use of taxpayer dollars, and to promote TQM awareness and implementation throughout the federal government. (Presidential Award for Quality 1994 Application The Federal Quality Institute.)

The award is given to as many as two organisations each year.

The Federal Quality Institute's Handbook identifies seven key factors which determine the success of quality efforts. These are:

1 Top management support.
2 Customer focus.
3 Long-term strategic planning.
4 Employee training and recognition.
5 Employee empowerment and teamwork.
6 Measurement.
7 Quality Assurance.

These seven key factors provide the basis for the criteria and scoring guidelines, and are used to judge federal organisations applying for the President's Award for Quality. The criteria also reflects elements of criteria set down by the US Malcolm Baldrige National Quality Award, and the Japanese Deming Prize.

Eligibility

Eligibility is dependent upon the maturity of the quality effort of the organisation which should be at least three to six years. Applying organisations must also meet the following criteria:

- they must be a part of the Federal Government;
- have no fewer than 500 full-time federal employees – and be autonomous with its own defined mission;
- provide products or services to the American public (with the exception of the Department of Defense organisations, whose primary customers are frequently other military organisations).

Administrative and or support organisations are not eligible to apply.

Each Department and executive agency may submit a maximum number of applications for the Presidential Award, dependent upon its size:

(i) Up to 50,000 employees – two applications.
(ii) Up to 95,000 employees – three applications.
(iii) Over 95,000 employees – four applications.

(iv)   Department of Defense may submit a maximum of three applications for each service (Army, Navy, and Air Force), and a total
of three additional applications for the other defence agencies.

Winners of the Presidential Award, may not reapply for four subsequent years, and an organisation may not apply for both the Quality
Improvement Prototype Award and the Presidential Award in the same
year.

Individual scoring categories

The individual scoring categories for the 1994 Presidential Award for
Quality are as follows:

- Leadership (125 points).
- Information and analysis (75 points).
- Strategic quality planning (60 points).
- Human resource development and management (170 points).
- Management of process quality (140 points).
- Quality and operational results (180 points).
- Customer focus and satisfaction (250 points).

A more detailed account of the criteria is laid down in Appendix I.

PRESIDENTIAL QUALITY AWARD WINNERS –
CASE STUDIES

Among the organisations that have received the award are the Naval
Air Systems Command, the Air Force Logistics Command and the
Internal Revenue Service (IRS) Ogden Service Center. The achieve-
ments of some of the winners as featured in an article by Karen
Benowski in Quality Progress, December 1993, are dealt with briefly
below.

The **Naval Air Systems Command** won the award in 1989. The
command acquires, develops and supports naval aeronautical and
related technology systems for naval operating forces. A quality initiative began in 1984 when some of the naval aviation depots in the command implemented quality improvement projects. A consequence of
this was the introduction of a command-wide quality programme in
1988. TQM has now become embedded in both their short- and long-
term strategic plans.

The **Air Force Logistics Command** won the award in 1991. By

1992 the Air Force Logistics Command and Air Force Systems Command joined forces to become the Air Force Material Command (AFMC). This body is responsible for researching, developing, testing, acquiring, delivering and logistically supporting Air Force weapon systems. The AFMC has a long history of quality; starting in the 1970s when Quality Circles were introduced. In 1987 a more structured approach was taken and the command embraced the TQM philosophy, naming the effort, 'QP4'; Quality is People, Process, Performance, and Product. Today their quality initiative is referred to as the Quality Air Force initiative, and as part of this initiative the command's headquarters and each of its 16 centres have completed a full self-assessment using the Baldrige Award criteria.

In 1992 the **Internal Revenue Service (IRS) Ogden Service Center** was the first civilian organisation to receive the award. The Center is responsible for processing functions such as answering taxpayers' inquiries and solving their problems. The senior management at the center were introduced to quality in 1984 and not long after this quality principles were introduced throughout the center by its Total Quality Organization effort.

THE QUALITY IMPROVEMENT PROTOTYPE AWARD (QIP)

The Quality Improvement Prototype Award (QIP) is designed for organisations that have recently begun the quality transformation process. Although some of the concepts illustrated by this award correspond quite closely to those of the President's Award, and will merge, after 1995 with the criteria set down by the Presidential Award for Quality it will still be useful to look at the award criteria and the organisations that have received the award. One of the fundamental differences between this award and the Presidential Award for Quality is that it does not incorporate some of the more advanced concepts of quality, which are required by the President's Award. Up to six awards may be given in one year.

Eligibility

Applying organisations must meet the following criteria:

- be a part of the Federal Government;
- have no fewer than 100 full time, Federal employees;

- be autonomous, with its own defined mission;
- provide products of services to customers outside the organisation's own agency (except for Department of Defense organisations, whose primary customers are often military organisations); and
- provide mission related services or products.

Each Department and executive agency may submit a maximum number of applications for the QIP Award, according to its size. The following guidelines have been set down;

(i)   Up to 20,000 employees – two applications
(ii)   Up to 50,000 employees – three applications
(iii)   Up to 95,000 employees – five applications
(iv)   Department of Defense may submit a maximum of five applications for each service (Army, Navy and Air Force), and a total of four applications for the other defence agencies.

The criteria for the QIP Award embody the same key concepts of quality management which have previously been listed for the President's Award, however, the individual scoring categories do differ.

Individual Scoring Categories

The individual scoring categories for the Quality Improvement Prototype Award are as follows:

- Top management leadership and support (20 points).
- Strategic quality planning (15 points).
- Customer focus (35 points).
- Training (10 points) and recognition (5 points).
- Employee empowerment and teamwork (20 points).
- Measurement and analysis (15 points).
- Quality assurance (30 points).
- Quality and productivity improvement results (50 points).

A more detailed account of the criteria for the 1994 Quality Improvement Prototype Award is laid down in Appendix I.

QUALITY IMPROVEMENT PROTOTYPE AWARD
WINNERS – CASE STUDIES

Among the organisations to receive the award are; the Arnold Engineering Development Center (AECD), Arnold Air Force Base, Tennessee, the Naval Aviation Depot, Cherry Point, North Carolina, the Aeronautical Systems Division, Air Force systems Command, Wright-Patterson Air Force Base, Ohio and Public Services and Administration, Patent and Trademark Office, Department of Commerce. Some of these organisations and their achievements, based on information provided by the FQI, are discussed briefly below.

In 1989 and 1992 the **Naval Aviation Depot** won the award. By introducing a quality initiative they have increased their market share of aircraft maintenance work from $249 million in 1988 to more than $400 million. Since 1988, they have also realised $185 million in savings and cost avoidance.

In 1992 the **Public Services and Administration, Patent and Trademark Office, Department of Commerce** won the award. By implementing a quality programme they managed to reduce the in-process error rate of filing receipts by over half. Other achievements have been decreasing the response rate of mailing filing receipts to applicants from 38 to 18 days, and increasing the incoming document productivity by 63 per cent over four years and in so doing saved $1m.

The **Arnold Engineering Development Center (AECD), Arnold Air Force Base**, Tennessee won the award in 1993. Their workforce of 3,500 is made up of approximately 400 Federal employees. The center comprises of the following structural elements; military, civilian and three private sector support contractors. There are 250 center teams that have worked on quality improvement and planning and accomplishments have included savings to customers of more than $7.8 million in two years by increasing their efficiency.

OBSTACLES TO TQM IN US FEDERAL GOVERNMENT

Federal Government Agencies are still faced with problems that represent obstacles to the implementation of TQM. Some of these were reflected in a survey carried out by Coopers & Lybrand in 1989 of some 602 federal executives which indicated that although there was widespread acceptance of, and familiarity with modern quality management, there was evidence of problems and missed opportunities. Barely half of the respondents were measuring customer satisfaction, and about one third had no plans to do so. Many middle managers saw TQM, at best, as additional work, and at worst as a threat. Other obstacles were considered to consist of the lack of dependable ways to measure quality, and a deeply ingrained sense of the way things have always been done. (Total Quality Management: the USA & UK Compared, Public Money & Management October–December 1992, John Brockman).

Such problems are reflected upon further by a former Director of the Federal Quality Institute in the October 1992 (Vol. XIV. No. 3) issue of Looking Ahead, a quarterly publication of the National Planning Association in Washington DC. as follows:

> The discipline of a competitive global market place that provides incentives for radical change to business and industry managers is missing in government;
>
> With the average tenure of government's top executives (presidential appointees) around 18 months, federal agencies have difficulty maintaining the integrity of long-range change efforts;
>
> Centralized and sometimes restrictive control of federal administrative support system–procurement, personal auditing, space, information, and finance–create extra layers and limited agencies ability to be flexible and responsive;
>
> The division of responsibility between executive and legislative branches requires endless negotiation and coalition-building around budget, legislation and regulations, deflecting attention from service delivery considerations.

In spite of these problems, however, Federal organisations do have an exceptionally good framework for the facilitation and implementation of TQM. A fact which is underlined by the role played by the Federal Quality Institute, the emphasis on recognised awards for quality achievements and finally, the knowledge that there is a legally binding obligation to implement the principles of TQM.

APPENDIX I

PRESIDENTIAL AWARD FOR QUALITY

1994 AWARD CRITERIA

CATEGORY

POINTS

1 LEADERSHIP
125

Leadership examines executives' personal commitment and involvement in creating and sustaining an organizational vision and customer focus orientation, as well as clear and visible quality values. It also examines how the vision, values, and customer focus orientation integrated into the management system, labor relations and external partnerships, and are reflected in the way public responsibilities are addressed.

1.1 Executive Leadership

a. Describe executives' commitment, personal involvement and visibility in quality related activities. Include:
   (i) reinforcing customer focus
   (ii) creating an organizational vision, quality values and setting expectations
   (iii) planning and reviewing progress toward quality and operational performance improvement goals
   (iv) recognizing employee contributions
   (v) communicating quality values outside and throughout the organization.
b. Provide a brief summary of the organization's vision, quality values and customer focus policy.
c. Describe how executives regularly communicate and reinforce the vision, quality values and customer focus orientation with managers and supervisors.

1.2 Managing for Quality

a. Describe how the organization's vision quality values, and customer focus orientation are translated into requirements for all managers and supervisors.
b. Summarize the principal roles and responsibilities of managers and supervisors within their units, and how co-operation with other units is fostered.

c. Describe how the vision, quality values and customer focus orientation are communicated and reinforced throughout the organization.
d. Describe how performance is reviewed with regard to quality and operational performance improvement plans, and how work units that are not performing according to plan are assisted.
e. Describe how mutual involvement with union leadership is addressed in the implementation of quality values and customer focus.
f. Describe how the organization partners with customer organizations, contractors, suppliers and other external organizations, and how your organization and its partners work toward common goals.

1.3   Public Responsibility and Community Citizenship

a. Describe how public responsibilities are integrated into quality policies and improvement practices.
b. Explain how citizenship responsibilities in key communities are fulfilled.

POINTS

2   INFORMATION AND ANALYSIS   75

Information and Analysis examines the scope, management, and use of data, information and measures, and how they are used to drive quality and operational performance improvement. It also examines the adequacy of the organization's data, information, and analysis system to support improvement of customer satisfaction, products, services and processes.

2.1   Scope and Management of Quality and Performance Data and Information

a. Describe the criteria for developing measures, selecting data and information for use in quality and operational performance improvement (eg, cycle time, productivity, waste reduction).
b. List key types of data and information used and briefly outline the principal purposes of each in improving quality and operational performance. Describe how measures relate to plans and goals as described in Element 3.
c. Explain how reliability, consistency, validity and ready access to data are assured.

2.2   Similar Provider Comparisons and Benchmarking

a. Describe how benchmark data and comparisons with similar providers are used to help drive improvement of quality and operational performance improvement.
b. Provide a brief summary of the current scope and principal uses of

various types of comparative and benchmark data, including product and service quality, business processes and support services (eg finance and accounting, information services, public affairs, procurement, facilities management, administrative services), employee-related activities, and supplier-related activities.

2.3 Analysis and Uses of Organization-Level Data

a. Describe how quality and customer data are aggregated with other key data, analyzed and translated into actionable information to: resolve customer-related problems and determine key customer-related trends to support reviews, decision making, and longer-term planning.
b. Describe how operational performance are aggregated with other key data, analyzed and translated into actionable information to: make short-term improvements in organization operations; and determine key operational trends to support reviews, decision making and longer-term planning.

POINTS

3 STRATEGIC QUALITY PLANNING 60

Strategic Quality Planning examines the organization's planning process, and how key quality improvements are integrated into overall planning. Both the organization's short- and longer-term plans are examined, as well as how quality and operational performance improvement goals are deployed to all work units.

3.1 Quality and Operational Performance Planning Process

a. Describe how strategies, plans and goals are developed to address quality (including customer focus and satisfaction) and operational performance improvement for the short-term (one to two years) and longer-term (three years or more). Describe how plans consider:

(i) customer requirements and expected evolution of these requirements
(ii) capabilities (including human resource development) to address key requirements or technological opportunities
(iii) supplier capabilities
(iv) realigning work processes to improve operational performance
(v) productivity improvement and reduction of waste
(vi) performance of similar providers. Describe how plans are aligned with the vision, values, and customer focus orientation described in Element 1.

b. Explain how plans are deployed to all work units, suppliers and key partners, and how resources are committed to meet the plan requirements.

c. Describe how the planning process is improved.

3.2   Quality and Operational Performance Plans

a. Outline both the organization's principal short- and longer-term quality (including customer focus and satisfaction) and operational performance improvement plans and goals. Include: a summary of key requirements as key operational performance indicators deployed to work units, suppliers, and key partners; a brief description of resources committed for key needs (eg capital equipment, facilities, education and training, and personnel).
b. Provide a two to five year projection of the most important quality and operational performance improvement indicators.

POINTS

4   HUMAN RESOURCE DEVELOPMENT AND MANAGEMENT   170

Human Resource Development and Management examines how the entire workforce is enabled to develop its full potential, and to pursue quality and operational performance improvement goals. It also examines efforts to build and maintain an environment for workforce excellence, which is conducive to increased involvement, personal and organizational development.

4.1   Human Resource Planning and Management

a. Briefly outline the key elements of the organization's HR plan for:

   (i)   employee involvement
   (ii)   education and training
   (iii)   workforce mobility and diversity
   (iv)   organization re-structuring and work re-design
   (v)   rewards or recognition, or compensation
   (vi)   performance management and feedback. Explain how these elements are integrated with the overall quality and operational performance improvement plans and goals, as described in Element 3.
b. Describe how HR operations and practices are improved.

4.2   Employee Involvement

a. Describe the types of involvement mechanisms available for all individuals and groups (employees and managers), and how they contribute to the organization's quality and operational performance improvement goals.
b. Explain how the organization increases employee involvement. Explain how an environment is created that supports increased empowerment, personal responsibility, and risk-taking; and how such an environment fosters creativity and innovation.
c. Describe the key methods and indicators used to evaluate the effectiveness and extent of involvement. Provide trend data (three to six years) for the

most important indicators of the effectiveness and extent of workforce involvement, across the spectrum of grade levels and types of employees.

4.3 Employee Education and Training

a. Explain how employees' needs for quality and related education and training are determined (including how employee input is used), and how these needs are integrated with the organization's quality and operational performance improvement plans.
b. Briefly describe the types of quality and related education and training provided for the entire workforce, and how they are delivered and reinforced.
c. Describe the key methods and indicators used to evaluate the effectiveness and extent of quality and related education and training. Provide trend data (three to six years) for key indicators of the effectiveness and extent of education and training, across the spectrum of grade levels and types of employees.

4.4 Employee Performance and Recognition

a. Describe the organization's approaches to employee performance, feedback, reward and recognition, and how they support the attainment of quality and operational performance improvement goals.
b. Describe the key methods and indicators used to evaluate the effectiveness and extent of employee performance, feedback, reward, and recognition. Provide trend data (three to six years) for key indicators of the effectiveness and extent of reward and recognition activities, across the spectrum of grade levels and types of employees.

4.5 Employee Well-Being and Satisfaction

a. Explain how special services and employee opportunities (eg, flexible work hours, counselling) and well-being factors (eg, health, safety, ergonomics, other environmental considerations) are included in quality improvement activities.
b. Provide trend data (three to six years) for key indicators of employee well-being and satisfaction.

POINTS

5 MANAGEMENT OF PROCESS QUALITY 140

Management of Process Quality examines the systematic process used by the organization for continuous improvement of quality and operational performance improvement. It also examines design and management of process quality for all work units, the management of internal customer-supplier relationships, supplier and intermediary quality, and quality assessment.

5.1 Design and Introduction of Quality Products and Services

a. Describe how new and/or improved products and services are designed and introduced to meet or exceed customer requirements (as described in Element 7). Describe how processes are designed to produce and deliver products and services, and how measurement systems are developed to track process performance.
b. Explain how designs are reviewed and validated, taking into account product and service performance, process capability, and supplier and intermediary capability.

5.2 Process Management: Product and Service Production and Delivery Processes

a. Describe how key production and delivery processes are managed to meet product and service design requirements.
b. Describe how the internal customer–supplier relationship is managed so that requirements and expectations for production and delivery processes are understood and met. Include an explanation of how feedback and complaints are obtained and used, and how information and assistance are made readily available.
c. Explain how root causes are determined for significant variations in processes or outputs, and how corrections are made and verified.

5.3 Process Management: Business Processes and Support Services

a, Describe how key business processes and support services (eg, finance and accounting information services, public affairs, procurement, facilities management, administrative services) are managed to meet customer and/or organization quality and operational performance requirements.
b. Describe how the internal customer–supplier relationship is managed so that requirements and expectations for business processes and support services are understood and met. Include an explanation of how feedback and complaints are obtained and used, and how information and assistance are made readily available.
c. Explain how root causes are determined for significant variations in processes or outputs, and how corrections are made and verified.

5.4 Supplier and Intermediary Quality

a. Describe how the organization defines quality requirements and selects suppliers based on these requirements; explain how requirements are communicated to suppliers and/or intermediaries (those groups used to reach the organization's ultimate customers). Include a brief summary of the principal quality requirements for key suppliers and/or intermediaries, and the key indicators used to evaluate their quality.

b. Describe the methods used to assure that quality requirements are met by suppliers and/or intermediaries.

5.5   Quality Assessment

a. Describe how the organization assesses the quality and performance of its key systems, processes, and practices and the quality of its key products and services.
b. Explain how assessment findings are used to improve key products and services, systems, processes, practices, and quality requirements for suppliers and intermediaries.

POINTS

6   QUALITY AND OPERATIONAL RESULTS   180

Quality and Operational Results examines the organization's trends and quality levels for products and services, operational performance, business processes and support services, supplier and intermediary quality, and comparison/benchmark data.

6.1   Product and Service Quality Results

a. Provide trend data (three to six years) and current levels for key measures of product and service quality, as described in Element 2.
b. Provide current quality level comparisons with appropriate benchmarks, as described in Element 2.

6.2   Operational Performance Results

a. Provide trend data (three to six years) and current levels for key measures of operational performance, as described in Element 2.
b. Provide current operational performance level comparisons with appropriate benchmarks, as described in Element 2.

6.3   Business Process and Support Service Results

a. Provide data (three to six years) and current levels for key performance measures of business processes and support services, as described in Element 2.
b. Provide current performance level comparisons of business processes and support services with appropriate benchmarks, as described in Element 2.

6.4   Supplier and Intermediary Quality Results

a. Provide trend data (three to six years) and current levels for the most important quality indicators of key suppliers and intermediaries.

7   CUSTOMER FOCUS AND SATISFACTION

Customer Focus and Satisfaction examines the organization's knowledge of external customer requirements, and how relationships with customers are established and maintained. It also examines the methods used to determine customer satisfaction, and the trends and current levels of customer satisfaction.

7.1   Customer Expectations: Current and Future

a.   Describe how the organization determines current and future requirements and expectations of customers. Describe how customer groups are determined; and the process for collecting information (eg, what information is sought, how often, methods used). Explain how this is shared with relevant employees.

b.   Describe how the process for determining customer needs and expectations are improved.

7.2   Customer Relationship Management

a.   Summarize key requirements for maintaining and building relationships around key processes and transactions that bring employees into contact with customers. Explain how key quality indicators are derived from these requirements.

b.   Describe service standards derived from the quality indicators addressed in 7.2a. Explain how these standards are deployed to all relevant employees, and how they are tracked.

c.   Explain how the organization follows up with customers on products, services and recent transactions to seek feedback and to help build relationships.

d.   Describe how the organization follows up with customers or products, services and recent transactions to seek feedback and to help build relationships.

e.   Describe how formal and informal customer complaints and feedback received are aggregated for overall evaluation and used through out the organization. Describe how complaints and problems are resolved promptly and effectively.

7.3   Commitment to Customers

a.   Describe the types of commitments that are made to promote trust and confidence in products, services and relationships, and how these commitments are communicated to external customers.

7.4 Determination of Customer Satisfaction

a. Describe how customer satisfaction is determined, including the methods, processes and measures used, and their frequency. Measures of customer dissatisfaction may also be described.
b. Describe how the methods, processes, and measures used to determine customer satisfaction are improved.

7.5 Customer Satisfaction Results

a. Provide trend data (three to six years) and current levels of external customer satisfaction or dissatisfaction (eg, complaints, claims, repeat service or litigation, official telephone calls or letters of inquiry).

7.6 Customer Satisfaction Comparison

a. Compare customer satisfaction results directly with those of similar providers or using information such as service awards, recognition/ratings by other organizations, surveys, etc.

QUALITY IMPROVEMENT PROTOTYPE AWARD

1994 AWARD CRITERIA

CATEGORY

POINTS

1 TOP MANAGEMENT LEADERSHIP AND SUPPORT   20

This category examines how all levels of senior management create and sustain a clear and visible quality value system along with a supporting management system to guide all activities of the organization.

a. Describe the roles of the key executives (head of applicant organization and senior managers) in quality management activities. Include specific examples of sustained, visible and personal involvement in the development of an effective quality culture.
b. Summarize the organization's policy on quality and describe how 'ownership' of the policy by senior management was accomplished and how it is reinforced. Include key strategies used to involve all levels of management and supervision in quality.
c. Describe how senior management communicates its quality vision to all levels, functional units, and employees. Include recent actions that demonstrate the importance of quality values to the organization.
d. Describe how management has established a value system and environment in which individuals and group actions reflect a continuous improvement attitude. Include actions taken to evaluate the extent to which quality values have been adopted throughout the organization.
e. Describe specific steps senior management takes to create close co-operation across functional and divisional lines and in different locations to ensure consistent quality improvement throughout the organization.
f. Describe how senior management seeks and obtains the support, co-operation, and participation of the organization's union (if applicable).
g. Describe how the organization's quality policies and improvement efforts reflect its commitment to public health and safety, environmental protection and ethical conduct.

POINTS

2 STRATEGIC QUALITY PLANNING   15

This category examines the organization's quality planning process, quality plans, and how all key quality requirements are integrated into overall planning.

a. Indicate whether operational (one–two year) and strategic (three–five year) goals and objectives for quality improvement exist across the organization that relate directly to the organization's mission, and to the vision and values described in Element 1. Give examples of the most important goals and objectives.

Note: In Element 6 you will describe the measures associated with organizational goals and objectives, and in Element 8 the results achieved relative to these goals and objectives.

b. Give specific plans for quality improvement relating to the most important goals and objectives described in sub-element a.

c. Describe the process used to establish operational and strategic quality improvement goals, and how goals and objectives are integrated into organization-wide planning and budgeting process. Describe how quality improvement plans are implemented and managed on a routine operational basis.

d. Describe how employees, customers, and suppliers participate in the planning process.

e. Describe the principal types of data, information and analysis used in planning, such as customer requirements, process capabilities, supplier data and benchmark data.

POINTS

3   CUSTOMER FOCUS   35

This category examines the organization's overall customer service systems, knowledge of internal and external customers, responsiveness and ability to meet requirements and expectations.

a. Describe the methods used to obtain a knowledge of external customer requirements and expectations, how this information is shared with relevant employees and how the employees use it.

b. Describe the methods used to identify internal customers, determine their requirements, and how this information is shared with employees and how the employees use it.

c. Describe internal and external customer feedback systems, including procedures for handling customer complaints, and how feedback information is used to improve products and services.

d. Describe the organization's service standards derived from internal and external customer requirements and expectations. Indicate how performance relative to these standards is tracked and used to ensure that customer needs are met.

e. Describe the organization's external customer interface practices (eg, how customer-contact employees are empowered to resolve problems). Describe any special training for customer-contact employees.

	POINTS
4 TRAINING AND	**10**
RECOGNITION	**5**

This category examines the organization's efforts to develop the full potential of the workforce for quality improvement, as well as its efforts to use rewards and incentives to recognize individuals.

a. Describe the organization's education and training strategy for quality improvement and how this strategy is integrated with the goals and objectives described in Element 2. Describe approaches used to provide education and training (eg, just-in-time training, train-the-trainer).
b. Describe how the education and training described in sub-element a. is based on a systematic needs analysis.
c. Describe the types of training provided for all levels of management in support of quality goals. Provide the number of managers who have received this training since the beginning of quality management implementation and the total number who are eligible.
d. Describe the types of training provided for employees in support of quality goals. Provide the number of employees who have received each type of training since the beginning of quality management implementation and the total number eligible for each.
e. Describe how contributions to goals and objectives described in Element 2 are recognized and rewarded. Indicate whether and how team, group and peer recognition are used.
f. Provide trend data for the past two or more years in employee recognition (ie, per cent of both employees and managers recognized by both individual, group and team recognition).

	POINTS
5 EMPLOYEE EMPOWERMENT AND TEAMWORK	**20**

This category examines the effectiveness and extent of workforce involvement in quality management, and the approaches used to enhance employee empowerment.

a. Describe the organizational strategy for involving and empowering the entire workforce (including union members) to achieve quality goals and objectives described in Element 2.
b. Describe the specific approaches used to enhance employee empowerment (authority to act).
c. Describe specific means available for members of the workforce (both employees and managers) to become involved in quality management activities, both as individuals and on teams and in groups.
d. Provide trend data for the past two or more years related to workforce

involvement for each type of activity described in sub-element c. Express individual involvement as a percentage of the total workforce. Provide number of teams/groups operating in each year.

POINTS

6 MEASUREMENT AND ANALYSIS
15

This category examines the scope, validity, use and management of data and information that underlie the organization's quality management system; how the data is used to support improvement; and the process for developing measures.

a. Describe the process for developing measures. Describe how measures relate to goals and objectives in the strategic plan as described in Element 2.
b. State whether measures relating to goals and objectives in the strategic plan exist; provide most significant measures.
c. Describe the organization's base of data and information used to measure progress toward goals and objectives. Indicate the scope of the data it contains (eg, relating to customers, suppliers, internal processes, program and administrative areas).
d. Describe the processes and/or technologies the organization uses to ensure that key data is accurate, consistent, valid, timely and available to those who need it.
e. Describe how and by whom data and information are analyzed to support quality improvement (eg, to identify problems, determine trends, evaluate performance of key processes). Give specific examples.
f. Describe the organization's approach to selecting areas to benchmark and organizations to benchmark against; the types of data collected; and the ways that comparative data is used for improvement.

POINTS

7 QUALITY ASSURANCE
30

This category examines the systematic approaches used by the organization to design, assess, control, and improve processes and inputs to produce quality products and services. Emphasis is on prevention rather than detection.

a. Describe how new or improved products and/or services are designed and introduced to meet or exceed customer requirements , as described in Element 3 and how processes are designed to produce and/or deliver these products and/or services.
b. Describe the principal means used by the organization to:

   (i)   ensure that processes are adequately controlled to meet design plans and customer requirements

    (ii)   identify and solve root causes of specific problems that disrupt processes

    (iii) continuously improve processes

c. Describe the principal approaches used to assess quality (eg, systems, audits, product or service audits). Indicate the frequency of such assessments and how the findings are translated into prevention and improvements.

d. Describe how the quality of materials, components, information, and services furnished by external suppliers is assured, assessed and improved.

POINTS

8   QUALITY AND PRODUCTIVITY IMPROVEMENT RESULTS   50

This category examines the measurable results of the organization's quality improvement efforts. Data tables and graphs summarizing trends and achievement should be utilized as much as possible.

a. List at least three of the most significant indicators of the organization's mission performance as described in Element 6; provide trend data for the past two or more years. Explain any adverse trends.

b. Provide trend data for the past two or more years, indicating the level of external customer satisfaction with the quality of major products and services.

c. Provide trend data for the past two or more years for key organizational measures of quality, timeliness, or productivity (other than those listed in sub-element a.). In addition, provide trend data for the past two or more years for in-process (eg, rework rate) and end-item (eg, defect rate) measures. For each measure listed, describe actions taken to produce those results.

d. Provide trend data for the last two years for performance of major external suppliers.

6

THE CHARTER INITIATIVE AND UK PUBLIC SECTOR QUALITY

Introduction

In July 1991 a ten-year programme of what has been described as, 'radical reform', was introduced into the UK Public Sector. The Citizen's Charter White Paper, (Command Paper Cm 1599, date of Publication, July 1991), not only provided all public sector organisations with a framework for the delivery of a 'better' standard of service to the citizen, it also introduced an award scheme that actively recognises excellence in delivering public services by individual public sector organisations.

This chapter looks at the principles of the Charter Initiative as encapsulated by, for example, the Citizen's Charter and the Charter Mark Award Scheme. It describes how public sector organisations implement these principles in their practical day-to-day management.

EVOLUTION OF THE CHARTER INITIATIVE

Although the Charter Initiative represents a major move away from the traditional style of the internal management as well as the external delivery of and by public sector organisations it did not appear overnight as many people assume. As far back as the late 1970s reforms were implemented which were aimed at increasing both the efficiency and effectiveness within public sector organisations. Three initiatives provided a basis for the development and structure of the Charter Initiative. These were the Efficiency Scrutinies, the Financial Management Initiative (FMI), and the Next Steps programme. The three initiatives are outlined briefly below:

1 In 1979 *Efficiency Scrutinies* were introduced into the public sector. The objective was both the recommendation and implementation of measurable financial improvements within a two-year period.

2 In 1982 the *Financial Management Initiative (FMI)* was introduced. The overall purpose of the FMI was to improve management in the Civil Service by ensuring that all managers knew and understood what their objectives were, how their achievements would be assessed, and that overall responsibilities would be defined to ensure best use of resources.

3 In 1988 the *Next Steps* programme was introduced into the public sector. It was designed to improve both management and the delivery of services to the public through the creation of Agencies to carry out executive functions of Government.

THE PRINCIPLES OF PUBLIC SECTOR AND THE CITIZEN'S CHARTER

The White Paper laid down a set of wide-sweeping proposals incorporating such themes as; quality, choice, standards and value, upon which the public service should manage itself and the delivery of its services to the end user.

The fundamental principles upon which the public sector is based were identified by the Citizen's Charter White Paper as; Standards, Information and Openness, Choice and Consultation, Courtesy and Helpfulness, Putting things Right, and Value for Money. A further explanation of these principles as put forward by the White Paper is given below;

Standards

Setting, monitoring and publication of explicit standards for the services that individual users can reasonably expect. Publication of actual performance against these standards.

Information and openness

Full, accurate information readily available in plain language about how public services are run; what they cost, how well they perform and who is in charge.

Choice and consultation

The public sector should provide choice wherever practicable. There should be regular and systematic consultation with those who use services. Users' views about services, and their priorities for improving them should be taken into account in final decisions on standards.

Courtesy and helpfulness

Courteous and helpful service from public servants who will normally wear name badges. Services to be available equally to all who are entitled to them and run to suit their convenience.

Putting things right

If things go wrong, an apology should be given, along with a full explanation and a swift and effective remedy. A well-publicised and easy to use complaints procedures should be implemented with an independent review wherever possible.

Value for money

Efficient and economical delivery of public services within the resources the nation can afford, and an independent validation of performance against standards.

In essence the Charter Initiative attempts to provide a structured framework for the external customer in which targets are set, published, monitored and maintained. The external customer knows what kind of service they will receive and employees know what kind of service to deliver – theoretically at least. The question remaining for public sector organisations to address is *how* they move away from theory to practical implementations of the principles set down by the Charter Initiative? The answer to this question is dealt with in the following sections of this chapter with practical case study examples of how specific public sector organisations have put the theory of the Charter Initiative into the day-do-day running of their organisations.

IMPLEMENTATION – PUTTING THE PRINCIPLES OF THE CITIZEN'S CHARTER INTO PRACTICE

Perhaps one of the more practical and important channels through which dissemination of the principles of the public sector takes place is through specific Charters that relate to individual public sector organisations. At time of writing there were 39 published Charters ranging from the Patient's Charter, and the Court's Charter to the Passenger's Charter. A list of published Charters to date can be found in Figure 6.1.

United Kingdom: England, Scotland, Wales & Northern Ireland

Contributors' Charter
Employers' Charter
Taxpayer's Charter HM Customs & Excise
Taxpayer's Charter Inland Revenue
Traveller's Charter HM Customs & Excise

Great Britain; England, Scotland & Wales

Benefits Agency Customer Charter
Child Support Agency Charter
Jobseeker's Charter
Passenger's Charter
Redundancy Payments Service Charter

England & Wales

Courts Charter

England Only

Aiming Higher: London Underground's Customer Charter
Charter for Further Education
Charter for Higher Education
Council Tenant's Charter
Parent's Charter
Road User's Charter

Scotland Only

Council Tenant's Charter for Scotland
Further & Higher Education Charter for Scotland
Justice Charter for Scotland
Parent's Charter for Scotland
Patient's Charter for Scotland

Wales Only

Charter for Further Education
Charter for Higher Education
Council Tenants' Charter for Wales
Parent's Charter for Wales
Patient's Charter for Wales

Northern Ireland Only

Bus Passenger's Charter
Child Support Agency Charter
Tenant's Charter for Northern Ireland
Courts Charter for Northern Ireland
The Citizen's Charter for Northern Ireland
Parent's Charter
Charter for Patients & Clients
Railway Passenger's Charter
Royal Ulster Constabulary Charter
Social Security Agency Charter
Training & Employment Agency Charter

Figure 6.1 Published Charters

Examples of how standards, information and openness, choice and consultation, courtesy and helpfulness and putting things right are encapsulated by different Charters are dealt with below; (Raising the Standard: Britain's Citizen's Charter and Public Service Reforms).

Standards

British Rail Passenger's Charter, introduced in May 1992, lays down specific targets in respect of punctuality and reliability of each line. British Rail also publish 'Trackrecord' which illustrates actual performance against these standards.

The Patient's Charter was launched in October 1991. It provides patients with timed hospital appointments, and a waiting time guarantee whereby patients are guaranteed admission for virtually all treatments within two years of being placed on a waiting list by a consultant.

Information and openness

Next Steps Agencies publish annual reports of progress against published targets, Police and Prison Inspectors' reports are published.

Choice and consultation

The Inland Revenue publish a wide range of taxpayers' views of the service they receive and their ideas for improvements.

Courtesy and helpfulness

The wearing of name badges has now been implemented into many public sector organisations, these include police services such as South Yorkshire, the Employment Service, Customs and Excise and some Fire Brigades.

Putting things right

Gas, electricity and telephone services pay compensation for failure to meet specified standards.

There are also internal mechanisms for redressing complaints that customers have about services. The Citizen's Charter Complaints Task Force, established in June 1993, ensures that the complaints systems used by public sector organisations operate in line with the principles set down by the Citizen's Charter. Other external bodies such as

Inspectorates ensure that key areas of public services such as the police service are delivered in an efficient and effective way. The privatised utilities such as gas, telecom, electricity and water also remain subject to inspection and checking. The Competition and Service (Utilities) Act 1992 also provides for the regulation of privatised utilities. It:

- sets and monitors standards;
- helps make customers aware of standards;
- provides for compensation where guaranteed standards are not met;
- improves complaints procedures; and
- facilitates greater competition in the provision of water and sewerage services.

THE CHARTER MARK AWARD SCHEME

The Charter Mark Award Scheme established an award that actively recognises and seeks to encourage performance against the principles of public service. The scheme established by the Citizen's Charter White Paper (Cm 1599), is administered by the Charter Unit which is part of the Office of Public Service and Science within the Cabinet Office. Applications are judged by members of the Citizen's Charter Advisory Panel. Members of the panel are selected from both private and public sector organisations.

In the first year of the award, 1992, 36 Charter Marks were awarded to a diversity of public sector organisations ranging from the police service, schools, and hospitals to local authorities and privatised utilities. In 1993, there was a significant increase in applying organisations and in the number of Charter Marks that were awarded; 411 applications were received and 93 Charter Marks were awarded.

Criteria and eligibility

Applying organisations must be able to demonstrate their performance against the principles laid down by the Citizen's Charter. They are also judged against more detailed criteria, relating to standards, information and openness, choice and consultation, courtesy and helpfulness, putting things right, value for money, customer satisfaction, measurable improvements in the quality of service over the first two or more years, and plans to introduce or have in hand at least one innovative enhancement to services without any extra cost to the taxpayer or consumer.

Appendix II sets down in more detail the 1994 award criteria.

Judges' decisions are based on the overall application of a public sector organisation which should be no longer than ten pages. Other checks are also carried out, for example in the case where the applying organisation provides a particular service which is maintained by regulation of a privatised utility, judges will automatically seek the view of the relevant regulatory body such as; OFFER, OFWAT, OFGAS, and OFTEL.

The Charter Mark Scheme is open to all organisations within the public sector; this includes Governmental Departments, Agencies and non-departmental public bodies, nationalised industries, schools, further and higher education institutions, the courts, police and emergency services, Training and Enterprise Councils, local authority services and privatised utilities.

Local authorities and privatised utilities

There are special rules governing local authority applications. Since local authorities provide such a large and diverse range of services, applying organisations are required to submit their applications for Charter Marks from individual service departments or units – applications are not acceptable from applications covering a range of services. However, local authorities may submit applications from a service which has been contracted out – as long as the local authority has overall responsibility for that particular service. In effect this means that the local authority remains responsible for setting standards and for monitoring performance against those standards. Private sector contractors may not submit applications.

District Health authorities and Family Health Service authorities may apply where they can demonstrate that they are providing a service directly to the public.

Finally with regard to the privatised utilities such as gas, electricity, and water; where the particular utility is under the same obligations as public sector bodies, they are eligible to apply.

CASE STUDIES

Introduction

The final section of this chapter looks at a number of diverse public sector organisations that really do implement quality in the public sector. Examples are taken from a police service, a local authority, British Rail, and a National Health Trust.

SOUTH YORKSHIRE POLICE

Introduction

In 1990 South Yorkshire Police embarked upon a major programme of change. In recognition of the fact that permanent change can only result from careful planning and strategy an initial three-month 'fact-finding' mission was embarked upon. South Yorkshire Police spent time canvassing the views of their diverse stakeholders; consisting of some 250 group representatives from their community as well as police staff.

Three documents emerged from this initial investigative stage;

The Chief Constable's Ten Point Plan. (see Figure 6.2.)
An informal series of points indicating the way the Chief Constable 'wanted to do business' in the Force.

Six Hill Horizon. (see Figure 6.3.)
Setting out the future aims and objectives of South Yorkshire Police according to individual talent and capability.

Statement of purpose and values. (see Figure 6.4.)
Setting out the thoughts and expectations of South Yorkshire Police in relation to what they believe to be the purpose of the police, the core values which underlie what the police service does, and the way the police and the public might like to do business together.

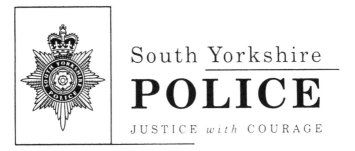

Chief Constable's "10 Point Plan"

1.   Emphasis on public service
2.   Staff care for customer care
3.   Human face
4.   Reasonableness of action
5.   Communication of doubt upwards
6.   Catching people doing right
7.   Regular meetings to establish common ground
8.   Do not waste any energy fighting each other
9.   Honesty with courtesy
10.   Allow individuality

Figure 6.2

South Yorkshire
POLICE
JUSTICE *with* COURAGE

SIX HILL HORIZON

Within five years, or as soon as practicable, to have a South Yorkshire Police Service which:–

- is more open, relaxed and honest with ourselves and the public

- is more aware of our environment, sensitive to change and positioning ourselves to respond to change

- is more clear about our role and our identity and is obviously justifiably proud of itself

- is more closely in touch with our customers, puts them first and delivers what they want quickly, effectively and courteously

- makes its decisions at the appropriate levels

- is the envy of all other forces

Figure 6.3

THE SOUTH YORKSHIRE POLICE SERVICE
Statement of Purpose and Values

OUR PURPOSE–

on behalf of the general public is:
- to uphold the Rule of Law
- to keep the Queen's Peace
- to prevent and detect crime
- to protect life and to help and reassure people in need

OUR VALUES–

In achieving our purpose, we must at all times strive to:
- act within the law, serving with integrity the ends of justice
- act fairly and reasonably, without fear or favour and without prejudice of any kind
- ensure that the rights of all citizens – especially the vulnerable – are safeguarded, regardless of status, race, colour, religion, sex or social background
- be courageous in facing physical danger or moral challenge
- be honest, courteous and tactful in all that we do and say
- use persuasion, common sense and good humour wherever possible as an alternative to the exercise of force and, if force is finally necessary, to use only that which is necessary to accomplish our lawful duty

OUR WAY OF WORKING–

In upholding these fundamental values, it will help us to be more effective in working together and with our communities if we:
- maintain the dignity of our office yet display humanity and compassion
- constantly practise high standards of personal and professional conduct
- remember that, although the office of constable carries power and authority, respect must be earned
- listen and try to understand the other person's point of view
- confront those who bully or exploit on behalf of those less than able to protect themselves
- act with a willingness to try new ways of working
- speak moderately, yet firmly and proudly of what we do well
- admit our failings promptly and apologise for our mistakes
- show determination and resourcefulness in helping others

"Justice with Courage"

Figure 6.4

Having put the information from the initial research undertaken onto a data base, the Senior Command Team, the top five officers at South Yorkshire Police, were able to put together a long-term programme for the implementation of change that addressed both cultural and structural aspects of both the police service and quality. Reliable methods of measuring and monitoring change at South Yorkshire were also taken on board. A fact that is clearly illustrated by their use of analytical University-based polls, door-stepping customers as they leave their police stations and random surveys of their many customers.

From strategy to implementation

South Yorkshire Police expected that a five to seven-year programme was required, but in-house surveys indicated that change at South Yorkshire had begun to accelerate at such a rate during year three that they were able to concentrate more on the structural issues of their programme.

By October 1992 their success in implementing quality was rewarded when they successfully applied for a Charter Mark Award. Their performance against and treatment of the 1992 criteria is shown opposite.

Concluding remarks

South Yorkshire Police really do embrace the principles of Total Quality within their organisation and recognise that there will always be room for improvement. A fact that is clearly illustrated by measuring themselves against the criteria set down by the European Quality Model. Even though at time of writing they are not eligible to apply for the European Quality Award they recognise its value as an internal Benchmark for measuring current performance and improving upon it.

INTRODUCTION:
THE SOUTH YORKSHIRE APPROACH

The Quality of Service initiative is not new to the South Yorkshire Police. Indeed, our own staff played a major part in the Operational Policing Review, conducting the survey of the views and opinions of police officers about the future shape of policing. It was the disparity between those views and the ones expressed by the public which led to the ACPO Strategic Policy Document – 'Meeting Community Expectations'.

Quality police services have to be delivered by front line officers. Our approach has been that quality is not something that can be produced by Headquarters decrees or the setting up of a specialist department. It has to be grown gradually and perceptibly within the organisation, by those responsible for service delivery.

Our aim has been to lead all our staff through a communications strategy, which takes them from unawareness, through the intermediate steps of awareness, comprehension and conviction, to action. People cannot be expected to implement anything which they do not believe in or understand.

We accept that the identified key service areas and core functions of the ACPO working group are at the very heart of our job, and that improvements in these areas will make a real impact on the provision of quality police services.

Customer consultation is a key feature of our initiative. Everybody has a customer and front line officers form an integral customer group for others within the organisation. Servicing their needs through the Supplies, Administration, Transport or Prosecutions Departments is vital to ensuring that they are equipped to service the needs of the public. The Quality of Service initiative in South Yorkshire embraces all of the organisation – frontstage and backstage.

Conviction grows out of quality design and innovation – out of releasing the tremendous potential that exists among our staff to tackle problems affecting their area of the organisation. Nobody knows better about the business of policing than those officers actually doing the job. Perhaps here lies part of the answer to 'chopping the Goliath of police bureaucracy down to size – by giving people the slings and stones to do it'.

South Yorkshire Police is determined to become a more efficient and responsive force. This Charter Mark application testifies to this process and the commitment within the service.

The Charter Standards are individually set out and the text includes references to examples where implementation is taking place to assist the Charter Unit in validation of the submission.

PUBLICATION OF THE STANDARDS OF SERVICE THAT THE CUSTOMER CAN REASONABLY EXPECT, AND OF PERFORMANCE AGAINST THOSE STANDARDS

The South Yorkshire Police is a large and diverse organisation, serving a wide range of communities and individual needs. Our view is that the essence of standard setting lies in the contract formed between the police and the public. These can then be translated into meaningful achievable measures and targets, which staff understand and accept the importance of meeting.

Local staff who have gone through the whole process of customer consultation, developing a customer orientation and deciding on relevant standards are far more committed to such standards than ones which have been universally applied and dictated from the centre.

As part of our quality initiative local 'quality' groups have been formed throughout the organisation to 'design in' quality into police services. These are also reinforcing the local nature of policing and our contract with the local communities. These all serve to increase the understanding and conviction of officers who implement the initiative.

Examples include:

- control room standards, including telephone answering time, a standard response – name, location and agreeing a contract with the caller for police response and response time (Attercliffe, Sheffield);
- contact and support during the course of the investigation, including notifying the complainant of the accused's first appearance before the courts (Rotherham CID);
- correspondence acknowledgement within three days of receipt and the provision of a contact point and name of person dealing (West Bar, Sheffield);
- officers at incident locations will give a contact telephone number and Command and Control incident number for any follow-up enquiries (West Bar, Sheffield);
- Headquarters Drug Squad have published 'A Guide to Drug Enforcement in South Yorkshire';
- Scenes of Crime – all officers have been provided with an A5 size booklet of advice and helpful hints regarding the range of service provided.

Performance against the standards are measured by supervisors, regular public consultation and the established independent means of review listed in this document.

EVIDENCE THAT THE VIEWS OF THOSE WHO USE THE SERVICE HAVE BEEN TAKEN INTO ACCOUNT IN SETTING STANDARDS

Customer consultation is enshrined in our Mission Statement '... an organisation which is more closely in touch with its customers ...

Internal and external consultation is taking place throughout the organisation – some formalised and some ad hoc and spontaneous.

- Examples of formal consultation include:
  - large scale contact by way of a Force customer survey of 1,400 members of the public. This will present not only a global picture across the county, but also a sample in each sub-division to assist local commanders in standard setting, the use of resources and setting priorities. At the same time, an in-house survey of all our staff will take place, examining such issues as organisation, management, morale and areas for improvement;
  - weekly questionnaires are sent to a random sample of customers about their use of the service and areas for improvement (Doncaster);
  - articles published in local newspapers which included a return coupon inviting the public to comment on police services and areas for improvement (Wombwell, Barnsley);
  - a sample survey of 200 victims of burglary on the service they received and how it can be improved. The survey included a question relating to what the victim considers to be the most important use of police resources (Barnsley, CID);
  - at station open days, a sample of the public are asked to complete a questionnaire which asked specific questions on standards of service (Hackenthorpe, Sheffield);
  - a victims of crime survey which tested the views of the public on how a report of crime had been dealt with by the police (Hammerton Road, Sheffield);
  - how the relatives of the victims of fatal road accidents can be supported (Operations and Traffic);
  - a recent scrutiny into property management asked the public their opinions on how the police should be involved in handling property.

- In-house surveys have included:
  - Operations and Traffic surveyed all sub-divisional commanders and staff about the service they require from the Traffic Department;
  - the Training Department has surveyed 10% of the Force concerning their wants and needs and are using this data as the basis for meeting customer expectations.

CLEAR INFORMATION ABOUT THE RANGE OF SERVICES PROVIDED, IN PLAIN LANGUAGE

While some members of the public may require information on the full range of services available, others will be particularly interested in those which relate to their personal interest or problem. These are often directly related to their reason for contact with the police – for example, burglary, domestic violence or concern over drugs. There is a range of 'composite' texts and materials and some more specialist information.

- Composite texts include:
  - the Annual Report of the Chief Constable;
  - a recently filmed video entitled 'Justice with Courage' – a 20 minute presentation documenting our work – to be used at schools, community groups and other forums;
  - consultation took place with 250 organisations in South Yorkshire, the Police Authority, and all officers and civil support staff to form the Force's new Statement of Purpose and Values. This is a published document against which the South Yorkshire Police Service is prepared to be measured.

- Specialist information includes:
  - the use of local newspapers and publications to detail the range of services available, including opening hours of rural police stations and the work of community officers in rural areas (Doncaster);
  - the Child and Sexual Abuse Unit has published a code of practice on the investigation of child abuse for the information of the police and public;
  - the Traffic Division produced a comprehensive booklet on the range of services provided, including traffic patrol, accident investigation, traffic management and speed enforcement;
  - Crime and Community Services have published a comprehensive guide on the multi-agency approach to problem solving and initiatives in the South Yorkshire area. This includes 'watch schemes', such as Hospital Watch, listing the aims of the schemes and key contact points;
  - victims of crime receive letters giving further guidance and support and information on the range of service available to them, including victim support and crime prevention (Sheffield and Barnsley).

Perhaps the most effective way, however, is for the public to enter one of our 'Cop Shops', situated in shopping centres and manned by police officers, promoting personally the full range of services we offer.

COURTEOUS AND EFFICIENT CUSTOMER SERVICE, FROM STAFF WHO ARE NORMALLY PREPARED TO IDENTIFY THEMSELVES BY NAME

The delivery of courteous and efficient customer service forms an integral part of our Statement of Purpose and Values. A declared aim is '... to have a service which is more closely in touch with our customers, puts them first and delivers what they want quickly, efficiently and courteously.'

Every effort has been made to communicate and further the understanding and application of that mission to ensure that the words become reality.

The point of first contact with the public is crucial – whether in the station foyer, on the telephone, in the street or in the home of a victim of crime.

- Name badges have been introduced in Sheffield and the rural areas of Doncaster. Officers from the Crime and Community Services and the Driving School – who work and travel throughout the South Yorkshire area – will also wear the badges. In total, some 566 staff will be taking part in this pilot scheme to test reaction and resolve any problems, before they are issued to all staff.

- Reception staff at the Headquarters foyer are now identified by photograph and name board.

- A common standard for telephone answering includes the name of the member of staff taking the call, and the station or department – a standard greeting – and the forming of a contract with the caller concerning the nature and timing of police response.

- Other efforts to 'personalise' our service include the use of business cards when calling at homes of victims. These are also used in Commercial Branch when dealing with members of the business community.

- Personalising the service also relates to the physical environment in which transactions take place. A major consultancy has been undertaken, aimed at creating a more friendly environment in such areas as station foyers, where many initial contacts are made and perceptions are formed.

WELL SIGNPOSTED AVENUES FOR COMPLAINT IF THE CUSTOMER IS NOT SATISFIED, WITH SOME INDEPENDENT REVIEW WHEREVER POSSIBLE

The procedures for registering official complaints against the police are contained in legislation in the Police and Criminal Evidence Act 1984. In 1985 the Police Complaints Authority, the independent arbiter/overseer of police complaints and means of review, was established. The Police Discipline Regulations are similarly a part of legislation.

Within the South Yorkshire area there is a well established Discipline and Complaints Department which, as far as possible, deals with all recorded complaints. This allows the maintenance of a common, professional standard of approach. A number of initiatives have been introduced by the department. These include talking to the police and public, computerisation of the administrative processes to enhance efficiency, and the creation of 'out offices' away from public buildings and Headquarters, where complainants may find an environment in which it is easier to discuss their complaint. Our record of dealing with complaints is well documented in the Annual Report and is validated by HMIC thematic inspection.

The procedures for informal resolution of complaints were reviewed recently and officers attending training courses receive instruction on these matters.

It is also accepted that there are areas of service provision where members of the public do not wish to register a formal complaint, but remain dissatisfied with the service they have received. These may be complaints about systems and procedures, rather than individual named officers. Others may wish to remain anonymous. There are several well advertised methods open to them:

- sub-divisional surgeries and forums – meetings are well publicised in local public buildings and the press and to which all members of the public in that area are invited;
- local community constable surgeries – these are advertised in the Doncaster Division using the paid for and free newspapers. In addition, every village in the Thorne area now has a dedicated officer who attends village meetings;
- suggestion boxes are being installed in the foyers of all police stations for members of the public to include their comments on the service they have received;
- where questionnaire surveys of customers have been conducted, both internally and externally, there is always space for the customer to add comments on the quality of service required.

INDEPENDENT VALIDATION OF PERFORMANCE AGAINST STANDARDS AND A CLEAR COMMITMENT TO IMPROVING VALUE FOR MONEY

Outside independent validation of our performance is provided by Her Majesty's Inspectors of Constabulary. They have a key role to play in assessing our performance and efficiency as an organisation.
To quote from his report in June 1992:

> 'The South Yorkshire Police, with an enlightened Chief Constable, strengthened command team and a very willing work force, is now at the dawn of a new era. It enjoys good and active support from the Police Authority, whose current and future involvement in initiatives concerning quality of service, policy analysis, performance indicators and equal opportunities is recognised.'

The service maintains a close link with HMIC through the Policy Analysis Unit. The unit uses the HMIC Matrix of indicators for validation and comparison of our performance with national standards, regional and 'family' groupings. Our commitment to providing value for money is shown by our scrutiny programme linked to HMI's office. Completed scrutinies include those on the Driving School, the vehicle fleet and handling of property. A full programme of cost saving recommendations has been implemented.

Performance indicators also provide a source of validation. Our view is that such measures must be meaningful, helpful and not exhaustive of limited resources – that is, they should support the quality initiative and not drain resources away from it. A Performance Review Department will start work on Monday, 27 July 1992.

Our Research and Development Department provides validation of ongoing work and value for money initiatives, using accepted methods such as activity analysis. Projects have included the use of crime desks for reporting crime, the optimum utilisation of manpower and the introduction of operational support units – file preparation units releasing expensive operational man hours back to operational policing.

Technical validation in such areas as the Operations Room is provided through the telephone system and command and control computer.

ONE INNOVATIVE ENHANCEMENT TO OUR SERVICE WHICH HAS BEEN INTRODUCED WITHOUT INCREASING THE COST TO THE TAXPAYER OR CUSTOMER

Below are details of a scheme which has been introduced and developed at no expense to the taxpayer.

During 1991, the suggestion scheme was relaunched to encourage such innovation. In 1992, the emphasis was on proper recognition and ownership of good ideas. This included the presentation of certificates by the Chief Constable and the Chairman of the Police Authority to the best suggestions received during 1991–92. The Safelink scheme was cited as the best suggestion (see below).

Quality circles have been formed and nurtured, leading to improved and more frequent communication, better use of an increasingly knowledgeable workforce, savings from problem solving and quality commitment, and more dedication to the organisation and greater identification with its goals and priorities.

- SAFELINK

    Safelink developed out of incidents of racial harassment where an Asian family had to run the gauntlet of racial abuse to reach a public telephone. The project began with the loan of an operational police portable telephone, leading to an increased sense of security, safety and well being.

    Further investigation revealed that the technology existed to enhance the scheme using a panic button – a double advantage of allowing a person under attack to summon assistance and also to cater for non-English speakers.

    A sponsorship deal allowed a trial of 16 units, connection fees, monthly rental, air time and calls being secured with no expense to the taxpayer.

    Advantages of the scheme include the fact that the potential victim can have close contact with the police without tying up operational officers, is not restricted to a particular location, has an increased sense of safety and security and can call the police and explain the type and urgency of the response required. The caller can also be contacted by telephone to allow updates and give reassurance.

    The adaptable scheme has been used for the victims of racial harassment, domestic violence and sexual abuse, witness protection, prison releases and families threatened with a firearms attack.

    Phase two of the development links to a national charity called Language Line. This allows a telephone based linguistic service to all South Yorkshire residents, again of obvious benefit to non-English speakers.

CONCLUSION

A further extension of the Safelink scheme is a personal attack alarm system which is now in operation in South Yorkshire. It gives a simple and practical example of how the implementation of Charter standards can produce beneficial results.

For years, the police has geared its expertise in alarms towards protecting property, not people. We in South Yorkshire listened to our public – some of whom were in need of personal protection – and hence the Safelink scheme was introduced. This, however, has been improved upon by the Force Alarms Officer who has designed a pendant-style personal alarm. At the touch of a button this provides direct communication with the police control room where all sounds can be heard and recorded for evidential purposes. This allows the control room to give constant information to officers approaching the scene.

In summary, we listened to the needs of our customers and responded. The service and standards relating to it were fully publicised. This courteous and efficient service has reduced fear of the very serious risk of crime in special circumstances and is just one of the ways the South Yorkshire Police strives for continuous improvement in the service it provides.

LOCAL CHARTER STANDARDS

Introduction

One of the most important channels through which many of the obligations of Central Government are carried out is through local authorities. In the UK local authorities are responsible for providing a diverse range of services to the local community, and since the publication of the White Paper a number of local authorities have produced their own local Charters, reflecting, not only the local authority's obligations, but the needs and expectations of the community that it serves.

Local Charters are based upon the framework of central Charters which have enabled local authorities to produce their own charters tailored to local needs and circumstances.

The case study that follows was written by the Assistant Chief Executive of Braintree District Council, and is indeed an example of a local authority that delights the customer.

BRAINTREE DISTRICT COUNCIL
'THE COUNCIL THAT HAS EVERYTHING'

Not our words, but the title of an article by Clare MacLure in the *Local Government Chronicle* (April 1993). Following the award to the Council in 1992 of a Charter Mark, and in early 1993 of an Investor in People Award and the PA/SOLACE 'Total Quality Award', Clare MacLure made the following comment:

'Anyone trying to develop a comprehensive list of initiatives or benchmarks which might indicate a lively, well-managed, progressive or politically correct council might just about cover what goes on in Braintree.'

Since then, of course, Braintree Council has also received a second Charter Mark and the Management Today/Arthur Andersen Service Excellence Award for Not for Profit Organisations. Most satisfying of all, the Council was nominated to represent UK Local Government in a prestigious international competition, sponsored by the Bertelsmann media conglomerate, to find 'the best managed Council in the world'. While the Council did not win the award, Braintree was recognised to be a world leader in quality management, customer focus and investment in people. So how has all this come about?

Braintree means business

Braintree has been committed, for more than ten years, to developing a strategic management philosophy focusing on customers and quality. To describe this we have coined the term 'Total Management Approach'.

This new approach began in earnest in the early 1980s, to confront a traumatic event in the local economy. In 1984, the district's largest employer – Courtaulds Ltd – having been associated with Braintree for more than 200 years, made the decision to close all its factories in the area. Over 4,000 people were made redundant virtually overnight. The Council had very limited resources but was committed to intervene, and reviewed what contribution it could make. The Council concluded that our most effective role would be as a catalyst for investment, and that this would be achieved by offering a quality response – accurate, immediate and above all positive – to anyone who might be a potential investor in the District. This, initially economic development, strategy went under the name 'BRAINTREE MEANS BUSINESS'.

Figure 6.5

It immediately became apparent that such a strategy could not be limited narrowly to economic development, but needs to be corporate, and apply to all customers. One key focus for this was to establish a set of 'core values' for the Council.

Core values

There is nothing sophisticated about such a list. Many organisations now have them. They were very rare, however, in 1985 when they were introduced (and, curiously, are still scarce in local government). At one level, these Core Values are only a 'wish statement'. At that time, they were certainly a statement of intent on behalf of the Council. Yet the fact remains that they have stood the test of time and are still, ten years on, the key principles on which the Council works. And current documents – including the Council's code of conduct for staff and councillors – still emphasise their pivotal importance.

In fact, these simple Core Values acted as the focus for a raft of initiatives throughout the 1980's on:

- customer care
- people development

- service quality
- organisational development
- performance management etc.

These were essentially continuous, evolutionary changes happening in parallel in many parts of the organisation. There is a very powerful quote from Jan Carlzon, Managing Director of Scandinavian Air Service (in Tom Peters' *'In Search of Excellence'*):

'We don't aim to be 1000% better at any one thing. We aim to be 1% better at 1,000 things'

This sums up Braintree's approach at that stage perfectly.

And indeed, such an approach can take a you a long way. A major market research exercise commissioned by the Council from MORI in 1989 gave very powerful feedback. Comparing Braintree with 24 other Councils, for whom MORI had carried out similar surveys by that time, the survey gave the following results (see Figure 6.6).

MORI SURVEY 1989

● Friendliness	1st
● Efficiency	2nd
● Helpfulness	2nd
● Accessibility	2nd
● Being Interested	2nd
● Promptness	2nd

KEY SERVICES

● Refuse Collection	1st
● Housing Repairs	1st

OVERALL SATISFACTION	1st

BRAINTREE

DISTRICT COUNCIL

Figure 6.6

This established Braintree as one of the leading Councils in the country.

Since 1989, we have been seeking increasingly to develop our approach from one based essentially on leadership and enthusiasm to a more integrated 'total quality' approach.

QUALITY MODEL

SETTING STANDARDS
- Active listening
- Marketing Research

QUALITY ASSURANCE
- ISO 9000/BS 5750 for all services

QUALITY GUARANTEES
- BDC Citizen's Charter: 'Your Guarantee of Quality'
- Customer Charters/Contracts

REMEDYING DEFECTS
- BDC Complaints System

BRAINTREE

DISTRICT

COUNCIL

Figure 6.7

Total quality

The movement to a more integrated approach stemmed from the recognition that while standards were demonstrably high – the MORI Survey was sufficient evidence of this – we were not always consistent. In particular, there was no way of guaranteeing the good service we were offering every time. We recognised – and our Customer panels told us – that our customers wanted to know what standard they could expect, and to be sure they would get it.

The Council approached a number of quality gurus, notably Crosby Associates, but decided that the solution did not lie in consultants, but in refining the Council's own quality strategy. We developed a simple process model of quality. The starting point was the Council's Quality Policy, formally adopted in 1990:

Braintree Council aims to deliver defect-free products and services to our customers, both internal and external, on time and within budget.

In other words, 'Right first time, every time . . .'

Quality approach

Setting Standards: The starting point is delivering services to a standard which customers want. This is essentially a process of market research and 'active listening' to customers, so that standards can be upgraded, or indeed downgraded, to meet the express customer expectations.

Quality Assurance: Having established that the standards being offered are what our customers want, the next issue is consistency, and this is where quality assurance (and in particular BS5750) is relevant. BS5750 is the recognised world-wide benchmark for quality assurance, and offers effective external validation of the reliability/consistency of service procedures.

The Council turned to the British Standards Institute – the brand leader in this country – and set out an ambitious objective: to achieve registration under BS5750 for all the Council's key services, a total of 70 in all. Following intensive preparation, the first services were registered in January 1993, and the final phase of 30 services in September. Braintree is the first Council in the world to have all its key service procedures quality assured (see Figure 6.8).

Chief Executives

    Complaints
    Electoral Registration
    Strategic Management
    Public Relations
    Safety & Planning

Housing

    Community Care
    Maintenance
    Repairs
    Management
    Computer
    Allocations
    Advisory & Enabling
    Sheltered

Personnel

    Management Services
    Training
    Payroll
    Personnel
    Witham Technology Centre

Development and Planning

    Building Control
    Architectural
    Development Control
    Forward Planning

Corporate Services

    Computer
    Reprographics
    Legal
    Land Charges
    Purchasing
    Help Desk
    Programme
    Licensing
    Post Room
    Committee

Commercial Services

    Stores

Property Services
Refuse Collection
Horticulture

Finance

    Facilities Management
    Estates and Valuation
    Accountancy
    Audit
    Creditors
    Housing Benefit
    Revenues
    Other Income
    Cashiers

Environmental Services

    Pest Control
    Recycling
    Dog Wardens
    Food (Environment)
    Health & Safety (Enforcement)
    Environmental Engineering
    Meat Inspection
    Health Promotion
    Pollution (Noise/Air)
    Housing (Public Health)
    CCT

Community and Leisure

    Bramston Sports Centre
    Cemeteries
    Energy
    Notley Sports Centre
    Riverside Centre
    Halstead Sport
    Halstead Pool
    Braintree Leisure
    Halls
    Museum
    Parks & Amenities
    Enabling & Community Service
    Transport

Figure 6.8 List of Braintree services registered under BS5750

Quality Guarantees: Having determined the standards, and with pro-cedures quality-assured for consistency, it then becomes very straightforward to guarantee these service delivery standards to our customers. In Braintree, this takes the form of a Charter – 'Your Guarantee of Quality' – setting out what our customers can expect in terms of their day-to-day dealings with the council if they visit, telephone or write to the Council for any reason. Under this 'umbrella' Charter are a series of Customer Contracts which set out in detail:

- *the nature of the service being offered.* Eg refuse collection.
- *the specific standards of the service.* Eg for refuse collection, we DO NOT guarantee that we will never miss collecting a dustbin from every household; this would be untenable. We DO guarantee that if we fail to collect a dustbin and the customer contacts the Council before noon, we will send a vehicle specifically to collect the missed bin the same day; if after noon, we will collect by the following morning.
- *what to do if there is a problem.* For refuse collection, contact numbers are given, and the Council's complaints system is explained in case the customer is dissatisfied.
- *how our customers can help us to provide a quality service.* Eg for refuse collection, by not locking gates, by tethering dangerous dogs etc!

Refuse collection is a good illustration because it is simple. For other services, such as planning (development) control, it is less straightforward but certainly achievable (in that case by recognising that there are two key sets of customers: the applicant, and those potentially affected. There is a separate Customer Contract for each).

In all these cases, the Contract is not a pious statement of intent; it is a real guarantee, which our customers can understand and which we can deliver EVERY TIME. For refuse collection, for instance, we know we can deliver the standard because we monitor in detail the number and distribution of missed bins daily, and what resources need to be devoted to special collections. Out of 44,000 collections each week, we currently miss on average 25 (0.06%), though this varies from around 15 to 60. Our management target is to reduce missed bins to fewer than 50 PER MONTH (0.03%). But this is NOT a customer target, because it is unenforceable when seen from the point of view of the individual customer. In fact, we have so far NEVER failed to meet our customer target for refuse collection.

Remedying Defects: Every organisation makes mistakes, and it is foolish to pretend otherwise. In fact, Braintree welcomes mistakes where these show that new ideas and approaches are being introduced and tried out: it is a sign of an innovative culture. In the same way, we welcome complaints and use them as an important tool for service improvement. There is a simple but rigorous complaints procedure – 'I Would Like to Make a Complaint! – which has been used by the Local Government Ombudsman as a model system for local government. Every member of staff and Councillor is briefed on how to receive and act on complaints. All complaints received by the Council are listed on a monthly schedule and are considered ndividually by the Council's Management Team.

Together, these provide a powerful model, providing a focused approach to quality which everyone in the organisation can understand and can contribute to.

But does it work?

This is all very well, but does it deliver? In recent years, Braintree has moved in the direction of external assessment and 'benchmarking' as an important measure of management effectiveness. This has included submitting for various awards. The results have been surprising:

- Selection of Braintree as one of the 16 best managed councils in the country, in a peer group survey and assessment by the University of Birmingham (July 1992)
- Charter Mark, in its inaugural year, for the Council's Housing services; one of only 11 councils to receive this Award (October 1992)
- Investor in People Award for our commitment to staff training and development; only the second council in the country to receive the Award (January 1993)
- PA/SOLACE Total Quality Award in its inaugural year, recognising that Braintree is the leading UK council for quality (May 1993)
- Nomination to represent UK local government to compete in the Carl Bertelsmann Competition to find the best managed Council in the world (September 1993)
- All Council services registered under BS 5750 (September 1993)
- Second Charter Mark, for the Council's Planning and Development Services (October 1993)
- Management Today/Arthur Andersen Service Excellence Award (Not for Profit Organisations) in its inaugural year (May 1994)

While these are important validations of the Council's management approach, they are insufficient as measures of overall performance. Local government does not have profit as a bottom-line indicator. The nearest equivalent is net customer satisfaction. During last summer, therefore, we commissioned Foresight Market Research Ltd to carry out a further detailed survey to measure the Council's performance, in particular relative to the MORI Survey described above, carried out in 1989. The findings gave the following direct comparisons (see Figure 6.9).

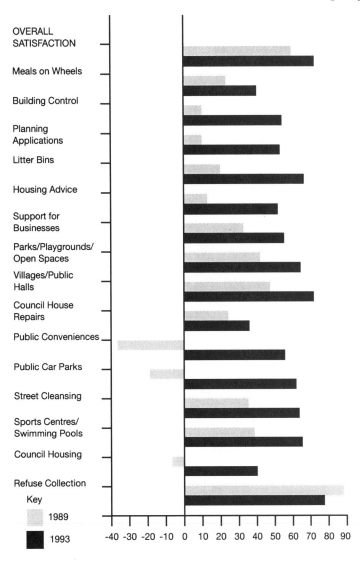

Figure 6.9 Net satisfaction with Council services

On virtually all Council services, and against a substantially less favourable national economic backcloth, customer satisfaction levels have improved over the four years, in some cases very substantially. The key trend is the virtual elimination of net dissatisfaction with services, and this can be directly attributed to our quality approach.

For the 'customer care' indicators, where we scored highly in 1989, again the Council's performance has been maintained or improved see Figure 6.10:

	% 1989	% 1993
When you last contacted the Council did you find it . . .		
● Helpful	74	83
● Efficient	72	72
● Interested in your problem	67	70
● Quick in dealing with your problem	61	61
How difficult was it getting to the right person . . .		
● Easy	72	85
● Difficult	23	14
And were you satisfied with the final outcome . . .		
● Satisfied	67	71
● Dissatisfied	28	21

Figure 6.10 Customer satisfaction

These are the true measures of performance, and give me confidence that Braintree now really does mean business!

ROBERT ATKINS
ASSISTANT CHIEF EXECUTIVE
BRAINTREE DISTRICT COUNCIL

Braintree District Councils Housing Services Charter Mark Application 1992

CRITERION 1

Setting standards

For many years Braintree District Council has set quality and performance standards, communicated them to the public, monitored the performance and acted on the experience gained.

> 'Having had dealings with officers from several local Councils, I have had no better, professional and honest, straightforward, direct answers than from Braintree.' Mr D. Ardback, Timber Preservations

Performance indicators within the Planning and Development Department are monitored against agreed service standards which accord with Audit Commission best practice. Examples include:

● All Building Control plans examined within 3 weeks.
● Investigation of priority enforcement complaints within 24 hours.
● Determining 75% of planning applications within 8 weeks.

Key targets are reviewed quarterly and reported to the Planning and Development Committee.

Customer contracts

We are one of the first Planning Authorities in the Country to produce a series of customer contracts for specified services.
    The following customer contracts are enclosed with our submission:–

● The Development Control Service – 1: **Applicants and Agents.**
● The Development Control Service – 2:
  Customers affected by development proposals.
● The Building Control Service.

The contracts explain for example, where and when customers can find out about a particular planning application (including outside normal working hours) and the performance targets the Council sets itself in order to provide an optimum level of service and reach a decision within an appropriate period of time.
    Contracts are supplied at Council Headquarters, Area Offices and dispatched where applicable to correspondents who write to the Council about planning applications and to all applicants.

Publicising our performance

Performance statistics are published quarterly and reviewed at Planning Committee meetings. Members are able to question specific targets or their degree of achievement. Where a target has not been achieved an explanation will be provided and, where feasible, corrective action will be specified. Local newspapers take a close interest in these reports and in the Planning Committee's Annual Plan from which service levels are derived. Additional information is also provided by way of press releases, the Council's own free newspaper and technical advice leaflets.

CRITERION 2

Information and openness

Communication with customers is an integral element of Customer Care. This is achieved by a variety of different methods:–

The Reporter is a free quarterly newspaper delivered to every household in the District. It provides information and advice on Council Services and new developments.

The Quality Life Catalogue provides a comprehensive directory of all Council Services and where to obtain advice. This includes:–

- Development Control
- Building Control
- Conservation/Landscape advice
- Action on dangerous structures
- Forward Planning

Advice leaflets are produced covering a vast range of planning services. These include the Department's **Planning Handbook** which sets out the work of the Department, its functions, development opportunities and useful contact points.

> 'The standard of cooperation and service by Braintree Building Control is far better than other Councils I have encountered.'
>
> *Mr B, Braintree.*

A **Business Opportunities Handbook** sets out useful advice and information on development opportunities within the District. As do the:–

EURO SIGNPOST
JOB SIGNPOST and
GUIDE TO THE DISTRICTS ECONOMIC PROFILE

Further advice leaflets deal with:–

HOUSE EXTENSIONS
UNDERSTANDING PLANNING RULES
COUNTRYSIDE MANAGEMENT PROJECTS
TREES ON DEVELOPMENT SITES
A GUIDE TO BUILDING CONTROL SERVICES and
CONSERVATION GUIDANCE

Plain English

All public documentation is reviewed and revised where necessary to ensure that plain language is employed. A most recent example is the planning application form which has been reprinted to make it easier for applicants to understand.

All leaflets and brochures are provided with the primary aim of being easy and simple to read. Many will be published as a direct consequence of needs identified by customer surveys; a current example being a guide to domestic house extensions. All our standard letters and forms have been reviewed in order to cut out "bureaucratic gobbledygook."

CRITERION 3

Choice and consultation

Market research

Each section of the Department carries out a customer survey for at least one service area every year. These are used to make improvements to the quality and range of services where appropriate. Examples of those include:–

In 1991 a survey of members of the public who comment on planning applications revealed a need for more information about how planning decisions are made. As a result, a free leaflet "Have Your Say" was printed and provided to correspondents with their acknowledgement. This leaflet is currently being revised to incorporate recent improvements to decision making procedures.

In the same year, a building control survey identified a need for more site inspections. This has been improved by establishing a radio network which allows building inspectors to provide a faster and more responsive service.

> *'Excellent service and we would like them to continue their friendly warm welcome.'*
>
> *Mr C, Witham.*

Customer surveys of reception and building control in 1992 revealed a high degree of satisfaction with the services provided. For example:–

73% were very satisfied with the quality of service.

80% said that staff were very helpful in dealing with enquiries.

We target groups of customers i.e. objectors, architects, public bodies to ensure that all users of the planning system are given an opportunity to comment.

Communication

One of the most often expressed concerns about the planning system relates to communication between the Council and customers. Surveys and questionnaires are thus targeted at as many groups as possible and it is often the case that their needs must be addressed in different ways: PARISH COUNCIL relationships have been improved by:–

- The introduction of publicity procedures for planning proposals which go beyond those laid down in legislation (for example by providing sets of application plans automatically and allowing sufficient time for comments).
- By setting up planning and building control surgeries at out-stations to improve access to advice.
- By providing more comprehensive information about planning decisions and how they are reached.

For applicants and the public, new procedures ensure that:–

- They are automatically informed when a planning application is to go to Committee as well as given full information on the nature of the decision.
- They are told how they can address the appropriate Area Planning Committee by asking a question or making a statement.
- Area Committees meet within the area they serve.

> *'I feel sure that you have helped to create a better atmosphere in which planning staff, Committee members and those of us working on planning matters outside the official framework will be able to communicate in the future.'*
>
> *Mr H, Braintree.*

Economic development

Discussions with local companies, Chambers of Trade etc indicated a strongly felt need for improved liaison between the business community, the District Council and the various business support agencies such as ESSEX TEC and the D.T.I. We accordingly set up the Braintree District Business Forum. With four meetings a year to discuss issues of mutual concern, these have proved highly successful with over 100 business people attending recent meetings.

The Council also operate a 'Customer First' suggestion scheme and a satisfaction card to generate feedback on the service that has been provided.

Consultation

Our consultation procedures are designed to ensure that everybody who has interest in their environment has a chance to comment on a variety of planning issues. Some consultees are notified as part of the statutory process. The vast majority are consulted in order to ensure that concerns and interests are taken on board as much as possible even though planning decisions will not meet everyone's wishes.

CRITERION 4

Courtesy and helpfulness

For many years Customer care has been a major element of the Council's Corporate Strategy. Our first core value is: "WE ARE CUSTOMER ORIENTATED".

We are proud of the friendly, helpful and efficient service we provide to the public. We believe that we lead the way by giving customer care top priority in the Council's activities and to do this we provide a comprehensive approach to service development, internal organisation/systems, training and staff development.

To ensure that staff are fully conversant with all aspects of customer care:–

- Induction sessions for all new staff emphasise the Council's commitment to customers and quality.
- Customer service is an integral element of the target setting, performance measure and review process which takes place at staff appraisals.
- Customer care training is provided for all front line staff. This deals with telephone techniques, plain English, coping with aggressive customers etc.

Staff provide their names in correspondence and over the telephone, wear name badges and, at reception areas wear uniform. Regular surveys test visitors reaction to reception arrangements and procedures.

Accessibility

In some cases, access to the Planning Department can be difficult for customers during the day and so a number of measures have been introduced to solve the problem. These include:–

- **Out of hours inspections of plans** – Arrangements are publicised for planning applications and other documents to be inspected at unsocial hours.
- **Surgeries** – Advice surgeries have been running for some years at 2 out stations
- **Preliminary Advice** – Where potential applicants need advice prior to submitting a planning application they can do so, at no charge at the Planning Department and at out-stations.
- **Copies of Plans** – Where customers can show that they are unable to view planning applications by normal means or through their Parish/Town Council, copies will be sent to them.

CRITERION 5

Putting things right

The Council have operated a defined complaints procedure for nearly ten years. A deliberately broad view is taken of what constitutes a complaint. In the Planning Department all responses good or bad are initially identified as "customer feedback" and, whether in writing, telephone or in person, all staff are able to deal with them.

The procedure is set out in a leaflet 'Our Aim is Quality' which is distributed to all staff and Councillors.

The complaint should be replied to within 7 days. If it is a complicated case, an interim response should be provided within 7 days and the customer subsequently kept informed of progress.

If the customer is not satisfied with the response, the Chief Executive will review the case and decide on any further action.

If still dissatisfied, the Chairman and Vice Chairman of the Council will consider the case, action taken and provide an appropriate response.

The Local Government Ombudsman

Customers can of course take their case to the Ombudsman and the procedure for doing this is explained in the leaflet. The Council's own procedure often avoids the need to refer cases to the Ombudsman.

Every month, a summary of all complaints against the Council is compiled and reviewed by the Council's Corporate Management Team. Complaints are reviewed every 2 months by elected Councillors at Policy Committee meetings.

The Planning Department has its own internal vetting procedure for complaints whereby all cases are reviewed monthly by the Department Management Team. This process provides a means of continuity at all levels which enables us to improve our service to customers.

CRITERION 6

Value for money

As part of the Council's Corporate Strategy, a Strategy Guidelines Report is prepared each year to provide specific guidelines on areas for particular achievement during the following year. This report also provides direction to Committees in preparing their Annual Plans and the budget process.
The Planning Committee Annual Plan:-
i)   Considers within the framework of the Strategy Guidelines Report service targets for the forthcoming year.

ii) Identifies other service priorities and issues facing the Committee and recommends changes.

iii) Recognises the opportunities and challenges facing the Committee.

The Plan reviews service targets relating to budget guidance, customer interests, quality, economic development, environment, housing, transport, service reviews, etc.

The budgetary position is reviewed quarterly at Planning Committee meetings together with all key performance indicators. Actual expenditure levels are examined against income levels and budgetary variations, where they occur, are considered and action taken.

The extent to which performance levels are achieved (or not) and targets met are reviewed through both the quarterly monitoring reports and the performance appraisal/performance related pay process.

In addition to the exercise of budgetary control through internal service reviews, service costs are examined by the Audit Commission who, in their 1992/93 estimates found that in Development Control:–

- Net expenditure per head was £2.0 against a 'family' average of £2.9.
- The cost of determining each planning application was on average £150 against the 'family' average of £243, and as a result the cost of the development control service per 100,000 population was £100,000 less than the family average.

These savings were achieved despite Braintree receiving 13.3 planning applications per thousand people when the Audit Commission equivalent family average figure is 12.0.

> 'Staff employed are courteous and well informed.'
> District Auditor, November 1992.

In performance terms Braintree currently determines just over 80% of planning applications within 8 weeks compared to the family average of 60% in 1991/92 (Source: CIPFA Planning and Development Statistics 1992 DoE).

In 1992 the District Auditor carried out a value for money study of our Development Control service as part of the Council's 1991/92 audit of accounts.

The study commended the Department for:–

- The provision of pre-application discussion and advice.
- Consultation procedures to inform the public.
- Provision of information on Committee meetings.
- Providing weekly planning surgeries at Witham and Halstead.
- Making provision for the public to view plans if they cannot attend during office hours.

- Providing advice notes for the public.
- Efficient acknowledgement of planning applications more quickly than recommended by best practice.
- Carrying out a plain English review of documentation.
- Carrying out development design audits with Councillors to consider the extent to which developments comply with planning policies.
- Running an Environmental Heritage Award Scheme which recognises good development, environmental enhancement etc, which is funded by private sponsorship.

In addition the study noted that development control procedures comply with best practice in respect of:–

- The commitment to quality through the introduction of customer contracts.
- The move to seek accreditation under BS5750 for development control systems.
- Carrying out customer satisfaction surveys.

Development Control procedures in Braintree comply with guidelines and best practice recommended by the Audit Commission in their study "Building in Quality, A Study of Development Control", – 1992, the Department of the Environment/National Planning Forum Charter Guide "Development Control" – 1993 and the "Guidelines for the Handling of Planning Applications" produced by the National; Development Control Forum in 1988.

These endorsements illustrate our commitment to quality services. In addition Braintree Council:–

- Won the PA/SOLACE Award as the top UK Council for quality.
- Has been listed as one of the 16 best managed Councils in the country by INLOGOV.
- Is the sole UK entrant for the Bertelsmann Prize for the best world wide local government.

CRITERION 7

Customer satisfaction

As indicated in Section 3, the Council has developed a marketing strategy which specifies the need to listen to and learn from our customers.

Every year, the Planning Department carries out at least 4 market research surveys of different customers. The results are analysed, reported in full to Committee and, whenever possible, improvements are made. Both favourable and unfavourable comments are quoted in

Committee reports even though the planning system cannot meet the requirements of all its customers.

> 'Your excellent customer service is second to none and is sincerely appreciated.'
>
> Building Company, September 1991

The feedback from client groups enables each department to instigate 10 x 1% self sustaining improvements to their services each year.

These may be income generating services, customer contracts, improvements to systems plus numerous procedural improvements identified through the development of quality assurance systems.

Customer Panels

The Braintree District Business Forum referred to previously under Criterion 2 has proved to be a highly successful vehicle for fostering dialogue and partnership between the business community, the Council and various public agencies providing business support. It is organised by a Steering Committee comprising all interest groups. The role of this Committee has developed so that it now provides a very effective consultative panel on local economic affairs.

A customer panel has also been established to oversee the development of a new neighbourhood development south of Braintree.

The Great Notley Liaison Forum was established in 1991, meets at least quarterly depending on circumstances and is comprised of the developer, local Councillor, Chairman of the Planning Committee and local Parish representatives.

The work of the Liaison Forum has provided a vital link in the chain of communication between local people, the Council and the developer.

A Landscape and Countryside Liaison Group has been established to discuss and review planning policies which effect the rural environment. The Group is comprised of Councillors, Officers, Ramblers, NFU, countryside groups etc and meets quarterly.

CRITERION 8

Quality of Service Improvements

The Council fully encourages change and innovation linked to both customer care and quality. Our policy for quality services states that:–

"Braintree District Council aims to deliver defect-free products and services to our customers, both internal and external on time and within budget.

To meet this target, the Council is securing accreditation to BS5750/ISO9004 for appropriate services with the intention of securing registration of the whole Council for BS5750 under BSI's company wide scheme by October 1993.

The Building Control Service was the first in the country to secure B.S.I. certification in March 1993. The remainder of the Planning Department is expected to do so by August 1993.

A Corporate Quality Improvement Team has been established to drive the initiative and individual quality teams within each Department provide a link with every member of staff to ensure that each individual is not only aware but contributes to the process.

The Council has a formal internal suggestion scheme. In addition each Director has to secure a series of improvements and report these to the Performance Appraisal Panel each year.

The following improvements were introduced this year:–
1.   Customer Contracts for Development Control and Building Control.
2.   Improvements to Area Planning Committee – Introduction of public question time, changes to agenda format, and information to the public.
3.   Advertising income obtained from promotional brochure and advertising local services.
4.   Establishment of public entertainment licensing system (Previously carried out by Essex County Council).
5.   Effective introduction of new Development Control/Building Control computer system.
6.   Improvements to economic development strategy through links with Department of Trade and Industry and handling of inward investment enquiries.
7.   New system introduced in October 1992 to improve Development Control/Building Control Liaison.
8.   Service level agreements for Building Control customers extended to small housing developments.

Public Question Time

The public question time procedure at Planning Committee meetings was originally introduced on an experimental basis in 1991 and has subsequently been confirmed – with refinements – as a consequence of surveying users of the system, the public, officers and members. The meetings take place within the area of the District they serve and the public can question Members and Officers (or make a statement) on any matter of Council business or an issue of local concern.

'ONE STOP SHOP FOR BUSINESS'

CRITERION 9

Great Notley garden village service level agreement with Countryside Properties plc

Braintree District Council took a bold decision in the late 1980's to plan for growth in the next ten years by focusing new development on large sites close to the existing towns. This would allow the District Council to negotiate contributions from landowners and developers for infrastructure and community facilities, including affordable housing, community and leisure facilities, highway improvements etc.

> *'We are convinced White Courts will become the focus of national interest and something of a blueprint for accommodating growth in a sensitive area.'*
>
> Roger Barrett, Director of Planning,
> September 1992.

Countryside Properties plc have now received planning permission for a major new neighbourhood south of Braintree on a site of 430 acres. The site – Great Notley – will provide 2000 new homes, business park, 100 acre country park and is subject to legal agreements providing community facilities to the value of approximately £16m. The design philosophy for the development emphasises the importance of a high quality landscape setting for the new housing areas coupled with an imaginative approach to road layouts to keep average speeds down to 20mph or less.

It was well known that Countryside Properties had almost exclusively used the NHBC for building control service since they were awarded 'approved inspector' status for new dwellings. Even before the granting of planning permission the District Council was well aware that a substantial amount of fee income was at stake (approximately £400,000 at current rates) and that to win over the Company's work a unique and attractive offer had to be put together.

An initial approach in early 1990 to Countryside Properties suggested they might be interested in using our Building Control service, but only if the Council could offer an overall package which would co-ordinate all its relevant services as well as those of other outside agencies such as the County Council and Water Company. The Company pointed out that on large projects in other areas they had experienced fragmentation of local authority interests and therefore favoured a project-led team approach co-ordinating all the different regulatory services.

A project team of all relevant departments and agencies was set up and in January 1991 submitted a draft Agreement to Countryside Properties. Following lengthy negotiations, formal signing of the final Agreement took place in March 1993. While negotiations were taking place, the team vetted a trial submission to test the practicality of the arrangements.

The Agreement is a statement of intent and is specifically not a legally binding relationship between the two organisations. It is additional to and does not substitute for the legal responsibilities of either party.

> *'Braintree's progressive attitude and their reasonable approach to private sector investment put them head and shoulders above other authorities.'*
>
> *Savills Property Agents,*
> *August 1992.*

All relevant Council services are covered by the Agreement, which sets out standards and levels of performance including response times where appropriate.

Services covered by the 'One Stop' Agreement:

Planning Control	Amenity & Leisure
Environmental Health	Estate Roads
Building Control	Street Naming & Numbering
Legal and Land Charge Services	Main Drainage & Water Supply

Central to the arrangement is the nomination by both the Company and the Council of a 'Project Officer' in each organisation, leading their respective development teams. During the actual construction stage of the development, the Council's team will provide a continuous site presence, ensuring effective co-ordination of all relevant services.

This Agreement which is, as far as we know, unique, clearly fulfils the following principles:

- the Agreement was a direct and specific response to a potential customer's identified need,
- there was some resistance within Countryside Properties to the idea of using local authority Building Control services, but the Company were eventually persuaded by the persistence and determination of the project team,
- it has involved a team of people across a wide range of services, both inside and outside the District Council,
- the District Council has responded to all problems the Company identified from dealing with local authorities on large sites and will continue to amend working practices in the light of experience,
- providing specific contact points on both sides to ensure a co-ordinated response to the complex range of issues that merge on any large scale development such as this,

- there is a continuous dialogue both within the project team and between the District Council and Countryside Properties.

Although the development is only just starting on site, the benefits of a co-ordinated response are already being seen in negotiations on infrastructure and the initial phases of the scheme.

'My Company has had a long relationship with the Council. During that time my colleagues and myself have noticed the ever-increasing ability of the Council to deliver a comprehensive and quality service to its customers.

We have found that all the officers we have negotiated with tackle their professional and managerial duties in a highly effective and efficient manner. It clearly seems to me that this culture of excellence has been instilled into the whole organisation, including its members.

I feel sure that the District Council will not only maintain but improve upon its commitment to total quality.'

Alan Cherry, Chairman,
Countryside Properties plc,
September 1992.

ANGLIA RAILWAYS

Introduction

Anglia Railways operate InterCity trains between London, Ipswich and Norwich, and local train services in Norfolk, Suffolk and parts of Cambridgeshire. In 1993 they became the first British Rail service to be awarded a Charter Mark Award for improvements to their InterCity route.

They are clearly representative of an organisation that is committed not only to the delivery of a high-quality service, but to continually improving that quality service in response to customer needs. This fact is reflected by the variety of channels which they use, both to gauge passengers' views about the service and provide information for self-assessment. See Figure 6.11.

Amongst these are customer surveys, letters/customer correspondence (which provide vital management information), customer surgeries (where members of the public have the opportunity to meet managers), and links with Travellers Associations, the Rail Users Consultative Committee (RUCC), media and local councillors. Anglia Railways has only existed in its current form since 1 April 1994; prior to that the organisation was known as InterCity Anglia and had responsibility only for the InterCity services for which it was awarded the Charter Mark. Excerpts from Anglia publications shown here, date from 1993 and therefore refer to InterCity Anglia.

The impact of the Passenger's Charter

The Passenger's Charter sets out some of the service standards which Anglia aims to achieve. These relate to train performance, ticket office standards and customer relations. The Passenger's Charter also indicates when customers are entitled to discounts or compensation when things go wrong.

The InterCity Anglia Annual Report to Customers 1992/93 (Investing in your Railway) detailed how the organisation had performed against Passenger's Charter standards and other key criteria. It also looks at how investment was being targeted sensibly. The report is summarised below, illustrating some of the steps taken which not only pleased travellers, but also formed the basis for the subsequent application and award of a Charter Mark.

Reliability – InterCity services achieved over 99% reliability throughout the year. Problems caused by locomotive unreliability – measured by the number of minutes delay incurred through locomotive failures – were reduced by 30% compared to 1991/92.

KEY AREAS OF CUSTOMER SERVICE

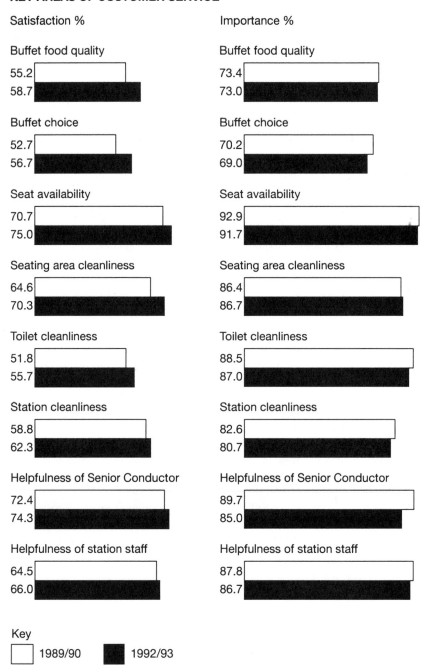

Satisfaction %

Buffet food quality
55.2
58.7

Buffet choice
52.7
56.7

Seat availability
70.7
75.0

Seating area cleanliness
64.6
70.3

Toilet cleanliness
51.8
55.7

Station cleanliness
58.8
62.3

Helpfulness of Senior Conductor
72.4
74.3

Helpfulness of station staff
64.5
66.0

Importance %

Buffet food quality
73.4
73.0

Buffet choice
70.2
69.0

Seat availability
92.9
91.7

Seating area cleanliness
86.4
86.7

Toilet cleanliness
88.5
87.0

Station cleanliness
82.6
80.7

Helpfulness of Senior Conductor
89.7
85.0

Helpfulness of station staff
87.8
86.7

Key
☐ 1989/90   ■ 1992/93

Figure 6.11

Punctuality – Although problems remained, performance was improving steadily with Anglia expecting 87% of its InterCity trains to arrive within 10 minutes of their advertised arrival time by the end of 1993. (Anglia gives discounts to Season Ticket Holders whilst performance is below 87% – as laid down in the Passenger's Charter). The Passenger's Charter target of 90% was the next step, although performance was already very encouraging with the 90% target exceeded over the two month period between mid-June and mid-August 1993. Indeed the overall performance for 1993/94 did ultimately exceed the target with an average of 90.7%.

Customer Correspondence – Over the 12 months to May 1993, 5286 letters were received by InterCity Anglia. Over 80% of these were replied to within 10 days – an improvement on the previous year's figure of 70%. The average response time was 6 days.

Improving the Product – Anglia implemented new initiatives to improve their product range. The introduction of a cheap day return fare (the London Day Out ticket), more advance purchase tickets, special promotions and better catering facilities were just some of the ways in which they responded to customers' diverse needs.

Improving the Service – Anglia took positive action to enhance their service, mostly in regard to customers' concerns and priorities – highlighted through research and passengers' correspondence. The first enhancement was the provision of accurate, timely and relevant information at every stage of the journey, and the introduction of a new handy Guide to Services providing comprehensive information for all customers using the route. This included a tear-off pocket timetable for regular travellers, which meets customer requests for a pocket size route timetable covering not just specific station departures, but full travel details for the route.

At stations and on trains, communication links were upgraded and enhanced. A new communications centre at Ipswich provides a focal point for co-ordinating information across the entire route. Messages are transmitted via pagers to Senior Conductors and station staff to ensure that they can keep passengers informed of any service alterations. Another new service introduced by Anglia was the Travel Check phone line which gives those about to travel or meet friends at the station up-to-date details of how trains are running.

Investing for the future – Investment has been focused on key areas eg. stations, infrastructure, trains, people, training and customer service. For example, £300,000 was spent refurbishing waiting rooms, new toilets, improving signage and exterior repainting. At the Train Maintenance Depot (Crown Point) in Norwich, new fault monitoring systems were introduced for rolling stock, better cleaning facilities provided and train reliability improved by 30%.

A £76m scheme to replace signalling equipment between London and Colchester is now under way, addressing the key section of line which most adversely affects train performance. As well as focusing on the external customer, Anglia has also been very much aware of the importance and value of the internal customer. Training is seen as an integral part of their strategy and training courses are run on a variety of subjects from technical issues to customer service. Further developments have also taken place with a new training school being opened at the Norwich Crown Point maintenance depot, a new briefing and training room at Ipswich and further training completed in safety management.

A Benchmark for Further Improvement – The Charter Mark application put together by InterCity Anglia follows overleaf, but it is worth noting that Anglia Railways' (as they subsequently became) commitment and action to improve their service didn't end in 1993 with the award of the Charter Mark.

The Charter Mark was an illustration of real, measurable improvements; a bench mark by which to monitor future developments and a spur to the Anglia team to continue their efforts to continually raise their standard of service to their customers. (Charter Mark winners have to re-apply for a Charter Mark after three years.) The Anglia team regard the Charter Mark not as an end in itself – customer service, customer satisfaction and increasing customer patronage are obviously the real issues – but a means by which progress can be both gauged and ultimately recognised.

Since the award in October 1993, further improvements have already taken place. These developments have been as follows:

- A new First Class lounge and a Standard waiting room at Ipswich station.
- A revamped forecourt at Ipswich station giving easier access and egress for customers by foot, bicycle , car, taxi and bus.
- Better information provision at Stowmarket and Diss stations.
- A new, more comprehensive guide for the local services, for which Anglia now has responsibility.
- New ticket opportunities for Anglia's customers.
- Better connections between the local and InterCity services.
- Better facilities and access for disabled travellers using local trains, by pioneering a portable ramp carried on the train.

In conclusion, it is interesting to look at Anglia Railways vision which encapsulates its business philosophy: 'To be a respected and successful East Anglian business recognised for its high standards of customer service.' Its customer service achievements so far seem totally consistent with this aspiration.

INTERCITY ANGLIA'S
CHARTER MARK APPLICATION 1993

STANDARDS

'Setting, monitoring and publication of explicit standards for the services that individual users can reasonably expect. Publication of actual performance against these standards.'

Setting standards

The twice yearly publication of a timetable immediately makes measurement of performance an important issue. This 'timetable promise' is measured in a number of ways and targets are set, and have been published, in our Passenger's Charter. The targets are demanding for us and will remain so as we seek improved performance from the railway infrastructure operator, Railtrack, from April 1994. The targets align closely to the areas of service which passengers tell us are important through specific research and our Passenger Monitor Questionnaire.

In many areas measurement is more difficult but our Fair Deal for Customers booklet makes clear our commitment to excellent customer service and indicates what our customers can expect.

Publishing of standards

A comprehensive statement of our performance standards is set out in the Passenger's Charter, available at all ticket offices. The Board's Annual Report highlights overall performance and we are now producing an Annual Report for our customers in East Anglia. This is seen as the most appropriate approach where data is drawn from local surveys and trends in data are the best indicator of customer requirements.

Publishing information on performance against standards

Information giving reasons for recent substandard performance is displayed at stations offering a clear explanation of events.

We publish every four weeks, data on directly measured items like train reliability and punctuality, at stations along the route.

INFORMATION AND OPENNESS

'Full, accurate information readily available in plain language about how public services are run, what they cost, how well they perform and who is in charge.'

Availability of information

Information on InterCity Anglia services is presented in many forms. The national BR Timetable and InterCity Guide to Services, together with the InterCity Anglia Guide each contain full details and are widely available. The BR Timetable may be found at stations, Information Centres, Booksellers and Libraries. Guides to services can also be requested by telephone and will be posted to customers. Posters and leaflets at stations give details of travel offers and other specialist advice, for example, travel and connectional arrangements for the disabled.

Telephone Enquiry Bureaux (TEB) are advertised in all literature and in the Phone Book and can give any assistance required. An 0800 telephone number is offered for tickets requiring advance purchase and TEB's will make arrangements for other ticket sales by telephone if requested. Information by telephone also includes a record ('talking') timetable, a Travel Check line giving current train running information and a weekend travel check line giving advice of any alterations to train services for those planning ahead. The quality and ease of obtaining information at stations and from TEB's is tested in our quarterly Passenger Monitor Question-naire; by a 'mystery caller' audit and through electronic monitoring of call rates.

Properly trained and briefed staff are on hand at stations and on trains to assist in providing and interpreting information for customers if this proves necessary. More recently Customer Welcome staff have been provided at key stations and interchanges to provide visible and pro-active assistance to travellers less familiar with our services.

We take our broader responsibilities very seriously and this is perhaps best illustrated by our publication of our Railway Code and Guide to Safety.

Comprehensiveness of the information that is published

A wide variety of publications provide information on aspects of our service and include our Conditions of Carriage, Code of Practice for dealing with customer comments and our Passenger's Charter. Customers therefore have access to information about the service they can expect and what to do if we fail to provide that service.

Where the service offered is subject to alteration, adequate advance publicity is given on posters, through the media and in many cases will be published in advance in the Guide to Services. In these circumstances additional staff are always posted at key locations to assist customers.

Feedback on the effectiveness of information provided is obtained in a number of ways. The Guide to Services is for example, mailed out to several thousand customers and comments are sought as to its appropriateness. Prior to its publication in May, a pilot of the Anglia Guide was published to enable us to consult with staff and customers to ensure that it met their needs. Feedback from staff in regular contact with customers is of a particular importance in making such assessments.

CHOICE AND CONSULTATION

'The public sector should provide choice wherever practical, there should be regular and systematic consultation with those who use services. Users' views about services, and their priorities for improving them, should be taken into account in final decisions and standards setting.'

Consulting the customer

1. Our Passenger Monitor Questionnaire is an extensive, quarterly tracking survey which reveals those aspects of our service which are of most importance to customers and asks for an assessment of our performance in each area. The greatest gaps between expectation and perception are then the focus for improvement.
2. Senior Managers meet the Rail Users Consultative Committee (RUCC) and sub Committees six times each year, and Committee officers informally 2/3 times each year. User groups (e.g. East Suffolk Travellers Association, Colchester Rail Users Group) are consulted informally 1–2 times each year to establish local priorities and gain feedback, particularly in respect of performance and timetable issues. Local Managers have a programme of 'meet the manager' style surgeries at each station to talk with regular travellers. Informal dinners on the train for small customer groups are held by the Director, allowing very focused discussions on topics of interests.
3. On specific topics consultation is undertaken in a variety of ways. Our handling of customer correspondence – by letter or comment form – is for example, followed up by questionnaires mailed to a sample of customers asking how well they thought we handled matters.

Using customer feedback to revise standards

Our service standards are reviewed annually, but currently the Department of Transport finally determines key targets.

We have been undertaking analysis of Passenger Monitor data to validate targets for punctuality, from responses given by customers. The importance ratings given have been calibrated against their experience of our service when surveyed. This is leading us to develop proposals for new performance standards based on the requirements 'revealed'. A second development will be to weight train service performance by the number of customers on board each leg of the journey to ensure the performance rating more accurately reflects customer experience. We collect loading data for every train.

The Passenger Monitor, its use of a rating system, and our analysis of the output, are all aimed to ensure standards are meaningful and accorded due priority.

COURTESY AND HELPFULNESS

'Courtesy and helpful service from public servants who will normally wear name badges. Services available equally to all who are entitled to them and run to suit their convenience.'

Courteous and efficient services accessible to all

Providing excellent customer service is the cornerstone of our business. The focus of staff is on ensuring that our service is of a consistently high standard so that customers choose to travel with us again. Our commitment to customer service is outlined in our 'Welcome to Anglia' posters at stations and published in our Guide to Services.

In support of this, customer service staff training takes a number of forms. Staff working on the train attend an annual two day briefing to update them on business developments and provide focused skills training, for example in public address which had been identified as a 'quality gap' by customers. Over the last year all staff coming into contact with customers attended a two day workshop in self awareness and interpersonal skills – Developing Our Positive Image. This is now being followed by a programme introducing individual coaching and support for these staff as part of an appraisal process. The Passenger Monitor assesses staff performance in specific areas of customer service.

Communicating with the customer

Name badges are always worn together with distinctive uniforms, and it is the norm for staff to give their names when answering telephone enquiries, and always in correspondence. Senior Managers also wear name badges when travelling on services.

Customers' accessibility to services

Through research, consultation and customer feedback our services have developed to best satisfy customer needs and commercial requirements. Train services have regular, even interval departures from London Liverpool Street and Norwich, the earliest departure at 0505 hours and the latest at 2330 hours. Ticket office opening hours are extensive and tickets to all destinations can be purchased on trains at other times without difficulty.

Special arrangements are in place for the disabled. Assistance may be arranged in advance by telephone and staff will be on hand at both ends of the journey and at any connections en route. Our computer reservation system records and passes on this information. Wheelchair-bound customers are accommodated on every train by using coaches where a seat folds away and access doors have been widened.

Improvements to service delivery continue to be made. On trains, an at seat service of refreshments now complements our restaurant and buffet offer, and a telephone is available to customers.

PUTTING THINGS RIGHT

'If things go wrong, an apology, a full explanation and a swift and effective remedy. A well published and easy to use complaints procedure with independent review wherever possible.'

Complaints procedure

We publish a Code of Practice for dealing with customer comments which clearly set out how to contact us – by letter, by comment form, by telephone and in person. It explains who to contact, how we will handle complaints when received and how we will deal with them to our customers' satisfaction. This document also describes the avenues to follow if you are still not satisfied with our response.

User friendliness of complaints procedure

We try to deal immediately with difficulties on the train. Senior Conductors can offer refreshments in the event of serious delays, free telephone calls and make arrangements for onward journeys and connections. Assistance on taking a complaint forward can also be given. In that event, our Code of Practice is aimed at making contact with us as easy as possible. This is being validated and our performance in handling complaints measured, by following up a sample of complaints to seek feedback on how we dealt with matters. Customer Relations staff have clear guidelines but are given discretion to enable them to deal promptly and fairly with complaints on their merits.

Effectiveness of complaints procedure

Our Code of Practice confirms that we will respond to written complaints within 10 days. Telephone messages will be followed up within 24 hours and dealt with similarly. Customer relations staff aim to give a full explanation of events, or to deal specifically with the issue raised, handling compensation in accordance with guidelines but using discretion to deal with more complicated problems. We aim to be consistent in our handling of complaints but with due regard to individual circumstances, for example special arrangements have been made for Season Ticket Holders.

All complaints are logged on a computer database and so may be analysed, identifying areas for particular attention. Senior Managers sample complaints and responses each month to review the nature and handling of a variety of problems. This use of a complaints data enables us to address clear weaknesses in service and specific problems. Where feedback is received on individual performance – good or bad – staff are interviewed. In this year's on train staff briefings, a full presentation on customer correspondence was given using many examples of customer feedback. This proved to be valuable in helping to improve awareness and so raise standards and will be repeated.

Independent review

Our Code of Practice advises customers of their right to take a complaint to the Rail Users Consultative Committee or London Regional Passengers Committee where it will be independently reviewed. Any matters referred to the Committees are followed up with us by letter or at our regular liaison meetings. This is an established arrangement which has proved to be a fair arbitration process.

VALUE FOR MONEY

'Efficient and economic delivery of public services within the resources the nation can afford and independent validation of performance against standards.'

Improving value for money

1. Over the last two years external supply contracts (and contracts with other parts of BR) for the provision of goods and services have been

reviewed progressively to ensure appropriate specifications are being met safely and at the lowest prices. Examples include the provision of express coach services at weekends when major engineering blockades have been necessary to undertake investment in infrastructure renewal; and provision of taxis to convey customers who have missed connections at Ipswich station.

2. Greater efficiency has in a number of instances, resulted from staff initiatives and outputs from Quality Improvement Teams. In many cases greater efficiency is linked to higher standards of quality and improved safety. Last year a chemical mixing room was set up at Norwich Crown Point train maintenance depot and placed under individual control. The result has been safer handling arrangements, higher standards of cleanliness through correct chemical mixing strengths and a 40% reduction in chemicals used saving over £25k each year.

The planning process

The InterCity Anglia timetable has been sustained through the recession but a cumulative 3% reduction in operating expenses has been targeted and more than achieved over the last three years. Delivery of the 1993/94 budget will see operating expenses reduced by 26% over 1990/91 in cash terms.

Productivity initiatives have resulted from improved management processes including regular manpower audits, and delegation of responsibility for budgets and financial control. Budgets are set and reviewed by source (what money is spent on) which has proved the most powerful way of ensuring value for money.

A recognition policy supports our business values and includes performance related pay for many staff as well as less formal ways of acknowledging the commitment of staff to quality improvement.

Efficiency improvements

1. A dedicated team has been established at Norwich to attend to InterCity Anglia customers. This change has produced greater alignment and focus and improved the service we offer, yet reduced staffing levels at the station by 10 posts.
2. An initiative to empower staff at Norwich Crown Point train maintenance depot has involved removing a whole layer of supervision, reducing costs by over £100,000 this year.
3. A competitive tendering process for all works contracts ensures we secure the best value from scarce funds available for asset maintenance and renewal and avoids a commitment to direct labour.

CUSTOMER SATISFACTION

We operate in a competitive market and our customer base is such that many of our customers travel with us only infrequently (once or twice a year). A consistent delivery of our service to the highest standards is therefore vital for the success of our business.

We measure customer satisfaction in a number of ways. Our Passenger Monitor Questionnaire not only asks for an assessment of performance in 30 separate areas, but asks also for an overall assessment. This is backed up by asking whether customers are more or less likely to travel again based upon their experience of our service on that occasion. This overall satisfaction measure has been showing a steady upward trend over the last two years, moving from a rating where 51% of respondents judged our service to be good or very good (85% good/very good/satisfactory) to a position in the last survey this year where the figures have risen to 66% and 91% respectively.

Our Passenger Monitor survey is a carefully structured document. Its application is carefully controlled, sampling trains to achieve a statistically valid and signficiant result. Over 500 questionnaires are completed on a rolling programme every 12 weeks, by an independent research company who analyses the data.

It has been our experience that the volume of customer correspondence correlates very closely with many of the measures of customers' satisfaction examined by our Passenger Monitor. It follows that we are also able to use analysis of the volume and nature of complaints as a measure of satisfaction.

Measurable improvements in the quality of service over the last two or more years

Customer priorities and the extent to which they are being met is the focus of our Passenger Monitor. As a tracking study, it allows us to identify changing priorities over time and trends in our performance against them. It also enables us to judge the effectiveness of our actions in addressing customers' perceptions of our performance. This research is central in determining our programme for management action to improve business performance. Specific research is also undertaken from time to time to focus on particular issues, both pre- and post-implementation. Recently we have tested new ideas on customers, for example, changes to our information leaflets and to our catering offer, to see whether they meet needs and expectations.

Changes in passenger monitor ratings 1990/91–1993

Quality Of Service Attribute	Customer Priority*	Performance Rating# 1990/91 Jan 1993	
Punctuality	1	53(72)	64(80)
Ease of Finding a Seat	3=	64(87)	82(94)
Journey Time	3=	53(82)	63(90)
Frequency of Train	5=	52(83)	61(90)
Cleanliness of Train	7	54(88)	66(95)

Notes

*Consistent data is not available for two of the top seven priorities currently (information at station, direct trains).

Figures are percentage of customers giving good/very good ratings (figures in brackets are good/very good/satisfactory ratings).

We operate in a very competitive market – with the private and company car, coach and rail alternatives available to customers. Leisure travellers have a range of options open to them which need not include rail travel. Customer requirements are therefore central to our business strategy. They are included in personal objectives, determining investment priorities both for asset renewal and business development, and are the focus for our staff training programme.

We have a policy of continuous improvement based upon measurement. We consider poor performance adds to our costs and a right first time approach eliminates such losses. In the area of train service reliability and punctuality, a customer priority, two processes illustrate our approach:–

1. A monthly Fleet Group reviews all delays to train services measured as minutes lost, due to problems with the trains themselves. This measurement allows basic causes of loss to be identified, prioritised and tackled. As a result the average weekly time lost due to problems with trains has fallen from 325 minutes in 1991/92 to 228 minutes in 1992/93 a (30% improvement), beating the target for achievement of 250 minutes. This target is now being tightened.

2. A train performance group looks in detail at all causes of delay, particularly instances of localised and repeated late running, to identify weaknesses in our timetable or the processes to deliver it. This group involves ground level staff in identification of the basic causes of delay and in seeking solutions.

PLANS TO INTRODUCE OR HAVE IN HAND AT LEAST ONE INNOVATIVE ENHANCEMENT TO SERVICES WITHOUT ANY EXTRA COST TO THE TAX PAYER OR CONSUMER.

InterCity Anglia communications centre

It has been apparent from customer surveys that one of the major causes of customer dissatisfaction has been the lack of current information on train services, particularly during times of disruption. The requirement is to assimilate and then disseminate information swiftly to those who are able to keep customers informed or take appropriate action to minimise disruption. This issue was the subject of a study by a Quality Improvement Team formed by staff on the route. Those closest to the issues therefore had an important influence on the solution.

A Communications Centre was established at Ipswich on 17th May 1993, operated by staff who had previously provided information to customers at Ipswich alone. With access to real time train information systems, their role has now been expanded to establish a link between train operations and information to customers. As a result it has been possible to provide not only a facility to give information to all staff along the route, but also to provide accurate up to date information to staff on every train whilst on the move. A paging bureau and radio pagers for all staff at key locations or in key posts provides the necessary link. The Quality Improvement Team also developed communications contracts for all such staff who now have a responsibility to advise the Communications Centre of events on the route. There is therefore a collective responsibility but clearly defined individual roles in this important area.

We also recognise that there is a need to provide information to other groups. A telephone information service updated hourly (Travel Check), provides current information on train running. This enables those intending to travel or those meeting passengers, to confirm arrangements before setting out. The improved flow of information has enabled us to restructure management and supervision along the route. Managers who were previously static are now part of the mobile team whose primary concern is customer service. Real time information now enables those Duty Managers to respond to events much more effectively. This change has improved the service offered to customers and reduced staff costs.

Information is critical to customer confidence in our service and these changes have provided significant improvements at lower cost, responding directly to customer needs. The knowledge and ingenuity of staff has been employed to come up with the appropriate solutions.

This approach is central to our Quality Strategy and staff are always able to make suggestions for improvement in any area through our staff suggestion scheme.

EAST GLOUCESTERSHIRE NHS TRUST

Introduction

East Gloucestershire NHS Trust (EGNHST) was established in April 1991 in response to the reforms that were taking place within the Health Service at that time. From its establishment EGNHST set down principles upon which their services would be based:

- A choice of comprehensive, high quality health care and services.
- Care provided through a range of hospital and community facilities, and in people's homes.

Commitment to these principles is clearly shown by the diverse range of services they provide to their customers, (approximately 218,000 people representing a largely rurally based community) including three acute, one elderly care and five community hospitals, a comprehensive range of mental health services for people with learning disabilities and community nursing services.

Between 1 April 1992 and 31 March 1993, the Trust treated over 32,000 in-patients, some 8,000 day cases, over 73,000 Accident and Emergency patients and saw over 17,000 out-patients. Together with approximately 40,000 attendances at day hospitals there were up to 325,000 patient contacts.

THE PATIENT'S CHARTER

On 30th October 1991, the NHS **Patient's Charter** was published. The Charter is a central part of the programme to improve and modernise the delivery of the National Health Service to the public. Two years later, in October 1993, the East Gloucestershire NHS Trust received one of only six **Charter Marks** awarded to NHS organisations by the Government in that year. This national recognition, which we very much welcome, comes as a result of the hard work and dedication of all Trust staff.

The **Charter Mark Scheme** acknowledges excellence in providing public services in accordance with the **Citizen's Charter**. Award winners must conform to a demanding set of standards in critical areas like communication, choice, civility, effective response to complaints and economy in the delivery of services. The Patient's Charter sets out seven existing national rights and three new rights from the 1st April 1992, along with nine standards of service which the NHS will be aiming to provide for you. The Charter also requires local Charter Standards to be set. We would like to tell you what you can expect from us in the light of the Charter. Don't forget you can help us by coming on time for appointments and by letting us know well ahead if you cannot attend a clinic or for operation.

SEVEN EXISTING RIGHTS

- To receive health care on the basis of clinical need regardless of ability to pay: **All our services will comply with your rights in this respect.**
- To be registered with a GP: **This is the responsibility of the Family Health Services Authority.**
- To receive emergency medical care at any time, through your GP or the emergency Ambulance Service, and hospital Accident & Emergency Department: **The Hospital Accident & Emergency service will provide emergency medical care when you require it.**
- To be referred to a consultant, acceptable to you, when your GP thinks it necessary, and to be referred for a second opinion if you and your GP agree this is desirable: **Your GP's referral will be to a consultant acceptable to you and a second opinion will be provided if agreed.**
- To be given a clear explanation of any treatment proposed, including any risks and any alternatives, before you decide whether you will agree to the treatment: **The consultant responsible for your treatment will ensure that the treatment proposed, including any relevant risks and alternatives, is discussed with you so that you can decide whether you will agree to any treatment.**
- To have access to your health records, and to know that those working for the NHS will, by law, keep their contents confidential: **We comply with the laws regarding confidentiality and access to your health records.**
- To choose whether or not you wish to take part in medical research or medical student training: **Your permission will be sought before you are included in medical research or training.**

THREE NEW RIGHTS

From 1st April 1992 you will have had three important new rights.
- To be given detailed information on local health services, including quality standards and maximum waiting times. **We provide Gloucestershire Health with information which they use to tell you what current quality standards and waiting times for treatment are. We are constantly working to improve the quality of services.**

■ To be guaranteed admission for treatment by a specific date, no later than two years from the day when your consultant places you on the waiting list. **We do not have any patients waiting for treatment for longer than ONE year. Currently 90% of patients are admitted within SIX MONTHS.**

■ To have any complaint about NHS services investigated, and to receive a full and prompt written reply from the Chief Executive. **Any complaint about services provided will be acknowledged and investigated promptly. We aim to provide you with a reply within three weeks; if we are unable to do so we will write and explain why. Replies will come from the Chief Executive.**

NATIONAL CHARTER STANDARDS

There are nine standards of service which the NHS will be aiming to provide for you:

■ Respect for privacy, dignity and religious and cultural beliefs: **We will treat you with due regard to your privacy and dignity and we will do our utmost to respect your religious and cultural beliefs.**

■ Arrangements to ensure that everyone, including people with special needs, can use the services: **We will ensure that all patients can use our services, making special arrangements if necessary.**

■ Information to relatives and friends about the progress of treatment, subject of course, to your wishes: **When your relatives and friends enquire about your treatment we will inform them of your progress, if we have your permission to do so.**

■ An emergency ambulance should arrive within 14 minutes in an urban area, or 19 minutes in a rural area: **The provision of ambulance services is the responsibility of the Gloucestershire Ambulance Trust. Gloucestershire is classified as a rural area.**

■ When attending an Accident & Emergency Department, you will be seen immediately and your need for treatment assessed: **If you have to attend the Accident & Emergency Department, you will be seen immediately by an experienced, qualified nurse who will assess the priority of your need for treatment by the doctor.**

■ When you go to an out-patient clinic, you will be given a specific appointment time and will be seen within 30 minutes of it: **When you attend for an out-patient appointment you will be given a specific appointment time, and it is our aim that you will be seen by the most appropriate member of the clinical team within 30 minutes of your appointment time. This occurs over 80% of the time, however in some circumstances this may not be possible, for example, the** doctor may be called to deal with an emergency. **Where your wait exceeds 30 minutes you will receive an explanation for the delay. The doctor may need the results of tests before he can discuss treatment with you, and this will be explained to you when you arrive at the out-patient clinic.**

■ Your operation should not be cancelled on the day you are due to arrive in hospital. If, exceptionally, your operation has to be postponed, you will be admitted to hospital within one month of the cancelled operation: **We aim not to cancel operations especially on the day set for admission. Sometimes, regrettably, this is a necessity. Arrangements will be made for your admission as soon as possible after the original date and within one month in the exceptional circumstances of a cancellation.**

■ A named qualified nurse, midwife or health visitor will be responsible for your nursing or midwifery care: **On admission to hospital or referral to community health services, you will be allocated a named qualified nurse, midwife or health visitor. In Hospitals, you will be allocated a 'Named Nurse'. In Midwifery, it will be the Community Midwife who books you initially but, on admission to St. Paul's Hospital, your named nurse will be another qualified midwife. In Community Services, it will be the District Nurse or Health Visitor. In Mental Health Services and Services for those with Learning Disabilities it will be the named Key Worker.**

■ A decision should be made about continuing health or social needs you may have, before you are discharged from hospital: **We will ensure that a decision is made about your requirements for continuing health or social care following an in-patient stay, before you are discharged from hospital. We will explain what these arrangements are to you and, if you wish, to your carers and relatives.**

LOCAL CHARTER STANDARDS

The Government has highlighted a number of aspects of service where they wish to see local standards set and publicised. In many of these aspects we had already taken action to review current standards, set new targets for improvement and to monitor progress against these targets. We are working with Gloucestershire Health to set, monitor and publicise standards in greater detail.

OUR LOCAL STANDARDS

These are our aims in five key areas:

- Waiting time for first routine out-patient appointments: **We will work towards everyone being seen by a consultant within 13 weeks of receiving the letter from your GP. At present, 82% of patients are. If your condition is described as urgent by your GP, you will be seen much more quickly of course.**

- Waiting times in Accident & Emergency departments after your need for treatment has been assessed: **We will aim at 30 minutes being the maximum length of wait. Please bear with us when doctors are called away to deal with emergencies in the Accident & Emergency Department, on wards or in operating theatres. In all cases of delay, you will be given an explanation for that delay. If treatment cannot be given within thirty minutes for exceptional reasons, your needs and priority will be reassessed.**

- Waiting times for taking you home after treatment where your doctor says you have a medical need for NHS transport: **The Gloucestershire Ambulance Trust make all the arrangements and are responsible for scheduling the vehicles. A Standard is difficult to set because ambulances may well be busy elsewhere when we call them. They will try to have you collected within 30 minutes. We will call an ambulance for you and let you know what is happening.**

- Enabling you and your visitors to find your way around the hospitals through enquiry points and better signposting: **A lot of signposting has been improved recently and we shall be doing more to make sure you can get from A to B easily. There are reception points in many of our hospitals already and our staff will gladly help with directions should you feel lost.**

- Ensuring that the staff you meet face to face wear name badges: **Everyone you meet will have a name badge. Don't be shy if you have to ask a name! We are here to serve you and we want our service to be as personal as it can be.**

MISSION STATEMENT
OUR PROMISE TO THE PUBLIC AND STAFF

OBJECTIVES | To provide a choice of comprehensive, high quality health care at hospitals in Cheltenham and Cirencester, at the associated community hospitals, through a range of community facilities and to patients in their own homes. Services will be free, accessible and will meet specified standards of quality as flexibly as possible.

PATIENTS | Patients will provide the Trust livelihood and will be put at the forefront of thinking in all areas of activity. The aim will be to develop and maintain excellent working relationships with all general practitioners with whom the Trust will work for the benefit of patients.

SCOPE | A full range of services will be provided to embrace health promotion, prevention and screening programmes as well as diagnostic and treatment facilities, inpatient and domiciliary services.

QUALITY | Only top quality will be acceptable. Information to patients will be improved. A Service Review Group will be established which will enable purchasers, general practitioners, patients, their relatives and the general public to communicate their views of standards of care provided.

STAFF | The Trust's most precious resource will be its staff. The Trust will provide an open and challenging environment in which staff of all disciplines will be able to develop their abilities to the full and contribute at all levels to maintaining excellence of care. The Trust will be a fair employer.

FINANCE | Financial resources will be earned on merit. The Trust will strive for efficiency and cost effectiveness. High quality services will be provided in return for a fair price. Prudent management will maintain financial stability and create surpluses which will allow a steady improvement in quality and quantity of services.

DEVELOPMENT | Opportunities will be sought to be innovative, consistent with the ever-widening scope of medical knowledge and proven benefits. There will be a flexible response to meeting new needs.

ETHICS | The highest ethical professional standards will be applied across the Trust's activities. The Trust will be entirely straightforward and deal openly with patients, purchasers, suppliers, Government Departments and the Community which it serves.

Their mission statement and their performance against both National and Local Charter Standards below, are indicative of their positive stance to both external and internal customer issues.

Perhaps one of the reasons for their success is their structured approach to quality which involves all levels of staff. This includes:

- the Quality Development Council which is led by the Chief Executive and which takes a strategic view of quality issues Trustwide and initiatives appropriate action;
- Quality Action Teams which give junior staff the opportunity to tackle practical problems directly; and
- a Patient's Charter Implementation Group, which is a small group of operational managers and professionals who review Trust performance and initiate any required action.

East Gloucestershire NHS Trust, The Charter Mark Award and Performance Against the 1993 Award Criteria

Building upon its already well established quality initiatives East Gloucestershire NHS Trust decided to apply for a Charter Mark an application covered the whole of the Trust. In May 1993 their first steering group meeting was held and by 30 June their application form had been submitted. This was followed by a visit from an inspector of the Citizen's Charter Office, and in October 1993 East Gloucestershire NHS Trust (EGNHST) were one of only seven Health Service organisations to receive a Charter Mark Award.

EAST GLOUCESTERSHIRE NHS TRUST
CHARTER MARK APPLICATION 1993
OUR RESPONSE TO THE QUALIFYING CRITERIA

Standards

We have developed a comprehensive system of **setting standards** appropriate to the services provided encompassing:

- professional standards relating to the quality of clinical care service
- standards relating to 'customer care' and patient experiences

In addition, we have **externally imposed standards:**

- set by Health Authorities, GP Fundholders and a range of statutory regulations
- our performance in relation to agreed standards is the subject of detailed checks every quarter
- the agreements between Health Authorities and EGNHST are public documents

How we match up to **clinical standards** is systematically reviewed:

- we run well-established 'audit' programmes through which staff measure how well they match up to professional standards and take action on areas where improvements are indicated. For example, a recent audit across the whole Trust on the Patient's Charter standard to see a nurse specified by name for each patient's stay in hospital, the 'Named Nurse', has resulted in action in areas where difficulties were found, learning from those parts of the Trust where we are doing well
- we have made good progress with the development of audit which involves staff from more than one profession collaborating in reviewing patient care
- a recent review carried out by one of our Health Authority purchasers has demonstrated external recognition of the high quality of our services, together with identifying areas for improvement

We developed a **Local Patient's Charter** which:

- was placed in every outpatient clinic in April 1992 and sent to every household (approximately 87,000) in east Gloucestershire in May 1992
- sets out our local as well as the national standards and publishes the performance which patients can expect from the Trust
- is displayed in key areas of the Trust, such as outpatient waiting areas and hospital wards

We are well-placed in providing services in line with Patient's Charter requirements. A particular achievement is the reduction of **inpatient waiting times:**

- we achieved a maximum waiting time for inpatient admission of nine months by March 1992, with overall inpatient waiting times which the Audit Commission recorded as the best in the country a few months ago
- we were invited by the NHS Management Executive to run a seminar on waiting list management for other hospitals from six regions in the country
- we have sophisticated computerised systems for making figures on waiting lists and waiting times quickly available to all Health Authorities, GPs in Gloucestershire and elsewhere, the Community Health Council (CHC), carers and volunteer representatives and the local press

The attainment of **accreditation** confirms that a hospital is meeting high standards specified over the whole range of its activity by a Regional Accreditation Team:

- our community hospitals at Tewkesbury (accredited 1991 and re-accredited October 1992) and Moreton-in-Marsh (accredited December 1992) have been successful in gaining **Community Hospital Accreditation**. Moore Cottage Hospital at Bourton-on-the-Water is being inspected in June 1993 and others are scheduled to follow.

Our services have received **external recognition**, both local and national, for example

- commendations for good design from the Cheltenham Civic Society for the new wing at Cheltenham General Hospital and Lexham Lodge Mental Health Resource Centre
- public toilets at Cheltenham General Hospital received a commendation in the national 'Loo of the Year' awards following a '24 hour sponsored re-decoration' in aid of the BBC's Children in Need
- Spa Award for high standards in hygiene, safety and customer comfort for Cheltenham General Hospital and Delancey Hospital catering departments
- Rose Bowl of Excellence for Cheltenham General Hospital catering department
- Heartbeat Award for contributing to the reduction of coronary heart disease for Cirencester Hospital catering department

Information and openness

The Trust is run in an open and accountable fashion. For instance:

- an annual meeting to review the Trust's progress is held for members of the public and an Annual Report and Accounts published
- the Trust Boards meet monthly and appropriate papers are published
- names of members of the Trust Boards and hospital managers, are widely publicised
- at ward level, patients are informed who is in charge and who is their 'named nurse' co-ordinating their care
- the inpatient handbook gives the name of the Hospital Manager
- discussion of Trust activity with local organisations
- frequent articles in local newspapers about Trust affairs
- publication of all complaints in summary form
- publication of patient satisfaction survey results

Following a review of inpatient information, a standard yet individual booklet was developed by staff. The 10 new handbooks

- have 'core' information on the outside pages, with the middle pages containing details specific to each hospital or service
- are sent out routinely with appointment information and given to emergency patients and carers/relatives where appropriate
- tell readers how to complain
- are reviewed and updated annually, and amended when particular changes occur
- are printed on recycled paper, in corporate Trust colours

All the comments we receive about the booklets are favourable.

Other examples of information for patients:

- we use many different **clinical leaflets** written by the staff themselves, to give patients written, in addition to verbal, information on specific clinical conditions or treatment
- some of our services produce **specific leaflets** giving details of the service, who does what and when, and what a first appointment might involve. For example, the Chiropody and Pediatric Service has recently produced a leaflet 'Information for New Patients'
- many wards and departments have **information boards** displaying names and photographs of the staff
- the verbal explanation and information given by Trust staff is reinforced whenever possible with **leaflets** and also **videos, audio cassettes, charts and models**
- Delancey Hospital, which specialises in Medicine for Elderly People, held two successful **Open Days;** one for professional colleagues in the Trust and private sector and one for members of the general

public. A display explaining the resource team concept at the hospital was included in the South West Regional Quality roadshow in January 1993

- Ophthalmology staff held an **Open Day** for patients on the waiting list for cataract operations, their relatives and friends. This was designed to inform and reassure about day case surgery. This initiative is being continued and extended throughout the Trust
- we produce a newspaper. **'Health News'**, which is delivered to homes in the east of Gloucestershire.

This newspaper features articles and pictures concerning service developments, who's who on the staff and generally what's happening in the Trust

- A pamphlet entitled **'Our Plans for the Next Five Years'** sets out our proposed service developments in a clear form. This has been widely circulated to Trust staff, Health Authorities, GPs in and around Gloucestershire, Service Review Groups, the CHC and other relevant agencies and individuals. The CHC has praised its clarity and easily understood language

We regularly ask patients for their views about both verbal and written information they receive, and have found very high rates of satisfaction.

There are very few residents in the east of Gloucestershire who are from ethnic minorities or whose first language is not English. However, for those patients, sometimes tourists, various choices/services are available, eg

- any choice for a special diet can be accommodated
- a register of all staff who speak languages other than English is held centrally and those staff are called on where appropriate
- religious/spiritual leaders of any religion/denomination can be called in on request
- the Trust policy and procedures for Care For Dying Patients include detailed information on issues related to various religions

We are sensitive to the needs of the community as a whole and take environmental responsibilities seriously, constantly reviewing the impact of our activities and their effect upon the quality of the local environment and greater global issues. We have:

- signed the Declaration of Commitment to responsible Energy Management produced by the Department of the Environment Energy Efficiency Office
- introduced policies about the use of Halogens, the use of tropical

hardwoods, and the management of trees
- successfully introduced schemes to recycle bottles, paper and toner cartridges
- introduced standards for building and engineering systems which are reducing the energy requirements of new buildings
- introduced a scheme of clinical waste disposal which meets the European standards three years in advance of the due date
- played an active part in the preparation of the South Western Regional Health Authority's 'Strategy for the Environment'
- used recycled or environmentally friendly paper in our publications (including this application!)

Choice and consultation

We operate various systems to find out the opinions and suggestions of, and to offer choices to our customers:
- patient satisfaction surveys
- complaints procedure
- Service Review Groups (see below)
- meetings with Community Health Council
- suggestions boxes

The application for Trust status included the intention to set up Service Review Groups. These groups have been running successfully for two years and:

- provide an opportunity for users of the Trust's services to gain information on and comment on the quality of services we provide
- meet regularly to discuss any items of concern or interest, such as waiting lists for inpatient treatment, waiting times for outpatient appointments, progress with meeting required standards of service and findings from consumer satisfaction surveys
- can help to resolve perceived deficiencies and identify good practice

The **Medical Service Review Group** of GP representatives has collaborated on topics such as standard-setting, development of clinical guidelines, the evaluation of a pilot project on electronic mail, the setting up of a one-stop vasectomy service and direct admission to general surgical waiting lists. They also helped in the preparation of a filofax compendium of all our services and specialists circulated to all GPs.

The **General Service Review Group**, which includes representatives from Health Authorities, the local Community Health Council, volunteer bureaux, Leagues of Friends, Carers' forum and WRVS, has addressed such matters as a lack of facilities for disabled people, a new signposting and zoning system, and also a new car parking scheme for Cheltenham General Hospital.

Clinical staff are invited to each meeting to discuss the service they provide, eg care plans for mental health services, cardiology services, ENT services, inpatient handbooks.

We place a high priority on taking **positive action** following discussion.

Every opportunity is taken to offer patients choices in the services they receive with, for example:

- daily choice of in-patient meals from a menu card
- preferences for time of outpatient appointment taken into consideration where possible
- preferences for date of admission taken into consideration where possible
- all a patient has to do to change an outpatient appointment is to ring up and ask (the telephone numbers are readily available)
- patients can choose their own music in some clinics and theatres

Courtesy and helpfulness

We maintain a positive approach to customer care:
- telephonists are encouraged to be welcoming and friendly
- all staff who come into contact with patients have been issued with name badges
- front-line reception staff wear uniforms
- volunteer staff regularly help out and assist patients in areas such as busy outpatient clinics
- there are reception desks at main entrances staffed by volunteers to help with patients' queries
- WRVS run refreshment facilities for patients, carers, relatives and friends

The patient satisfaction surveys carried out in 1991/92 and 1992/93 showed:

- extremely high satisfaction concerning helpful, courteous and friendly staff
- high reported rates of staff introducing themselves and being easily identified

A comprehensive **'Customer Care' training course**, together with refresher courses, has been available since 1990. These courses are:

- run by our Training Department
- regularly updated and revised to accommodate the needs of staff in different areas
- given a high priority by senior staff who give it particular emphasis. 500 staff have already attended

The **accessibility** of services to all patients is given a high priority:

- **local access** is provided for this largely rural population, many of whom have transport problems, by the network of hospitals and community services
- **good access** in terms of waiting is ensured by maintaining extremely short waiting lists for inpatient and most outpatient treatment
- our Environmental Audit Group reviewed the **physical access** into and around the Cheltenham General Hospital for disabled people, together with provision of disabled facilities such as WCs and car parking. The survey was carried out with advice from disabled people. Improvements included: automated doors, removal of cobbles, provision of a wheelchair ramp, enhanced disabled parking
- to ensure **equity of access** we operate only one waiting list: no NHS patient is admitted preferentially to any other except on grounds of clinical priority

Initiatives to increase convenience for patients include:

- more convenient timings for physiotherapy appointments are available at Tewkesbury Hospital
- one-stop vasectomy service at Tewkesbury Hospital

A **Trust Fund** has been established in memory of an EGNHST patient to enhance and develop communications between staff, patients and relatives. Many bids from staff have been received for funds to progress projects across the Trust with this overall aim in mind.

Appreciation of the staff, their courtesy and friendliness and good clinical care, is demonstrated by patients:

- verbally to staff
- letters of thanks to wards and departments
- letters to the local, and occasionally, national press
- letters and other gestures of appreciation were counted in June 1992 and June 1993. In one recent month 310 letters and gestures of appreciation were counted compared with 18 complaints received

Putting things right

In February 1992, we revised our complaints policy and documentation for dealing with complaints in a timely and appropriate manner.

The Procedure:

- was so **well received** by Health Authorities that one asked to use our Complaints Review System as an example of Good Practice for its other Provider Units

- sets a **standard of a 3-week response** time which is better than the more widely accepted 4-week period
- is effective – each complaint is acknowledged, fully investigated, relevant action taken, and the patient is sent a full and prompt written reply from the Trust Chief Executive
- is **open** – the nature of complaints, the way they are handled and the managerial action taken are reviewed:
  internally – by the Trust Boards, and two non-executive directors who review all complaints on a quarterly basis and satisfy themselves that the complaints have been promptly and sympathetically investigated and appropriate action taken where necessary. The complaints are also monitored for trends which may indicate a need for other action
  externally – by Health Authorities and the Community Health Council. The Service Review Groups also discuss complaints and how to put things right
- is **user friendly** – how to complain is explained in detail in patient information leaflets; patients may make their complaint in writing, by telephone or by talking it over with staff; Trust staff will assist patients to follow the complaints procedure, eg by contacting a senior member of staff, helping patients to put a complaint in writing
- involves **action** being taken to improve our services with subsequent checking through a fall in the number of complaints, eg signposting and carparking at Cheltenham General Hospital, development of patient handouts on common operations

Whilst complaints let us know when and where things have gone wrong from the patient's point of view, we receive very few complaints (48 complaints in the January to March 1993 quarter) when compared with the tens of thousands of monthly contacts with patients and their carers, relatives and friends.

Our staff recognise the importance of finding out how we might improve our services and we make use of a variety of avenues to gain more information than can be ascertained by the complaints

- patient satisfaction surveys
- Service Review Groups
- Annual meeting
- patients are encouraged to give informal feedback to staff on the quality of service they receive, either by discussing difficulties with staff at the time or by filling in a suggestions card to give comments, suggestions or compliments.

Value for money

We believe that we have a duty to provide highly efficient services from a strong, prudent and stable financial base. This approach is seen as fully consistent with the achievement of maximum service quality and quantity and achieves the best possible outcome for patients and taxpayers.

We ensure that a **proper balance** is struck between income and expenditure in the medium term:

- all staff and all physical assets operate at near capacity
- there is a keen awareness that long term success depends on the provision of excellent services at a fair price
- inefficiency in any part of the organisation is seen as a threat to the whole which must be tackled
- management structures are very flat with few general managers and an emphasis on enabling maximum freedom from clinical managers
- a system of clinical directorates has been established, with delegated budgets, led by a senior doctor, nurse and manager
- there are no restrictions on the use of delegated budgets save that patient services may not be reduced

Services **have expanded** over the past two years with a major increase in the number of patients from areas not previously served by the Trust:

- in 1992/93 for the local population, we exceeded treatment target numbers by 5%. However targets were exceeded by no less than 18% for patients from other areas
- the additional earnings have enabled fixed costs and overheads to be spread over more cases. As a result our prices have been reduced for 1993/94 by a full 7% with no loss in service quality

The extra patients are evidence of the value Provided by our clinical services in the eyes of Health Authorities, GPs and patients.

We have exceeded all our financial targets and have avoided any artificial restrictions on workload:
- indeed, in early 1993, it was possible to assist several Health Authorities with budget pressures by treating patients at no extra cost to avoid delaying treatment to the new financial year. Effectively the treatment was funded by efficiency gains.
- the Audit Commission has stated that the Trust has the lowest overall inpatient waiting list in the country, which is one factor in the Trust's ability to attract extra income.

We have market tested many of our services and now work with private companies in areas such as building maintenance, legal, computer software and internal audit services, as well as cleaning and laundry. The Trust's finance department has competed successfully to secure financial services contracts for three other NHS organisations.

Objective external assessments of our efficiency are undertaken by the External Auditors. Ernst and Young, through both regularity and value for money audits. In recent months, they have commented in writing that the Trust:

- is within the top 25% of hospitals for day surgery
- runs efficient pathology, property and energy management services
- has maintenance arrears less than half the average for the NHS
- is in a healthy financial position and has demonstrated its ability to manage its finances well (with no matters of concern)
- is operating efficiently and effectively and has adapted well to the change brought about by the introduction of the internal market
- has adopted a pro-active approach to value for money, with the Audit Commission's studies reflecting favourably on the Trust

The management and performance of the Trust is monitored by the NHS Management Executive South West. No difficulties have arisen and it is understood that the quality of our financial and general management is perceived as being as high as any in the South West and Wessex area. All our senior managers have moved to personal contracts which expose them to a reward system linked closely to success in achieving specific quality and other objectives.

OUR RESPONSE TO THE DETERMINING CRITERIA

Customer satisfaction

We give a high priority to finding out what patients think about our services, what they feel is done well and what we might improve. An important part of this is a comprehensive rolling programme of patient satisfaction surveys carried out across all inpatient, outpatient, Accident & Emergency and Community services.

The survey team collects independent high quality data on the perceptions of patients. The surveys have shown that satisfaction levels are very high.

Patients are invited to complete questionnaires which ask about Patient's Charter issues such as waiting times, privacy, dignity, courtesy, finding the way around the hospital and the facilities provided. In this way, the Trust's performance against Patient's Charter standards is assessed from the **patient's perspective**. They also contain specific questions relevant to the department concerned, or of particular interest to staff, plus lots of room for additional comments!

Reports on main findings of the surveys are considered by the Trust Boards and are published to Health Authorities, Service Review Groups and the local press. In most areas at least 90% of patients were satisfied with the service they received and, in some areas assessed, 100% recorded satisfaction. Patients had particular praise for the staff.

Although overall satisfaction levels were high, there is always room for improvement. Examples of areas highlighted by the surveys as being of patient concern which are being addressed as a high priority are:

- waiting times at a few outpatient clinics
- methods of explaining to patients about unavoidable delay in outpatient clinics
- facilities such as signposting, refreshments, more comfortable seating

An example of an area where action has been taken as a result of findings from the surveys in line with patients preferences is:

- early morning **physiotherapy** appointments so that patients can choose to attend before work: staff had expected that evening appointments would have been preferred!

The surveys have also demonstrated the effectiveness of improvements made in line with patients' concerns noted in last year's survey programme. For example: the new pay and display car parking system at Cheltenham General Hospital has dramatically reduced the number of complaints received; appreciation of improvements in facilities, such as the introduction of a vending machine in A & E at Cheltenham General Hospital, the provision of high-backed chairs for elderly people in outpatient clinics, and the alterations to the outpatient doors at Tewkesbury Hospital.

In addition to patient satisfaction surveys, the local **Community Health Council** visits our facilities on behalf of the local population:

- the reports concerning these visits are circulated to Community Health Council members and Trust senior management
- senior management replies to concerns raised and initiates any required action

Measurable improvements in the quality of service over the last two years

Our first two years have seen a number of notable achievements, in particular:

- the successful introduction of new arrangements which increased the **involvement of clinical staff** in management and minimised administrative costs
- **10 new consultant** appointments in a range of medical and surgical specialities in the last 2 years

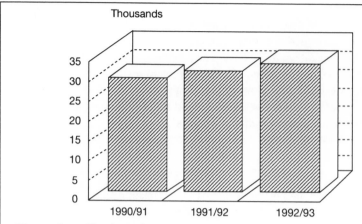

Figure 6.12 Number of in-patients

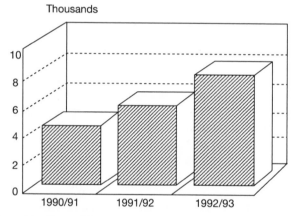

Figure 6.13 Number of day cases

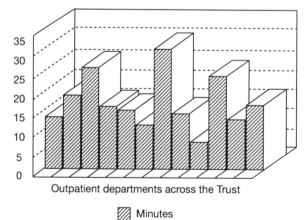

Figure 6.14 Average waiting times

- substantial and sustained increase in the number of **patients treated** and **reduction in waiting times**

We have set up various quality initiatives aimed to improve quality of service for patients, to meet their needs and offer choice whenever possible, for instance:

- in response to those terminally ill patients who wished to die at home but whose needs exceeded the capacity of the District Nursing Service, we set up a Palliative Care Support Scheme in March 1991, an evaluation of which has shown that the scheme:
  * meets the wishes of patients who prefer to remain at home, and their carers, giving a more realistic choice for patients between hospital and care at home
  * prevents unplanned hospital admission and gives greater relief to carers in terms of anxiety and stress
  * is welcomed by patients and carers, district nurses and GPs
  * gives excellent value for money
- an **Environmental Audit Group** progresses improvements to access and facilities for disabled people. At the Cheltenham General Hospital for example, more toilets for disabled people and the introduction of special telephones for people who are hard of hearing
- the **Quality Development Council** allocated £20,000 for funding quality initiatives, by inviting bids from our staff: this was particularly appreciated by direct care staff, who were able to respond to what patients told them about their experiences by setting up small projects to improve the quality of service provided

Projects funded included:
  * raising ground-level flower beds to enable elderly people with psychiatric disorders to do gardening from wheelchairs
  * introducing a nursing care plan (including maintaining dignity) for patients in operating theatres
  * catheter care leaflets
  * conversion of a laundry room to a multi-sensory room for people with learning disabilities
  * wipe-boards, cards and photographs to tell patients who is their named nurse

Following the success of this scheme, the Quality Development Council has allocated a further £20,000 in the 1993/94 financial year.

- employing a number of **clinical nurse specialists** who help to provide care to patients locally and in their own homes, in areas such as breast cancer, diabetes care
- developing exciting new ways of involving patients and staff with a local voluntary organisation called **Artshare**, who have a dynamic programme of creating art features in new facilities. This explores the value of provision of art and 3-D models to build confidence and provide a more therapeutic environment for patients in new purpose-built buildings

- setting up a **Bereavement Group** for people who have been recently bereaved to meet and share experiences and feelings with others in a similar situation and specially trained staff
- introducing a new **plastic surgery** service, based at Cirencester Hospital
- developing **pre-admission** clinics which evaluation has shown are appreciated by patients and the number of such clinics is being increased
- improving post-operative **pain control** by the purchase throughout the Trust of a number of machines which allow patients to control their own pain relief
- joint venture between our Sewing Room and Marks & Spencer to provide breast prostheses using mastectomy patients' own underwear
- improvements to the **physical environment** including upgrading of wards (e.g. sponsored painting), provision of murals for patients to look at whilst undergoing a scan
- offering additional **physiotherapy** treatment to clinically selected patients awaiting their first orthopaedic consultant appointment, helping to improve their quality of life and in some cases removing the need for further investigation or operative treatment

Plans to introduce or have in hand at least one innovative enhancement to services without extra cost to the consumer

The main emphasis and thrust of our plans for the next five years is to maintain and enhance the quality and range of services available, taking into account patients' interests and priorities:

- a new **cardiac catheterisation service**, for treatment of people with heart problems, with equipment funded by public donation (Trust Funds), will mean patients do not have to travel long distances to Bristol, Oxford, London or Birmingham. There will be savings for the taxpayer
- working more closely with GPs to develop **'shared care'** for patients with diabetes. This will produce an improved quality of service and cost no more
- increasing laparoscopic surgery leading to a much shorter stay in hospital and time off work. The equipment will be funded by public donations
- transfer of St Paul's Hospital **(obstetrics and gynaecology)** to the Cheltenham General Hospital site will improve the quality of clinical care and save money. This will create savings for use in other services

As this application has highlighted throughout we have a variety of systems for assessing the impact of changes in service from the point of view of both patients and professionals.

APPENDIX II

CHARTER MARK CRITERIA

CRITERION 1

STANDARDS

'Setting, monitoring and publication of explicit standards for the services that individual users can reasonably expect. Publication of actual performance against those standards.'
(Cm 2101)

Organisations should set and display standards for **key areas of performance** in a form which the citizen understands, publish information regularly on performance against those standards, and show how they are meeting their standards.

What the judges will be looking for:

Overall

- evidence that an organisation publicises its standards and performance in a way that brings them clearly to the customer's attention;
- evidence that standards are genuine customer service standards, set in terms of individual levels of performance and not simply management information targets;
- evidence that standards are challenging; and
- evidence of how the organisation is meeting its standards and that this information is readily available to its customers.

In particular

A. *Setting standards*

- Whether service standards are demanding, but realistic, given the resources that are available.
- Whether organisations are continually looking to improve on their existing standards.
- Whether service standards are meaningful to customers and reflect their priorities, have been set in consultation with users, and have been tested through customer surveys etc.

B. *Publishing standards*

- Whether service standards are published in a variety of ways, and are widely available to customers and potential customers.

C. *Publishing information of performance against standards*

- Whether performance information is published.

- How performance against standards is monitored, how often, and by whom. (Examples can usefully be given of the scope and type of data collected.)
- Whether customers are given an explanation of any adverse performance, together with details of corrective action taken.
- Whether performance data is fed into a cycle of continuous improvement.

CRITERION 2

INFORMATION AND OPENNESS

'Full, accurate information, readily available in plain language, about how public services are run, what they cost, how well they perform and who is in charge.'
(Cm 2101)

As a matter of course, organisations should provide individual users with all the information they need to be able to use the services available to them in a form that they can understand.

What the judges will be looking for:

Overall

- evidence that the organisation communicates effectively with its customers;
- evidence that information about services is presented to users in ways which are most appropriate to their needs;
- evidence that leaflets are written in plain language and are simple and clear. Where appropriate, they should cater for ethnic minorities and be available in braille or on tape etc; and
- evidence that the organisation makes positive efforts to get information into the hands of its users.

In particular

A. *Availability of information*

- Whether information is readily available, for example, in the form of leaflets and posters, and other means where appropriate. Evidence that organisations are aware of the specific needs of their customers and that, where appropriate, they produce literature for groups with special needs, eg those from ethnic minorities or people with disabilities.
- Whether customer awareness of the availability of information is tested.

B. *Information appropriate to customers' needs*

- Whether customers are provided with all the information they need to use the services available to them.
- Whether customer comprehension of the published information is tested through surveys, focus groups etc, and through routine monitoring.
- Evidence that the information covers the aspects of most importance to the customers.

- Do customers understand the information? Do they find it helpful? Does it cover all the things they want to know about services? How accurate is it?
- Whether results of customer surveys etc. are fed back into, and as a result improve, the published information.
- Whether the content of published information is assessed on a routine basis.

CRITERION 3

CHOICE AND CONSULTATION

'The public sector should provide choice wherever practicable. There should be regular and systematic consultation with those who use services. Users' views about services, and their priorities for improving them, to be taken into account in final decisions about standards.'
(Cm 2101)

Organisations should consult customers about services, monitor customer reaction to those services, and revise services accordingly.

What the judges will be looking for:

Overall

- evidence of regular, systematic customer consultation through surveys, questionnaires, meetings etc:
- evidence that consultation systems are effective;
- evidence of how customer feedback is used in revising and improving services as part of an ongoing process. Organisations should actively seek customer comments and have systems in place to monitor these and to effect changes where necessary; and
- evidence that the organisation makes efforts to give customers choice about the services they receive or the way in which these, services are delivered.

In particular

A. *Consulting customers*

- Whether consultation is direct, as well as with consumer groups.
- Whether consultation takes places on a regular basis.
- Whether consultation is carried out in the most appropriate ways.
- Whether *ad hoc* consultation is undertaken when necessary.
- Whether consultation is used to assess the customers' priorities.
- Examples of how services have improved as a result of consulting customers
- How effective are the procedures?

B. *Choice*

- How organisations ensure that customers have some choice over the activities or services they receive, or how these are delivered.

NB: Organisations should distinguish between consultation that it carried out as part of their statutory requirements, and that which goes beyond statutory requirements.

CRITERION 4

COURTESY AND HELPFULNESS

'Courteous and helpful service, from public servants who will normally wear name badges. Services available equally to all who are entitled to them and run to suit their convenience.'
(Cm 2101)

Services should be run to suit the convenience of customers, not staff. Services should be accessible to all, regardless of sex, creed or disability. Staff should wear name badges and give their names on the telephone and on letters.

What the judges will be looking for:

Overall

- evidence that the organisation puts the treatment of its customers first:
- evidence that staff appraisal procedures measure performance in customer service;
- evidence that staff give their names in correspondence and over the phone, and wear name badges;
- evidence that services are accessible to all customers; and
- evidence that customers feel they are receiving a courteous and helpful service.

In particular

A. *Courteous and efficient services*

- Whether a customer service policy is in place and is widely publicised.
- Whether training in customer service is given to all members of staff.
- Whether service delivery is reviewed as part of the staff appraisal process.
- Whether customers remark on the high level of service received.
- Is there a written policy on customer service? What customer-care training do staff receive? Are staff committed to delivering a high-quality service and encouraged to recognise the needs of their customers?

B. *Communicating with the customer*

- Whether name badges are worn and names given over the phone or in correspondence. What effect does this have on customers?

C. *Customers accessibility to services*

- Whether customers' needs have been assessed and efforts made to tailor services to those needs, for example physical adaptations to make services more accessible to disabled people and opening hours that have been changed to improve access
- Are offices 'user friendly'? Do opening hours reflect the needs of customers? Are customers with particular needs catered for?
- Whether methods of service delivery have been altered to make life easier for the customer, eg one-stop shops, mobile offices etc.

CRITERION 5
PUTTING THINGS RIGHT

'If things go wrong, an apology, a full explanation and a swift and effective remedy. Well publicised and easy to use complaints procedures with independent reviews wherever possible'
(Cm 2101)

Organisations should have easy-to-use and effective complaints procedures and, wherever possible, should provide the complainant with a means of independent review.

What the judges will be looking for:

Overall

- evidence that procedures are defined and published for dealing with complaints;
- evidence that these procedures are published and known to customers;
- evidence of the number of complaints received and how quickly they are dealt with;
- evidence that information about complaints is fed back into decisions about service delivery; and
- evidence of a means of independent review if a complaint cannot be resolved satisfactorily, and evidence that customers are made aware of the independent element.

In particular

A. *Complaints procedures*

- Whether there are clear written procedures for staff when handling complaints, with the emphasis on solving users' problems and not just complying with procedures. What can staff do to put things right?

B. *User-friendliness of complaints procedures*

- Whether complaints procedures are easy to access and use, with named individuals to complain to. Evidence that customers' views of procedures have been sought, and that customers are happy with the procedures.
- Whether front-line staff are empowered to respond to complaints, wherever practicable.
- How straightforward are the procedures? Can customers complain in writing, in person, and on the telephone? Are customers told how long it will take the organisation to investigate the complaint? Is a response promised?
- What research has the organisation undertaken to assess whether there are dissatisfied customers who have not complained, and if so, why not?

C. *Effectiveness of complaints procedures*

- Whether procedures specify time limits for investigating complaints. Whether they are met.
- Whether responses are aimed at solving problems rather than clearing officials of blame.
- Whether the effectiveness of complaints procedures is continuously reviewed and analysed to identify underlying factors. Are there systems in place for monitoring and analysing complaints?
- Whether complaints are used to improve services.
- What is the level of customer satisfaction with these procedures?

D. *Independent review*

- Whether a means for independent review exists.
- Whether the availability of independent review is publicised.
- Whether organisations use information from independent review to improve services.

NB: Free copies of *Effective Complaints Systems: Principles and Checklist*, published by the Citizen's Charter Complaints Task Force, can be obtained from:
Citizen's Charter Unit, Cabinet Office,
Horse Guards Road, London SW1P 3AL
Tel: 071-270 6348.

CRITERION 6

VALUE FOR MONEY

'Efficient and economical delivery of public services within resources the nation can afford. And independent validation of performance against standards.'
(Cm 2101)

Organisations should have the necessary systems in place to trigger and monitor a progressive improvement in value for money and quality of service, over an appropriate timescale. Achievements should be corroborated by some form of external, objective assessment.

What the judges will be looking for:

Overall

- evidence of sound financial management;
- evidence of forward planning to improve performance;
- evidence of value for money savings already made;
- evidence of objective performance-monitoring through the organisation's normal management information audit systems. These systems should measure quality as well as efficiency and economy; and
- evidence that the organisation's claims are supported by some form of objective assessment.

In particular

A. *Improving value for money*

- Whether there is a clear commitment to improving value for money within the organisation. This should be supported by specific examples.
- Whether organisations have been able to provide more cost-effective services as a result of market testing or contracting-out certain services.
- Evidence of value for money considerations, eg that the organisation is actively looking for efficiency savings and that savings have been achieved.

B. *The planning process*

- Whether quality and value for money measures are incorporated into the formal planning process
- Whether there are recognition, reward and performance measurements for individuals which support the organisation's quality objectives.

C. *Efficiency improvements*

- Whether there are examples to demonstrate that value for money savings are being achieved, and a commitment given to continue to seek such savings.

D. *Independent validation of performance against standards*

- Whether claims and achievements are validated by external audit or survey data, and examples given. The nature of the validation will vary, but organisations would normally be expected to use mechanisms already in place. Unbiased survey data would be an alternative form.

NB: Independent validation of the claims can be provided from a number of sources, such as existing audit reports or independent customer surveys.

CRITERION 7

CUSTOMER SATISFACTION

What the judges will be looking for:

Overall

- evidence that organisations can demonstrate customer satisfaction with the service.

In particular

- Whether key customer satisfaction measures are in place which identify both quantitative and qualitative improvements. Customer satisfaction should be assessed by the most appropriate means, eg customer surveys and questionnaires.
- Whether there is demonstrable evidence of annual improvements in the reported level of satisfaction.
- Evidence is given to show that, where customer satisfaction is not high, the organisation has acted to bring about improvements.

NB: We are looking here for the actual results of customer satisfaction surveys. There is no need to repeat information on customer consultation already provided in criterion 2.

CRITERION 8

MEASURABLE IMPROVEMENTS IN THE QUALITY OF SERVICE OVER THE LAST TWO OR MORE YEARS

What the judges will be looking for:

Overall

- evidence that improvements are in the key areas that have been identified as customer concerns;
- evidence that improvements are part of a concerted plan, rather than a windfall gain:
- evidence that customers are aware of and appreciate the improvements made;
- evidence that organisations are able to demonstrate a progressive, measurable, improvement in quality of service; and
- evidence that organisations are able to measure these improvements.

In particular

- Details of improvements made.
- Whether the organisation has achieved improvements in quality of service over one, two, or more years. Specific examples of these improvements should be given, together with customers' response, eg survey results, customer comments.
- Whether improvements have been made in areas identified by customers.

- Whether improvements are seen as part of a pre-planned programme.
- Whether improvements are relevant to the public.
- Whether the costs involved have been monitored.

NB: Organisations are free to show improvements in service over a number of years if this is appropriate, but should bear in mind that the assessors will be looking for evidence of continuous improvements in services. Organisations should look to provide evidence of improvements over at least a one-year period.

CRITERION 9

TO HAVE IN HAND, OR PLAN TO INTRODUCE, AT LEAST ONE INNOVATIVE
ENHANCEMENT TO SERVICES WITHOUT ANY EXTRA COST TO THE TAXPAYER
OR CONSUMER

What the judges will be looking for:

Overall

- evidence that organisations are looking to introduce changes which encapsulate the spirit of the Citizen's Charter, for example changes which develop service to the individual customer or empower the consumer:
- evidence that organisations have in place the systems to enable them to analyse the trade-off between quality, cost and other aspects of performance, and to set appropriate targets; and
- evidence that the innovations are being introduced at no extra cost to the taxpayer or the consumer.

In particular

- Details of the planned innovations.
- Whether these innovations recognise the concerns of the customers of the services. Whether users' views on the innovations are sought and schemes assessed against other priorities.
- Whether organisations have in place systems to allow them to monitor the quality and cost of the innovation.
- Whether the innovations will be introduced at no additional cost to the taxpayer or consumer.
- Whether there are opportunities for staff to contribute through suggestion schemes, hotlines etc.

Organisations should show clearly how customers have benefited, or will benefit from the improvements. There should be an explanation of the ways in which the innovations best capture the spirit of the Citizen's Charter initiative.

NB: The evidence provided against this criterion helps the assessors to judge how organisations propose to improve their existing services for the benefit of their customers. Organisations will not be eligible for a Charter Mark if they cannot demonstrate that they can meet this criterion and should draw attention to it in the summary on page 1 of their application.

7

MARKET TESTING AND COMPULSORY COMPETITIVE TENDERING

Introduction

The concept of contracting out core activities to an external body is not a new phenomenon. In the private sector this strategy has been used for some considerable time and within a wide diversity of both manufacturing and service based organisations. However, in the public sector, market testing and compulsory competitive tendering (CCT) has been used, until very recently on a smaller scale, whereby only auxiliary services such as cleansing and catering have traditionally been contracted out. The situation is now rapidly changing – brought about by a culmination of factors – a growing deficit in central funding, an increase in demand for a 'better' service from a more sophisticated customer combined with rising customer' expectations appear to have acted as catalysts in the growth of market testing within the public sector at both central and local government levels.

THE MARKET TESTING PROGRAMME

The overall responsibility for the market testing programme including policy and agreement of suitable activities to be market tested for Departments and Agencies is the Efficiency Unit in the Office of Public Service and Science. Their role is supported by a series of in-built management systems together with personal responsibilities of line management.

At the beginning of the 1990s, the market testing programme averaged at about £25m, however, the White Paper, 'Competing for Quality', (Cm 1730, November 1991) laid down new plans for the further involvement of the private sector, through competition, in the provision of services, in order to secure better value for money. This included plans for Central Government, the National Health Service and local authorities. In line with the requirements of the White Paper, Central Government was required to expand its current market testing activities to include new areas and departments were asked to make significantly greater commitments to the use of market testing and other Competing for Quality techniques. Health authorities, directly managed units and NHS Trusts were required to report on a yearly basis to the NHS Management Executive in respect of their plans and progress with market testing regarding existing contracts as well as new areas. New guide lines for local authorities were also laid down to broaden their scope for compulsory competitive tendering activities. (Compulsory competitive tendering is taken up later in the Chapter.)

The Government's plans for market testing in 1993 are illustrated by Figure 7.1. The table sets out the different Department/Agency subject to a market test together with the approximate value of activities, the approximate number of employees affected and the main activities to be market tested. A summary of results in relation to the 1993 programme can be seen in Figure 7.2.

THE PROCESS OF MARKET TESTING

Market testing is used as a tool within the public sector to assess whether either the in-house team or an external body, such as a private sector organisation, offers the best possible combination of value for money and quality of service.

In the public sector a process, referred to as, 'Prior Options', is initially used to ascertain which is the best approach to achieving better value for money for a particular activity. This involves certain considerations:

• Does the activity in question need to be performed?

If the answer is no, the activity is terminated, but where it is decided that the activity in question should continue the process continues:

• Could the activity be privatised?

Department/ Agency	Approximate value of activities to be tested £m	Approximate number of staff involved in this work	Main activities to be tested by 30 September 1993
Ministry of Agriculture, Fisheries and Food	42	850	Building and estate management Central office services General recruitment IT systems, services and development Investigation services Library services Milk hygiene enforcement RN surface surveillance Staff training Typing services Van services
Customs and Excise	53	2200	Consultancy services Customs cutters (marine branch) Debt collection Facilities management Gaming machine licenses Import and betting duty collection IT division (part) Internal audit Messenger services Statistical data keying Storage and distribution of office supplies Typing services
Ministry of Defence	323	12200 (includes 1800 service posts)	Accommodation and office services Elementary flying training Engineering services and support Fire services Freight delivery Grounds maintenance IT services Motor Transport In-service equipment support Nuclear weapon research and production facilities Operation of experimental aircraft fleet Vehicle maintenance
Department for Education	10	300 (includes effect of OFSTED changes)	Building, office and support services in DFE's London HQ Some information systems services Payroll services provided by Chessington Computer Centre Services provided to Teachers Pension Agency by the Paymaster General's Office

Figure 7.1 Government departments' market testing plans

Department/ Agency	Approximate value of activities to be tested £m	Approximate number of staff involved in this work	Main activities to be tested by 30 September 1993
Department of Employment	72	1900	Central Despatch Employment Rehabilitation courses Estates services IT Support of non-mainframe applications Jobclubs/Jobsearch seminars Payroll services Pensions administration Publications distribution Reprographics Security Typing services
Department of the Environment	58	700	Accommodation facilities management Accountants Central reprographics Conveyancing Designs, drawing and print services Economists Professional property services Registry services Training Workshops and stores
Foreign and Commonwealth Office	22	550	Buildings management Diplomatic service language centre Home security force (subject to confirmation) IT project management and training Installation of local radio networks and satellite communications Messenger services Overseas estate project management Research
Department of Health	20	600	Internal audit Internal management consultancy Library services Office services Selected statistical surveys and support Welfare foods scheme
Home Office	120	3850	Accommodation and office services Computing services Internal audit Pay services Police national computer (Hendon Datacentre) Prison Service College, training and facilities management Computing services Court escorts Dog service Education Prison establishments Warehousing, distribution and fleet management

Figure 7.1 Government departments' market testing plans – contd.

Department/ Agency	Approximate value of activities to be tested £m	Approximate number of staff involved in this work	Main activities to be tested by 30 September 1993
Inland Revenue	282	3350	Bulk mailing Catering Estate management services Facilities management Form design and procurement IT services Office support services Reprographics Typing/secretarial services Video production Writing of training material
Lord Chancellor's Department	30	1400	Building management and maintenance County Court Bailiffs (as part of a review of enforcement agents) Estate surveying services IT services Internal audit Pay Services Printing and form supply Public Record Office support services Statutory publications office Public Trust Office taxes division Public Trust Office typing services
Department of National Heritage	10	50	Building agent services (Royal Parks) Facilities management Gardens maintenance (Historic Royal Palaces Agency) Library services Office services National lottery Payroll
Northern Ireland	40	1550	Catering Computerisation Estate management Internal audit Machinery and vehicles maintenance Messenger services Some planning services Some road services Training Centres Typing Some water services

Figure 7.1 Government departments' market testing plans – contd.

Department/ Agency	Approximate value of activities to be tested £m	Approximate number of staff involved in this work	Main activities to be tested by 30 September 1993
Overseas Development Administration	7	300	Office services Overseas pensions administration
Office of Public Service and Science	11	200	Accommodation and office services Internal audit IT systems development Recruitment Research studies Security guarding Stationery Telecommunications services Training Welfare services
Scottish Office	15	1050	Certain office management services NHS audits Prison service stores and works Registers of Scotland – non-core activities Statistical services
Department of Social Security	127	6900	Accommodation and office services Accountancy services Archival storage Audit Catering Data entry Legal services Medical services and administrative support Resettlement centres Training
Department of Trade and Industry	80	1900	Accounting (Insolvency Service) Companies House Export Market Information Centre IT services Internal consultancy services Offshore geology programme Office and support services Oil and gas royalties Pay Ship radio licensing (Radiocommunications Agency) Trade marks examination research (Patent Office) Training

Figure 7.1 Government departments' market testing plans – contd.

Department/ Agency	Approximate value of activities to be tested £m	Approximate number of staff involved in this work	Main activities to be tested by 30 September 1993
Department of Transport	33	950	Despatch and mail handling at 　DVLA Drivers, Vehicles and Operators 　Information Technology Agency 　(DVOIT) Register of shipping and seamen Security at DVLA Survey and certification of ships Vehicle excise duty refunds
HM Treasury	4	200	Economic model building and 　development Internal audit Library Recruitment and training Reprographics and stationery Consultancy inspections service 　activities Treasury security guard (subject to 　confirmation)
Welsh Office	7	300	Building maintenance Catering Drawing office IT services Internal audit Office support services Staff training
Other Departments, Agencies and areas not covered above	83	2950	
TOTAL	**1449**	**44250**	

Figure 7.1 Government departments' market testing plans – contd.

If it is decided that a particular activity should be privatised then the necessary steps are taken to privatise, but where it is decided that the activity should remain the responsibility of Central Government, but does not need to be done by civil servants, a decision is made as to whether the service should be strategically contracted out. When this happens the activity that is carried out by either local authority or

Results of Test	Pretest Value of Activities (£m)	Number of Tests	Pretest number of Civil Service Posts	Reduction in Posts[1]
Abolished	22.8	25	753	397
Contracted Out (no in-house bid)	767.9	113	14,722	10,801
In-house Win	189.3	147	7,086	1,713
Contracted Out (with in-house bid)	87.4	82	1,591	1,054
Privatised	24.9	3	441	436
Untied[2]	11.7	6	144	33
Withdrawn (with efficiency gains)	15.2	13	409	153
TOTAL	**1,119.2**	**389**	**25,146**	**14,587**

1.   Reduction in posts refers to Civil Service posts, not the staff in them (not all will leave the Civil Service, some may be redeployed).
2.   Untied means the activity has been restructured without a formal test. The budget is allocated to the customers of the activity – it is for them to decide whether to use the internal service or not

Figure 7.2 Summary of results of 1992–93 market testing programme (programme completed by 31st December 1993).

Central Government is awarded to a private sector organisation – there is no bid from the in-house team. Examples of public sector organisations that contract out some of their services are British Rail and London Underground Ltd.

Where a decision is reached that the responsibility for an activity should remain within Central Government, consideration is nonetheless given to whether either the in-house team or an external party can carry out the service more efficiently. The activity is then subject to a 'market test'. Furthermore, if the activity is to remain in Central Government a decision could be taken that it should have greater independence with a performance targeting of an Executive Agency under the Next Steps programme. Where there is a question as to whether either the in-house team or an external party can carry out the service more efficiently the activity is subject to a 'market test'.

Having identified specific activities to be market tested, the scope and the precise nature of the particular activity is determined. At this point consideration is given to whether the activity being market tested should be grouped, and whether a strategic proportion of a particular activity should remain in-house so that, for example, advice to ministers on areas of policy can continue.

Bid specification and evaluation

One of the more crucial documents within the market testing process is the specification. It provides the basis upon which the contract/service level agreement is enforceable by setting down the service that the successful bidder, whether in-house or external, must supply.

Some of the key components that have been identified by the *Government's Guide to Market Testing* (1993) as follows:

- the scope and type of work to be undertaken; the output required, in amount/quantity; standards to be met; response times, and when and how the work will be measured;
- the frequency of measurement and inspection of the work at the work place;
- the responsibilities of the supplier and the department or agency;
- the anticipated start date for contract/service level agreement;
- the schedule for the supply of the service;
- any equipment, services, accommodation and materials which might be provided by the department or agency; and
- how changes in requirements are to be catered for.

A short list of suitable bidders is produced once the specification has been published and prospective bidders interests registered. Although there is not set criteria for assessing the bidders, information will have been collected in relation to both their competence and capability for carrying out and delivering the service. Bidders might also be required to be interviewed or be subject to a quality management system audit before a short list can eventually be finalised.

All bids, including the in-house bid are considered alongside each other together with additional in-house bids from in-house teams whose core function is to compete for business across Government Departments and Agencies. Other in-house bids are eligible if they come from another team within the Department or Agency provided that they have the capacity to carry out the service which is being market tested. In addition, or as an alternative, personnel, who are currently involved in the activity which is being subjected to market testing, may make a bid in the form of a management buy-out. Such bids are made upon the basis that the personnel involved will form their own private organisation if successful.

The process of evaluation is carried out by the bid analysis team. Determination of what constitutes the 'best' bid is based upon technical, contractual, financial and personnel issues. However, final selection is based upon the overall criteria – that it is the proposal that represents the best long-term value for money.

The assessment criteria that are used for evaluating bids are usually based upon capability; technical; quality; and financial assessments. These are described very briefly below:

- **Capability assessment** is used to determine whether the bidders are capable of delivering the service. Consideration is given to the bidder's experience, capabilities, and personnel including both management and supervisory support. In addition to which checks are made on the references which the bidder has supplied, together with employment policies.
- **Technical assessment** is used to determine whether tenders meet the requirements laid down by the specification.
- **Quality assessment** is used to determine whether the bidders can deliver the service to the quality standards where appropriate.
- **Financial assessment** is used to check that costings are realistic. This will include an assessment of the effects of any proposed inflation over the period which the service is being delivered for.

A simplified version of the market testing process is illustrated by the flowchart in Figure 7.3.

Monitoring the contract/service level agreement (SLA)

Dependent upon whether the in-house team or an external body is successful in obtaining the bid, a contract or service level agreement is awarded. Where the successful bid comes from a private sector organisation a contract will be awarded, but where the successful bid comes from an in-house team a service level agreement will be awarded. The reason for this is that the Crown is indivisible in law, making legal action impossible – however, both documents are based on the same principals.

Once the successful bidder has been awarded the contract/SLA it is essential that the service provided is monitored. This involves regular checks on the cost and quality of the service. In addition to which in the

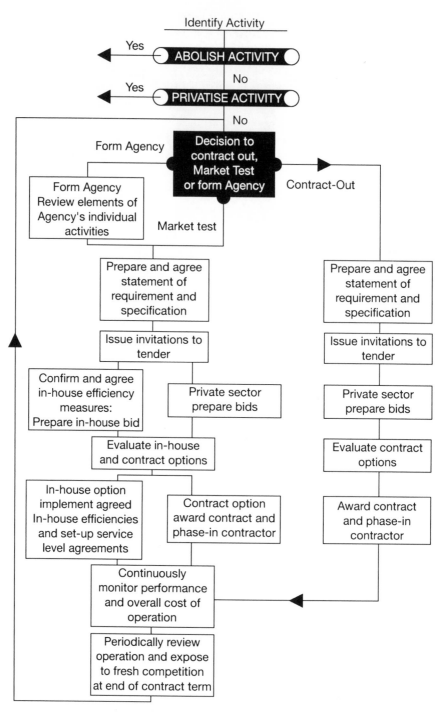

Figure 7.3

event of a serious breach or continuous non-performance specific clauses within the contract/SLA provide for termination.

Other checks are carried out by the National Audit Office (NAO) whose responsibility it is to provide information to Parliament on the financial aspects of public sector organisations. This includes information relating to the use of taxpayers' money, as well as the efficiency and effectiveness of the particular public sector organisation in question. This function continues even when a service has been contracted out to a private body, and where applicable can be provided for by requiring a right of access to relevant documents and information within the private sector organisation's contract.

COMPULSORY COMPETITIVE TENDERING (CCT)

As its name suggests, compulsory competitive tendering (CCT) is mandatory. It works along similar principles of market testing whereby a particular activity is subject to external competition. As in market testing, the in-house team are eligible to put forward a bid for the service which is being subject to external competition. The Government Department that has overall responsibility for CCT is the Department of the Environment.

Traditionally local authorities have subjected blue-collar activities to competition in accordance with legislation. The Local Government, Planning and Land Act 1980 requires the following activities to be subject to CCT;
New building
Building repair and maintenance
Highways construction and maintenance
This list was then extended by the Local Government Act 1988 to include:
Refuse collection
Street cleaning
Building cleaning
School and welfare catering
Other catering
Vehicle maintenance
Ground maintenance
Management of sport and leisure services
However, the publication of the consultation paper, 'Competing for Quality: Competition in the Provision of Local Services' provided for the expansion of CCT to white-collar activities within local authorities.

In addition to which, in November 1992, two further consultation papers issued by the Department of the Environment recommended that CCT would be extended in a phased programme to defined authorities' legal services, construction-related services, IT, finance, personnel and corporate and administration services.

The percentage of those services that will be subject to CCT are tabled in Figure 7.4 below.

Service	Proportion of the activity to be subject to CCT (%)
Construction related services (architecture, engineering, and property management)	65
Corporate and administrative services	15
Legal services	45
Financial services	25
Personnel	25
Computing	80

Figure 7.4

In addition to the above figures, support services for police and fire services, are also subject to CCT. The Citizen's Charter First Report 1992 estimated the overall figure as consisting of 40 per cent of the annual value of police vehicle maintenance and repair, and 90 per cent of the cleaning of police buildings. In addition to which, fire brigades were also required to market test their vehicle and equipment maintenance over the next three years. An exception to this is the maintenance staff who have firefighting duties.

Provisions against anti-competitive practices within the process of CCT are set down in the Local Government, Planning and Land Act 1980, the Local Government Act 1988 and the Local Government Act 1992. In addition to these requirements in May 1993 the Local Government (Direct Service Organisations) (Competition) Regulations 1993, was established to help local authorities to avoid against anti-competitive tendering. Where competition rules are breached legislation enables the Secretary of State to take action against a specific local authority.

POTENTIAL PROBLEMS ASSOCIATED WITH TRANSFER FROM PUBLIC SECTOR TO PRIVATE SECTOR

Transfer of undertakings (protection of employment regulations 1981) TUPE

Somewhat inevitably, there are always problems associated with reform, and there have been a few with market testing and CCT. Some of the problems have been linked to personnel and may only be described as 'people' problems. These have been connected to low staff morale linked to concerns at having to implement a programme which could lead to a change of employer or at worst loss of job. A fact which was underlined by a one-day strike in November 1993.

Other problems have been of a technical nature, with one of the more complex problems associated to the provisions of the Transfer of Undertakings (Protection of Employment Regulations 1981) TUPE which implements the 1977 European Acquired Rights Directive. The underlying issue that needs to be addressed by private sector organisations is whether TUPE applies in the situation where a service is contracted out to them following a market test or a compulsory competitive tender.

In the private sector when there is a transfer of an 'economic entity' from one employer to another the 1988 Regulations come into operation. Initially, when the government drew up the rules, the EEC directive was interpreted as applying only to the private sector, however, this view was superseded by a number of decisions made by the European Court of Justice which have indicated that the Act is applicable in certain circumstances, where a contract is awarded to the private sector from the public sector. This was underlined further in the test cases of Sophie Redmon v Bartil, and Rask.

The underlying problem is whether there has been transference of an 'economic entity'. In an attempt to overcome some of the complexity surrounding the Act, the Government issued a guidance document on the implications for market testing including local authority CCT of the Transfer of Undertakings (Protection of Employment) Regulations 1981. The document identifies the following situations as being 'likely' to invoke the regulations:

- where the new employer is unable to do the work without keeping on a group of key employees who can be regarded as an essential asset;

- where the new employer takes on substantially the same employees as recognisably the same organisational unit;
- where the former employer makes it a condition of the contract, or there is an understanding between the parties, that the new employer will continue to use the same employees for the same work (it is the government's policy that public sector organisations that invite tenders for the performance of public services should not impose such conditions except for reasons strictly related to the performance of the service in question);
- where, whether or not any employees are taken on, the new employer takes over the management or control of premises, assets or equipment which:
  - (i) were used by the previous employer to carry the activity in question;
  - (ii) are significant in relation to that activity; and
  - (iii) are managed or controlled by the new employer for the purpose of carrying out that activity.

According to the document, the Regulations are unlikely to apply:

- where the new employer conducts the operation substantially differently, without making significant use of previous staff, key employees, premises or equipment; or
- where the identity of the previous undertaking is substantially changed and any staff taken on by the new employer are incorporated into a different organisational structure.

There are serious consequences where the Regulations do apply – both in terms of financial and moral liabilities. To summarise, the new employer takes over liability in respect of employees' contracts of employment, including terms of pay, conditions of employment and union recognition. The new employer will also be responsible for an employee's unfair dismissal if it is connected to the transfer – unless for an economic, technical or organisational reason. Where the dismissal is connected to an economic, technical or organisational reason, the employee may be eligible for a redundancy payment, and when the redundancy takes effect after the transfer the new employer will be liable for such a payment. In addition to which, the new employer will be liable if the employee's overall terms and conditions of employment are unilaterally altered to the detriment of the employee. In such cases the employee will have a claim for constructive dismissal and/or breach of contract against the new employer.

Finally, not only is there a possibility of a financial cost to a new employer there is also a potential human cost. Private sector organisations may find themselves with the unpleasant task of making numerous redundancies in relation to the workforce they take over from the public sector, a factor that could cost them severely in terms of good working relationships not only with the employees they take on from the public sector, but in relation to employees that have nothing to do with the private sector transfer.

EXPOSURE TO COMPETITION AND THE ROLE OF QUALITY

One of the most fundamental concerns that people have had about market testing, compulsory competitive tendering and contracting out is whether they can ensure that what the end service customers receive is a quality service. Yet, how can this be achieved?, and is there an in-built mechanism within the processes of market testing, CCT and contracting out for ensuring that certain quality standards are met?

There are channels within the process of market testing for ensuring that a certain standard is met. One of the more effective ways of achieving this is through the bid specification. The importance of the bid specification has been stressed earlier in this Chapter, but to recap briefly; *the bid specification sets down standards to which service should be performed and so doing it provides a yardstick for measuring the service that is eventually provided by the successful bidder. Finally, it provides for termination in the event of non-contractual performance.*

Provision has also been made for securing a quality service by requiring bidders to provide a quality plan which contains essential information in relation to quality aspects of the service. This would include, for example, information as to how the service will be introduced, achieved and monitored.

Finally where quality accreditation is required, and where such a requirement does not restrict competition in an anti-competitive way, both external and in-house bidders need to have implemented or be in the process of implementing within their organisations, a recognised quality system such as BS 5750 or ISO 9000. Although BS 5750 and ISO 9000 are not in themselves indicative of providing a quality service or a quality product, it is indicative that the organisation understands the importance of the concept of a quality system.

By opening up what has been until now, a relatively 'closed' and somewhat bureaucratic institution to competition from the private sector there are undoubted advantages. Not only does competition ensure best value for money, it also has the ability to give both internal and external bidders the opportunity to be more innovative and to put forward proposals that actually do represent the provision of quality services to the end-user.

THE MOD MARKET TESTING PROGRAMME

Introduction

The MoD has a long tradition of contracting out and has the largest and longest standing market testing programme in Central Government. At MoD we are committed to obtaining maximum value for money for the defence budget and to make every penny count in supporting the front line defence capability. Market testing is a very important tool in achieving this objective – we intend to obtain the maximum involvement of industry in our market testing programme to ensure that tasks are carried out in the most cost effective and efficient manner possible. Essentially, our policy remains that work should be done in the private sector except where it can be demonstrated that it is more effective to keep the activity in-house or where there are proven operational reasons for maintaining the activity within the Department. Among the reasons for MoD's market testing policy are that it:

- enables MoD to concentrate on essential business;
- encourages competition, saving money and improving efficiency; and
- encourages managers to focus on the cost-effectiveness of the service.

Results to date

Following the issue of the Defence White Paper, 'Competing for Quality' in November, 1991, the MoD produced a market testing programme worth some £1.2bn over the period April 1992 to March 1996. The programme covers all areas of support activity, both civilian and military. During the first eighteen months of this period (to the end of September 1993), MoD carried out 36 tests involving 7,842 posts worth some £346m including the transfer to the public sector of management of the Atomic Weapons Establishment. 18 functions were directly contractorised and 18 were competed. The 18 competed tests resulted in 8 being retained in-house and 10 being contractorised, with up to 28 per cent savings in cost achieved. See Figure 7.5.

The way ahead – defence costs studies

The UK defence budget has come under ever increasing pressure over the last few years. In an attempt to meet the level of financial savings demanded following the 1993 Public Expenditure Survey, the Secretary of State set in place a series of Defence Costs Studies, some 33 in total, under the collective heading of 'Front Line First'. The aim of this is to identify areas where costs can be reduced to ensure that all expenditure is essential for operational effectiveness. These studies have reviewed various activities undertaken by the

MARKET TESTING RESULTS. MoD
Tests completed between 1/4/92 and 30/9/93

Value of Activities tested £m	Posts covered by tests	Main Activities tested
346.2	7842	Accommodation and office services
		Elementary flying training
		Engineering services and support
		Freight delivery
		Food distribution and supply
		Ground maintenance
		IT services
		In-service equipment support
		Nuclear weapons research and production facilities
		Operation of experimental aircraft fleet

Figure 7.5

Department covering a range of activities including amongst others; recruitment and manning, the Department's head office organisation, the Defence Estate and its work services, and the MoD's strategy for the repair and maintenance of its capital assets. One study was established to examine specifically market testing and contracting out, with a remit to determine the full potential for exposing non-core activities to private sector involvement.

The study concluded that the Department's market testing programme should be expanded with the ultimate aim of achieving an overall doubling of the programme, and also the size of individual market tests should be increased. Where individual activities were not of sufficient value to merit the cost of mounting the test they should normally be grouped together for testing purposes into larger packages to achieve the best use of limited resources. MoD intend to follow this policy in the future and also seek to obtain greater savings potential through the rationalisation of common services across budget holders – a process that is easier said than done!

The Defence Costs Study endorsed the idea of establishing the post of senior co-ordinator for the DoD market testing programme. In line with the Minister for Defence Procurement's preference for an industrialist to be appointed to enable a commercial awareness to be brought to market testing policy as well as improving the interface with the private sector, I was appointed to this post for a period of two years from Rolls-Royce. My terms of reference make me personally responsible to the Defence Procurement Minister for the delivery of a market testing and contractorisation programme which embodies the full potential to achieve improved efficiency and quality of service. I lead an organisation of specialists who work with the civilian and service budget holders to determine the scope of the tests, manage the programme and provide training and support to teams on both sides of the client/bidder 'chinese wall'.

Strategy for the future

The underlying criterion for all market testing activity is *value for money*. This does not just mean the cheapest option – it must also take account of quality of service and delivery offered, long-term impact, risk and long-term improvement strategy. Long-term value for money must be obtained without affecting the operational effectiveness of the Armed Forces.

To ensure that significant savings are made, best use of industry's facilities and capabilities through the development of a productive partnership in a competitive environment must be made. MoD intends to set up a forum that will permit regular discussion between the Department and senior industrialists.

The final element that forms part of market testing strategy for the future is the need for those within the Department to work towards increasing the cost-effectiveness and quality of those services provided in-house. This is driven by the imposition of the disciplines that would normally be associated with the contractual relationship between customer and supplier.

External and internal concerns about MoD's market testing initiative

MoD recognises that it is essential that industry should be closely involved in the market testing initiative and it was this need to hear the voice of industry that led to the appointment of two full-time commercial advisers in 1993. During discussions with industry, the commercial advisers were made aware of considerable frustrations and reservations within industry about the Department's market testing initiative. These concerns inhibited many major players from committing management time to seeking innovative ways of engaging with the programme. In order to establish the depth of feeling within industry the advisers conducted a survey of the major defence organisations. The initial findings of this survey were presented to the Minister for Defence Procurement Steering Group on Market Testing; a regular forum for reviewing progress at senior level. The report recommended that the Minister should press for the following improvements:

- a more ambitious programme;
- faster delivery of savings;
- more efficient process;
- better industry participation; and
- greater commitment at all levels in MoD.

A good understanding of the importance of market testing exists at senior levels within the Department, and we are anxious that this is translated into commitment which cascades down the management chain. There is no immediate and easy answer to the threat that many feel – but the best solution is to reduce uncertainty and to communicate the inexorable requirement for change in working practices and culture. Hopefully, this process of 'winning hearts and minds' will prove both productive and fulfilling.

Despite several well-attended market testing seminars for industry since November 1992, several organisations have complained about lack of programme visibility, particularly in the long term. In fact, MoD performance has varied widely between major budget areas. The army, for example, has an 'open-book' approach, with a database of industrial contacts exceeding 250 organisations. MoD intends to build on the best practice to date and increase the profile of the programme through proposed regular meetings with trade associations and by encouraging participation of the private sector in feasibility studies and in the formulation of statements of requirement.

Innovation – treatment of innovative bids

Many organisations have expressed concern with regard to the way MoD has treated innovative proposals. Scepticism has been shown about the treatment of such proposals within the Department. Commercial organisations have been reluctant to put forward innovative approaches when proposals are likely to receive a poor response or may only be considered if subjected to open competition during the tendering process. The Department recognises these concerns, but believes innovative bids to be of paramount importance within the market testing organisation to ensure that such proposals are adequately examined by the department and considered on the basis of value for money. MoD has announced revised contracts policy to concentrate on non-prescriptive statements of requirement, focusing on essential output. MoD are trying to make tender evaluation simpler, and to ensure that alternative solutions to the status quo are not regarded as non-compliant. MoD also embody the principles of the Treasury's Private Finance initiative in order to encourage unique and imaginative proposals where the appropriate balance of risk and reward is struck – single tender action may be possible.

Conclusion

Market testing within MoD can be viewed with a sense of achievement and expectation. The future climate of greater communication between all parties and a more business-like approach to planning and implementation should allow MoD to move forward with a much expanded programme that is realistically deliverable. The initiative will remain a major driver towards fulfilling our ultimate objective of a strong, affordable, front line defence capability supported in partnership with a sound defence industry base.

DR DEREK LEES
HEAD OF MARKET TESTING AND CONTRACTORISATION
MINISTRY OF DEFENCE

8

CONSORTIA APPROACH TO QUALITY

Introduction

It may reasonably be argued that never before has the UK public sector seen so much change. The Next Steps Initiative, Market Testing, The Charter Initiatives, and BS 5750/ISO 9000, as we have seen in previous chapters, are but some of the channels through which these changing requirements are being implemented. Some of the key issues related to these changing requirements have been collectively responded to in the form of consortium projects instigated by The Development Division of the Office of Public Service & Science (OPSS) in the Cabinet Office.

One underlying theme of the consortium projects has been the development of quality – internally within Departments and Agencies as far as training, awareness of quality issues and commitment from the top are concerned – and externally with regard to the provision of quality services that clearly reflect and respond to needs of customers.

To date there have been three consortium projects; Learning to Improve Customer Service (1988), The Development of Quality of Service Standards and Leadership (1991), and Management Development in Customer Focused Organisations (1994).

LEARNING TO IMPROVE CUSTOMER SERVICE

The first consortium project, Learning to Improve Customer Service developed in response to the launch of the Next Steps Initiative in 1988. A report, 'Basic Issues of Training in Customer Service and Quality Management', followed and the Training Development Division of the Cabinet Office (OMCS) put forward a pilot action learning project.

By September 1989, six Departments and Agencies had nominated themselves to take part in the project forming a consortium; Service to

Customers Action Team (SCAT).

The following Departments and Agencies took part in the project:

The British Library Science Reference and Information Service (SRIS)

The Laboratory of the Government Chemist (LGC)

The HM Land Registry (LR)

The Home Office (HO)

Employment Department (ED)

The two locations of the Department for National Savings (DNS)

A summary of the individual tasks addressed by the six Departments and Agencies is illustrated in Figure 8.1.

Department/Agency	Team task
The British Library Science Reference and Information Service (SRIS)	To develop a customer care strategy
The Laboratory of the Goverrnment Chemist (LGC)	To develop Total Quality Management within a newly formed Agency
HM Land Registry (LR)	To research external customers with the intention of developing 'customer-friendly' systems and procedures
The Home Office (HO)	To research staff and managers' perceptions of some of its internal services
The Employment Department (ED)	To focus on the initial educatory/communication process required to gain line management commitment before introducing a Quality Improvement project in a headquarter Information systems branch
The two Departments for National Savings (NS)	The development of specific quality/service improvement in relation to telephone communications and written correspondence

Figure 8.1 Consortium project: learning to improve customer service

Representatives from the different Departments and Agencies met on a monthly basis over a period of nine months to explore and implement their own strategies and actions in response to the Next Steps emphasis on the delivery of service.

Overview of the project

The overall team task was identified as the following;

'To co-ordinate and support projects to improve the quality of customer service within participating agencies/departments and produce a report to promote wider application.'

Findings from the project were grouped into the two key areas; *Customer Service and Quality Issues* and *Training and Development Issues.*

The consortium initially identified and analysed the close relationship between customer service and Total Quality Management (TQM). To solve confusion surrounding the definition of TQM, the factors that were common to organisations run upon the principles of TQM were identified, and from this information Departments and Agencies were able to make a start.

One of the major factors identified as being essential to the success of developing customer service, no matter how large or small the Agency or Department, was commitment from the top. Senior managers have the authority to improve and can therefore make significant improvements. Other important factors that were identified as being important in encouraging customer service and quality issues included; staying close to customers by using research, surveys, and by building a vision – setting down clear and focused values that were communicated to all personnel throughout the organisation – and, finally, by analysing systems and procedures for effectiveness in meeting requirements of customers.

Training and development issues were identified as being important channels through which responsibility for provision of the end-service provided was embraced by all Departmental and Agency staff. This was achieved at an early part of the project by involving all Departmental and Agency staff, thus creating a shared sense of ownership. Some of the channels through which this was achieved were:

- presentations to top management who wanted a better understanding of what improving service actually meant in practice;
- workshops to clarify the business vision and values;
- open staff meetings to identify what areas the project should deal with and their suggestions for improvements; and
- project teams to discuss and work through the same ideal as the SCAT participants, thus spreading the understanding of customer service and TQM.

Changes made to training and development of all staff as a result of the project included changes to the timing, content and format of training. In addition to which more specific areas such as telephone skills and letter writing were also addressed.

THE DEVELOPMENT OF QUALITY OF SERVICE STANDARDS

In November 1991, a second consortium project was established. The consortium was formed and led by the Development Division of the Cabinet Office, (OPSS). Members of the consortium consisted of 12 project leaders from the following 11 Departments and Agencies:

Benefits Agency (Central Derbyshire District)

Central Office of Information

Civil Service College (London Centre)

Employment Service

Health & Safety Executive (Research and Laboratory Services Division)

Home Office (Immigration Service)

Inland Revenue (Accounts Office, Cumbernauld)

Inland Revenue (Capital Taxes Office)

Lord Chancellor's Department (South Eastern Circuit)

Patent Office

Public Record Office

Department of Trade and Industry (North East)

A summary of the individual tasks addressed by Departments and Agencies is illustrated in Figure 8.2.

Overview of the project

Their primary objective was identified as to;

'encourage, co-ordinate and support projects . . . which will enable departments and agencies to achieve demonstrable and continuous improvements in the quality of service they provide.'

Department/Agency	Team task
Benefits Agency (Central Derbyshire District)	To set up a quality programme which will achieve sustainable and demonstrable improvements in the quality of service
Central Office of Information	To establish a series of measures of quality and effectiveness in campaigns managed by COI which may be used to define guaranteed levels of service throughout COI
Civil Service College (London Centre)	To carry out a pilot project in the London Centre of the Civil Service College to operate Quality Service Standards and identify and implement improvements
Employment Service	To identify and examine all links with external suppliers in the benefit and allowance payment chain. Establish mechanisms to gain progressive improvements in the quality of customer service
Health and Safety Executive (Research and Laboratory Services Division)	To encourage and promote activities within RLSD aimed at improving communications
Home Office – Immigration Service	To develop a quality of service improvement strategy for Immigration Service (Ports)
Inland Revenue – Accounts Office, Cumbernauld	To heighten awareness of the customer/supplier relationship and to encourage and support staff to seek improvements in the service provided to all customers (internal and external)
Lord Chancellor's Department (South Eastern Circuit)	To enable a better match to be made between the expectations of different groups of court users and local and regional management decisions by developing a methodology for user surveys which will provide information on needs and expectations
Patent Office	To establish the means to develop a customer-focused culture within the Trade marks Examination Units
Public Record Office	To carry out a programme of research and establish/ develop quality of service standards within the Reader Services Department
Department of Trade and Industry – North East	To create a climate amongst managers within which they can develop and adopt performance standards which fully reflect customer needs and aspirations

Figure 8.2 Consortium project: the development of quality of service standards

Their programme focused upon the development of standards relating to quality of service. This was achieved by establishing measures of quality of service which would then enable the setting of realistic standards derived from the priorities set down by their customers. With this in mind, research was carried out to establish customers' priorities. From this, current performance and targets for improvement of services could then be established.

Members of the consortium developed a twofold approach. They established measures which related to customers' understanding of the service and their degree of satisfaction with it as well as establishing measures which related to the effective delivery of the service, they were then able to use this information to set standards of Benchmarks for future performance.

The first stage was used to gather initial data which then acted as a base for the establishment of measurement and performance Benchmarks enabling members of the consortium to identify key issues to measure. Research was used to establish satisfaction measures, performance Benchmarks, and to provide information to enable improvement and innovations to be implemented. Members found it useful to consider four areas when measuring service quality. These were convenience of service, facilities and amenities available, provision of information and personal treatment.

Measurement against a set of standards is essential to the achievement of superior performance in any organisation, whether in the public sector or private sector. There were three categories of measurement that the consortium took into consideration when setting targets to be achieved. These consisted of product, process and customer satisfaction.

Product measures were defined as those measures which focus on the fundamental issues which an organisation believes are important to its customers. They are used to measure the satisfaction of the customer in relation to the processes of the service given to the customer. Satisfaction measures were defined as relating directly to the customer's interaction with the actual organisation itself, while process measures were defined as relating to the running of the organisation – those internal processes concerned with the operational efficiency of the service.

From this information specific targets could then be set in different Departments. For example, in relation to response times the Patent Office set a target of trying to reply in detail to correspondence within four to six weeks as well as issuing examination reports within three months. At the Accounts Office (Cumbernauld) a target was set of processing 100 per cent of Giro credits by the day following receipt. And in the Capital Taxes Office targets were set for 80 per cent of correspondence to be dealt within 28 days and 95 per cent within 56 days.

LEADERSHIP AND MANAGEMENT DEVELOPMENT IN CUSTOMER FOCUSED ORGANISATIONS

A third consortium project to be led by the Development Division in the Cabinet Office (OPSS) was formed in November 1993. The project concentrated upon the implementation of approaches to leadership and management development in support of quality of service improvements.

The consortium project involved the following Agencies and Departments:

Benefits Agency

Contributions Agency

Defence Analytical Services Agency

Health & Safety Executive (Research & Laboratory Services Division)

Industrial Development Board (Northern Ireland)

Information Technology Services Agency

HM Land Registry

Metropolitan Police Service

National Maritime Museum

Patent Office

Training Enterprise and Education Directorate (TEED)

Transport Research Laboratory

Welsh Development Agency

A summary of individual tasks undertaken by Departments and Agencies is illustrated by Figure 8.3.

Department/Agency	Team task
Benefits Agency	To identify and develop competencies for senior management in line with being a customer focused and quality organisation
Contributions Agency	To consult with senior managers and identify appropriate leadership and development issues to manage change effectively
Defence Analytical Services Agency	To explore leadership barriers to achieving customer driven strategic objectives and plan to overcome them
Health & Safety Executive (Research & Laboratory Services Division)	To address leadership and management skills to improve customer relations and communications within the organisation
Industrial Development Board (Northern Ireland)	To build on the 'commitment plus' strategy and develop quality conscious managers
Information Technology Services Agency	To support the implementation of Investors in People
HM Land Registry	To test and develop competencies in a pilot site to develop customer focused managers, and then cascade the learning
Metropolitan Police Services	To apply action learning principles to acquire and apply customer focused leadership skills
National Maritime Museum	To develop new leadership and management skills to support the new customer-facing organisation structure
Patent Office	To identify required management competencies and investigate options for accessing development opportunities to meet them
Training Enterprise and Education Directorate (TEED)	To develop team-working principles in line with developing as a learning organisation and achieving the IIP standard
Transport Research Laboratory	To identify and develop leadership competences which will fit with a move to a market driven culture
Welsh Development Agency	To consider the implications for the management of the Agency following the introduction of the client services function, and to recommend actions to maximise effectiveness

Figure 8.3 Consortium project: leadership and management development in customer focused organisations

Overview of the project

The main objective for consortium members was to;

'. . . encourage, co-ordinate and support projects within partici-
pating Departments and Agencies which will enable them to imple-
ment approaches to leadership and management development in
support of quality of service improvements; and disseminate key
learning outcomes for the wider benefit of the Civil Service.'

The main task to be addressed by consortium members was the development of managerial skills in the face of major changes within the
Civil Service. These changes were listed as follows:

- public expectations of prompt, high quality and value for money
  services;
- the need to maximise the use of constrained resources;
- the creation of Executive Agencies;
- the Citizens Charter Initiative; and
- the implications of market testing and privatisation.

To help organisations cope with these changes a seven-step approach
was identified:

1 Understand your organisation
- Review its purpose and core activities.
- Identify the views, needs and expectations of its customers.
- Assess the attitudes and understanding of its managers and staff.

2 Establish a clear vision
- Define and promote the organisation's long-term aims.
- Decide its character or style.
- Design an appropriate structure.

3 Identify the key competences
- Research the current competences of managers and staff.
- Relate these to the targeted aims and structure.

4 Identify the gap
- Define the new management and leadership skills.
- Ensure these are related to business objectives.

5 Establish a development strategy
- Decide priorities for action to close the gap.
- Identify development methods.
- Produce a targeted development programme.

6 **Implement the strategy**
   - Use all possible development and learning methods.
   - Seek to become a learning organisation.
   - Develop managers as change agents and change leaders.

7 **Review continuously**
   - Monitor progress and change.
   - Evaluate improvements and identify needs for further action.
   - Monitor changes in the external environment and adapt accordingly.
   - Look continuously for better ways of doing things.
   - Feed back new ideas and lessons learned into reviews of goals and performance targets.

THE CONSORTIUM APPROACH

Although many Departments and Agencies run their own highly successful quality and customer service initiatives without support from Development Division, the consortium approach is certainly useful. The essence of the process is that each participant gets the input of a management consultant in the running of their projects as well as peer and project management support. Useful learning outcomes derived from the experience of all the consortium participants are then traded on by Development Division to all Central Government organisations in the form of a consortium report.

9

THE APPLICATION OF BS 5750, ISO 9000 AND QUALITY SYSTEMS IN THE PUBLIC SECTOR

Introduction

The application of ISO 9000 within the public sector is relatively recent, and perhaps may be considered rather incongruous given its origins within manufacturing and particularly engineering industries. Is it just another administrative constraint placed upon employees, or can it assist with the quest for the continuously improving organisation?

The International Standard ISO 9000, together with its UK equivalent BS 5750 (BS EN ISO 9000), deals with the basic requirements for quality systems to ensure the existence of essential internal procedures, their control and documentation. While the Standard has its origins within manufacturing, it has now extended into all aspects of commercial and administrative life. Not only are service organisations of all types seeking and gaining certification to the Standard, there is also great interest within public administration. Thus we now have hotels, educational establishments, parts of the Health Service, the police force and many others, pursuing compliance with the Standard.

Despite the current increase by public and private sector organisations in aiming to achieve certification to the Standard, it is not without its critics. At its extremes ISO 9000 can lead to bureaucratic systems, with organisations concentrating on adhering to documented procedures and auditing actual practices against them, to the extent that originality, creativity, team-work, delegated authority and involvement, are stifled. While documentation of procedures and certification to ISO 9000 can provide a key element in the organisation's drive for improvement, the danger is that they are seen in isolation and apart from other initiatives which are required. This can lead to confusion and a too limited view whereby achievement of certification alone is seen as the end point of the improvement process.

What then is the role of Quality Assurance Standards in implementing quality in the public sector. What are the dangers, and how can it be used to re-enforce the quest for continuous improvement?

QUALITY ASSURANCE

As we saw in Chapter 2, Quality Assurance is not just a modern day topic, its origins can be found amongst manuscripts of civilisations who were at the forefront of scientific thought going back several thousand years BC. They contain documented accounts of quality standards required, particularly those related to buildings, and to the service required from the tradesmen and craftsmen of that time. For example, the specification of materials to be used in the project, the use of manpower and other resources, and the programme for construction, were all prerequisites for an agreement to proceed. Anyone who has seen pictures of buildings constructed at that time cannot fail to be impressed, not only by their magnificence, but also the time and effort which must have been put in to plan and effect the project.

Unfortunately there are examples, from more recent history, of the failure of structures which might well have been averted if the design procedures and construction methods had been validated prior to building. The Tay Bridge disaster in the second half of the nineteenth century is just one example.

As a consequence of Taylorism, organisations have tended to concentrate upon examining the finished service or product rather than on assuring the quality at creation. This has led to an excessive amount of time subsequently being spent on 'fire fighting'. Consequently, too often managers spend a great deal of time studying what is wrong with the actual *service* or *product*, rather than looking at what is wrong with the *process*.

The concentration of effort into detecting defects has a number of serious pitfalls. First, it is very *expensive*. We typically put our best, most experienced people into the role of inspector, rather than use them in the process itself. In addition, we carry out this final inspection at the stage when the service or product is at its most expensive and, perhaps, more importantly, at the most critical time, since the next process will be to deliver it to the customer. Failure at this point will almost inevitably lead to the customer being let down, with potentially serious consequences.

In addition, *even 100 per cent inspection is not foolproof.* Any inspection process, particularly that of visual inspection, is fallible, and cannot guarantee that defects will not be missed. Even if we increase the number of inspectors tenfold, we will not improve the quality one iota. While we may prevent more defects being provided to the customer, we may not actually prevent them being generated. Generally, quality cannot be 'inspected in', it must be 'built in'.

Furthermore, if the final inspectors miss the problem, the customer is almost certain to detect it. In many cases the customer will receive the service or item only once, whereas the inspectors may see thousands.

Perhaps the most serious problem, arising from too much reliance on final inspection, is that *it creates the atmosphere that it is acceptable to make mistakes* because someone else is checking. Inspection as a separate operation after the event, re-enforces the belief that, 'quality is nothing to do with me'. Why should a clerk, IT operator or cook, meet the requirements first time if someone else is checking, and therefore taking the final responsibility?

We therefore need to study the processes by which the customers needs can be satisfied, to devise ways in which these processes can be defined, measured and controlled, in order that we have some degree of assurance that the service or product will be satisfactory, without relying on detection at the end point.

In the past, customers – particularly large organisations – have taken a reactive approach by visiting the supplier and inspecting samples of services or products themselves, to ensure that they meet the specification. Often, the management within the supplier organisation have adopted a similar approach with their own suppliers. This was very time consuming and expensive. It also did nothing, or very little, to ensure that service or product to be delivered in the future would be satisfactory, since it relied totally on historical information.

In contrast, Quality Assurance examines the processes by which the service or product is supplied. By establishing a Quality Assurance System, the supplier can demonstrate that he has a process which has the *capability* of supplying the service or product. While this may not obviate the need for final inspection, it can reduce the level of that inspection. A Quality Assurance System gives the customer increased *confidence* that the supplier will deliver what has been requested.

The definition of Quality Assurance given in BS 4778 part 1 (1987), ISO 8402: 1986 is:

All those planned and systematic actions necessary to provide adequate confidence that a product or service will satisfy given requirements for quality.

The introduction of the Quality Assurance concept has enabled many customers to refocus the purpose of their visits to the supplier, they will now examine the adequacy of the quality assurance system rather than look purely at the product or service.

ADVANTAGES OF DOCUMENTING PROCEDURES

Implementation of an effective Quality Assurance System, and compliance with ISO 9000, requires an organisation to have a documented system. The form that the documentation takes obviously depends upon the nature of that organisation, but nevertheless the standard makes it clear that written procedures are essential for the control of essential activities.

A written procedure should define the purpose and scope of the activity that it controls and should specify what is done, by whom, and how, when and where. In everyday language we must:

- document what we do;
- do what we have written; and
- document that we have done it.

One of the difficulties encountered when establishing a documented Quality System, can be an aversion to documentation. The word itself evokes images of large, formalised scrolls, which are designed to make the organisation bureaucratic and to stifle initiative. However, people in all walks of life are familiar with, and often make use of, documentation. For example, they may leave a note at home (dinner in oven!), make a list of items to take on vacation (passport, tickets, toothbrush) or just produce an *aide-memoire* of 'things to do'. In essence, documenting procedures to support the Quality System is little different.

The major benefits of documenting the Quality Assurance System are:

- it is 'permanent' and acts as an *aide-memoire*, and also ensures continuity when personnel change;
- it provides an excellent basis for training, and therefore can give greater flexibility amongst personnel;
- it provides consistent instructions and a uniform basis for understanding;
- it ensures that any changes are effectively communicated throughout the organisation;
- it can be audited, ie we can verify whether what has been written

down is actually taking place; and

- it provides a basis for improvement in the methods of operation. In other words, as we write down the way we do things today, and clarify current processes, we can examine and discuss potentially better methods.

It is the final point here which is perhaps the most significant in terms of continuous improvement. After all, we cannot improve what we cannot understand.

This theme of a documented Quality Assurance System as a basis for continuous improvement was taken up by Mr Terry Harwood of HMSO, in a presentation at a Services Ltd/IFS conference on Ensuring Quality in the Public Sector;

> In any organisation there is an inevitable tension between two opposing needs, the need for stability and the need for change. Most people, for most of the time are involved in 'on-line' production or service delivery activities. These require stable systems under control in order to maintain consistent and predictable outputs day in day out at the required level of quality. At the same time, under external pressure – from customers, stake-holders and competitors – and in response to new opportunities, there is a constant need to improve the quality of existing products/services and plan new ones. These improvement and planning activities take place 'off-line', typically in teams. A Quality Management System based on BS 5750 provides a stable foundation of day to day quality assurance and a moving baseline to capture and hold the gains of quality improvement.
> BS 5750: The Need, the Process and the Way Forward, November 1993

The two things that most clearly characterise a Quality System based on the Standard are *controlled documentation of procedures* and *regular internal auditing*. Since these requirements cannot be met without some continuing allocation of resources, and as they are also at the heart of the more frequent criticism of BS 5750 – that it is bureaucratic and mechanistic – it is worth considering their intrinsic value.

Where we are able to define a right way of doing things, it is common sense to capture this in documentary form so that it becomes part of the organisational memory and it is left unaltered until deliberately changed. In addition to establishing consistency at the operating level, documentation of processes makes them clearly visible. Process documentation under proper control is of great benefit in managing change, since we are able to specify 'no process change without document change', and ensure that new ways of working are adequately communicated.

Controlled documented procedures are also a prerequisite for compliance auditing, since to assess whether we 'do what we say' clearly we must first 'say what we do'. Compliance auditing is a safety net, ensuring that any fallback in quality or system requirements is detected and standards are maintained. In the early days of implementation of a Quality System, the identification and correction of non-compliances to system requirements will play a significant role in the learning process that the organisation has to go through to get the Quality System up and running. However, if the only contribution of auditing thereafter is now and again to detect minor one-off non-compliances such as an incomplete record, it can quickly come to be regarded as a mechanistic activity of little value. It is important therefore that equal attention is given to ascertaining the general effectiveness of the Quality System. A good auditor, by bringing a view that is both independent and informed by knowledge of good practice, will make a valuable contribution to the continuing improvement of the system.

Thus a documented Quality Assurance System can provide focus, simplification and a cohesive approach to the operation of any organisation.

QUALITY ASSURANCE STANDARDS

Evolution towards ISO 9000 series of quality assurance standards

As discussed earlier Quality Assurance emanated from manufacturing organisations and therefore much of the language used is currently directed towards that sector. However, an understanding of its intention will assist in providing guidance to its application elsewhere.

During the Second World War many lessons were learned about the quality of supplies to the military. Some basic principles were formulated and NATO produced a series of documents, Allied Quality Assurance Publications (AQAP), which changed the emphasis from approved inspection by the purchaser, to complete control by the subcontractor, supplemented by audit surveillance by the purchaser. Subsequently, these were republished as a series of DEF STANS (Defence Standards) by the UK Procurement Executive of the Ministry of Defence.

In 1972, the Ministry of Defence published the 05-series of Defence Standards. These were based directly on the NATO AQAP documents and saw widespread application with military contractors and sub-contractors.

Also in 1972, the British Standards Institution published BS 4891: *A Guide to Quality Assurance*. This document was intended to introduce some standardisation for Quality Assurance requirements, and act as a basic guideline to organisations setting up their own Quality Systems. It was written in very general terms and was produced as a 'guide' and not as a 'standard'.

Some parts of British industry, in particular the Society of Motor Manufacturers and Traders (SMMT), believed that more specific standards were needed in a form applicable to industry in general. In 1974, BS 5179: *Guide to the Operation and Evaluation of Quality Assurance Systems*, was published. Although this was again written as recommendations, it provided a basis for the implementation of documented Quality Management Systems and was used for vendor and supplier rating schemes.

Sir Frederick Warner chaired a Government-sponsored committee which investigated standards and specifications in the engineering industries, and its subsequent recommendations led to the publication in 1979 of BS 5750 parts 1, 2 and 3. In 1981, BS 5750 parts 4, 5 and 6 were published as guides to the use of parts 1, 2 and 3 respectively.

Subsequently, the International Organisation for Standardisation (ISO) published the ISO 9000 series of Quality Systems Standards. The original BS 5750 was withdrawn and replaced with BS 5750:1987 to become identical with the wording of the ISO 9000 series. The Standards are also identical with the European Standards issued by the European Committee for Standardisation (CEN) having the prefix EN 29000.

The relationship between some of the key National, International and European Standards is provided in Figure 9.1. As of summer 1994, the BS 5750 standard is being relabelled as BS EN ISO 9000.

Purpose of key standards in the series

The key British Standards for Quality Assurance have been published as a number of 'parts'. This often causes confusion amongst those unfamiliar with these documents. In fact, these 'parts' can be regarded as separate Standards, but each has a different purpose or application.

1. BS 5750: Part 1: 1987 – Specification for design/development, production, installation and servicing

The Standard specifies Quality System requirements for use where a contract between a supplier and a customer requires a demonstration of

BS 5750, ISO 9000 and Quality Systems in the Public Sector   209

British Standard	European Standard	ISO Standard	BSI Title
BS 5750 part 0 section 0.1	EN 29000	ISO 9000	Principal concepts and applications. Guide to selection and use.
BS 5750 part 0 section 0.2	EN 29004	ISO 9004	(Principal concepts and applications). Guide to quality management and quality system elements.
BS 5750 part 1	EN 29001	ISO 9001	Specification for design/ development, production, installation and servicing.
BS 5750 part 2	EN 29002	ISO 9002	Specification for production and installation.
BS 5750 part 3	EN 29003	ISO 9003	Specification for final inspection and test.
BS 5750 part 4	No Equivalent	No Equivalent	Guide to the use of BS 5750 parts 1, 2 and 3.
BS 5750 part 8	No Equivalent	ISO 9004-2	Guide to quality management and quality systems elements for services.
BS 5750 part 13	No Equivalent	ISO 9000-3	Guide to the application of BS 5750 part 1, to the development, supply and maintenance of software.

Figure 9.1   The parts of BS 5750 and the corresponding European and international standards

the supplier's capability not only to supply, but also design or develop a service or product. In other words, the customer has used the 'fitness for purpose' definition of quality and has not clearly specified the detailed requirements of the service or product at the time at which the order was placed.

2. BS 5750: Part 2: 1987 – Specification for production and installation

This applies to products whose design have previously been established, and, compared to BS 5750 Part 1, assumes that the supplier is offering a service or product to a previously agreed specification or design. Therefore compared to Part 1, it has no provision for the Quality Systems elements for design control, or servicing.

It is identical to ISO 9002, 1987 which has the title 'Quality Systems – Model for quality assurance in production and installation'.

3. BS 5750: Part 3: 1987 – Specification for final inspection and test

The Standard is relatively little used and does not address either design or manufacturing quality assurance system requirements.

It is identical to ISO 9003, 1987.

4. BS 5750: Part 4: 1990 – Guide to the use of BS 5750: Part 1, Part 2 and Part 3

This Part of BS 5750 has been prepared to give guidance to organisations providing a service or product and wishing to ensure that they comply with BS 5750: Parts 1, 2 and 3.

However, it must be noted that it is a guide only and must be read in conjunction with the Part of BS 5750 with which compliance is being sought. Its aim, therefore, is primarily to assist those managing a business to achieve the requirements of BS 5750: Parts 1, 2 and 3.

5. BS 5750: Part 0:   *– Quality Systems*
   Section 0.1: 1987   *– Principal concepts and applications*
                       Guide to selection and use

This standard clarifies the distinctions and inter-relationships among the principal quality concepts and provides guidelines for the selection and use of a series of International Standards on Quality Systems that can be used for external Quality Assurance purposes.

It is identical to ISO 9000, 1987.

6. BS 5750: Part 0:   *– Quality Systems*
   Section 0.2: 1987   *– Principal concepts and applications*
                       Guide to Quality Management and
                       Quality System elements

It describes a basic set of elements by which quality management systems can be developed and implemented.

It is identical with ISO 9004, 1987 'Quality management and quality system elements – guidelines'.

*7. BS 5750: Part 8: 1991 – Guide to Quality Management and
Quality System elements for services*

This part of BS 5750 gives guidance for establishing and implementing
a Quality System within an organisation offering a service.
It is identical to ISO 9004–2, 1991.

8. BS 7000: 1989   – Guide to managing product design

This Standard gives guidance on the management of product design at
all levels, for all organisations and all products.

The content of ISO 9001

While it is not the purpose of this book to explain in detail the precise
requirements of the various Quality Assurance Standards, an outline
may provide the reader with a useful insight into the clauses contained
within ISO 9001. It must be stressed that these comments are for indication only; the Standard itself must be referred to for the exact statement of the requirements.

OUTLINE OF THE CLAUSES OF ISO 9001

1 Management responsibility

What are the organisation's policy and objectives for quality?
Is it effectively implemented and understood by everyone?
Have the roles and responsibilities for achieving the policy and objec-
tives been defined.
Is someone responsible for maintaining the Quality System?
Do management review periodically how well the system is operating?

2 Quality system

Have we written down the way we do things in order to achieve our
quality objectives and are they actually done?

3 Contract review

Do we understand clearly what the customer wants?
Can we do it?

If we cannot do precisely what the customers want, can we obtain their agreement to change the requirements?

4 Design control

We know what the customer wants, how do we go about designing it?
Has the correct number of staff been allocated?
Are there sufficient checks to ensure that the requirements have been met?
If changes to the original brief are made:

(i)   Are they recorded?
(ii) Is everyone who needs to be aware of them informed?
(iii) Does the finished design meet the requirements?

5 Document control

All key documents (eg instructions, procedures, specifications) must be authorised, ie signed and dated).

There must also be a mechanism to update these documents and remove old ones so that all relevant personnel only have the latest information.

6 Purchasing

We must specify exactly what we require of our suppliers and sub-contractors and check that they are delivering what was agreed.

We must monitor the performance of our suppliers, so that we know whether the products or services are meeting our requirements consistently.

7 Purchaser supplied product

If our customer supplies material to us for inclusion in their product, or if they supply us with their product for us to process further, we must ensure that it is handled in accordance with written procedures and that any loss or damage is reported to the customer.

8 Product identification

We must be able to identify product at all stages, ie what it was made from, when it was made, etc., so that if a problem is detected later, there is a possibility of tracing back to the source of the problem.

9 Process control

Do we have:

(i)   Written instructions on how to carry out the work?
(ii) Records of the process showing that it is proceeding according to plan?
(iii) Standards that we need to meet during the process?

10 Inspection and testing

We must inspect and test, in an appropriate way, materials on receipt in process and prior to release and keep records of the findings.

Any product (including raw materials) which does not meet specification must be clearly labelled.

11 Inspection, measuring and test equipment

Equipment which is used for checking or testing, must be capable of giving the organisation the accuracy required, and be reliable, ie it must be calibrated.

12 Inspection and test status

Do we know which items have been tested, which have been passed and which have failed?

13 Control of non-conforming product

Product which does not meet specification (including raw materials) must be clearly identified and its disposition (ie rework or scrap) be systematic.

14 Corrective action

We must use all available information (eg records) to help us improve our Quality System.

15 Handling, storage, packaging, delivery

Procedures are required to ensure that the product we are making or despatching to the customer, is stored, packaged and delivered in such a way that it will not deteriorate or be damaged.

16 Quality records

We must keep records to show that the required quality is being achieved and that the Quality System is working effectively.

17 Internal quality audits

Periodically, we must check to make sure everything in the Quality System is working as planned and identify any areas for improvement.

18 Training

Personnel performing particular jobs must have the necessary experience, skills and knowledge, and their training needs reviewed periodically.

19 Servicing

If servicing is specified in the contract, are there adequate checks that this has been correctly performed?

20 Statistical techniques

Where they are helpful, we must use such techniques to ensure that our products or services meet the customers requirements and to highlight areas for improvement.

ISO 9000 and service organisations

As mentioned earlier, the language of the Standard is not surprisingly somewhat biased towards the manufacturing sector. However, 1991 saw the introduction of BS 5750: Part 8 'Guide to quality management and quality systems elements for services' (equivalent to ISO 9004–2: 1991). This document seeks to encourage organisations to manage the quality aspects of their service activities in a more effective manner, but recognises that manufacturing companies also provide internal services in their marketing, delivery systems and after-sales activities.

It recognises that the successful application of quality management to services provides significant opportunities for:

- improved service performance and customer satisfaction;
- improved productivity, efficiency and cost reduction; and
- improved market share.

To achieve these benefits, a Quality System for services should also respond to the human aspects involved in the provision of a service by:

- managing the social processes involved in a service;
- regarding human interactions as a crucial part of service quality;
- recognising the importance of a customer's perception of the organisation's image, culture and performance;
- developing the skills and capability of personnel; and
- motivating personnel to improve quality and to meet customer expectations.

The Guide is applicable to all forms of service whether solely of a service character or in combination with the manufacture and supply of a product. While written principally with respect to external customers, it can also apply to internal customers for overall achievement of the required quality.

Examples to which BS 5750: Part 8: 1991 ISO 9004–2: 1991 may be applied are:

Hospitality services	– Catering, hotels, tourism, entertainment, radio, television, leisure
Communications	– Airports and airlines, road, rail and sea transport, telecommunications postal, data
Health services	– Medical staff/doctors, hospitals, ambulances, medical laboratories, dentists, opticians
Maintenance	– Electrical, mechanical, vehicles, heating systems, air-conditioning, buildings, computers
Utilities	– Cleansing, waste management, water supply, grounds maintenance, electricity, gas and energy supply, fire, police, public services
Trading	– Wholesale, retail, stockist, distributor, marketing, packaging
Financial	– Banking, insurance, pensions, property services, accounting
Professional	– Building design (architects), surveying, legal, law enforcement, security, engineering, project management, quality management, consultancy, training and education

Administration – Personnel, computing, office services
Technical – Consultancy, photography
Purchasing – Contracting, inventory management and distribution
Scientific – Research, development, studies, decision aids

While it is not possible here to provide a detailed description of the contents of this invaluable document, three aspects which it contains are of particular significance.

First, it lists characteristics of service and service delivery and provides examples of characteristics that might be specified in requirement documents ie:

- facilities, capacity, number of personnel and quality of materials;
- waiting time, delivery time and process times;
- hygiene, safety, reliability and security; and
- responsiveness, accessibility, courtesy, comfort, aesthetics of environment, competence, dependability, accuracy, completeness, state of the art, credibility and effective communication.

Second, it emphasises that the customer is the focal point of the three key aspects of a quality system. As illustrated in Figure 9.2, customer satisfaction can only be assured when there is a harmony of interaction

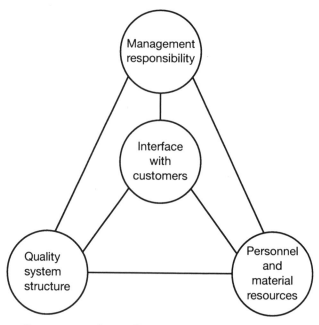

Figure 9.2 Key aspects of a quality system. (Reproduced from BS 5750 Part 8: 1991)

between management responsibility, personnel and material resources and the quality system structure.

Third, it states that Quality System procedures should be established to specify the performance requirements for all service processes including the three main provisioning processes (marketing, design and service delivery) which can be shown to be operating in a service quality loop, as illustrated in Figure 9.3.

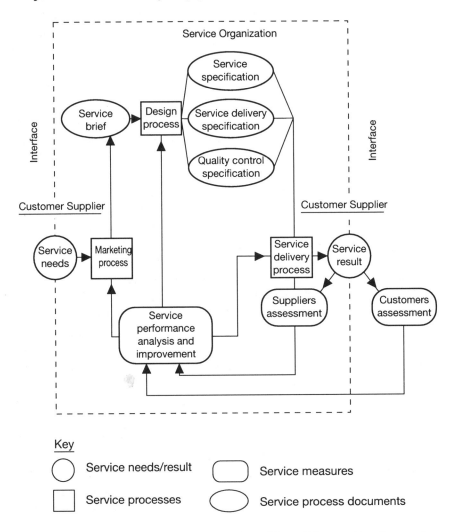

Figure 9.3 Service quality loop. (Reproduced from BS 5750 Part 8: 1991)

IMPLEMENTING A QUALITY ASSURANCE SYSTEM

The implementation of a Quality Assurance System, should be approached in a systematic way, as illustrated by Figure 9.4.

The starting point should be to *examine the organisation's current and planned activities in order to establish the terms and scope of the Quality System.* The interpretation of the requirements within the context of the organisation must be clarified. The next stage is to carry out a *critical review and audit of the organisation's operations against the requirements of the Standard*, in order to identify areas of compliance and non-compliance.

This initial assessment enables an understanding to be gained of existing documentation and planned activities, particularly those relating to organisational improvement and will identify any particular needs of personnel in specific areas. This is essential in order to avoid conflict on implementation timescales and resources, and will also ensure that the implementation of a Documented Quality Management System is complementary to, and supportive of, existing programmes. Following this, a modular approach should be adopted, covering the different areas and activities within the organisation. This will ensure that all parts of the organisation receive coverage and reduce the possibility of serious omissions. The findings of the initial assessment, should be compiled into a *written report* setting out an implementation plan.

The plan must be discussed with senior management and will outline for each area the steps that need to be taken to enable the Quality System to be developed to the required standard. At this stage senior management will need to assign responsibilities and ensure that necessary resources are available. Training requirements will also be highlighted.

Before commencing the process of documentation it is essential to make all personnel aware of the need for the plans to gain, BS 5750/ISO 9000 registration. This can be achieved by a series of short awareness workshops covering all personnel. In particular, there is a need to emphasise that implementation of the Documented Quality Management System and registration to BS 5750/ISO 9000 is only a part, albeit an important one, of the overall process of Continuous Improvement.

Throughout the implementation phase the adequacy and effectiveness of the documented procedures must be closely monitored. Staff at all levels should be encouraged to scrutinise procedures and instructions relating to their own activities and to provide feedback. Only in

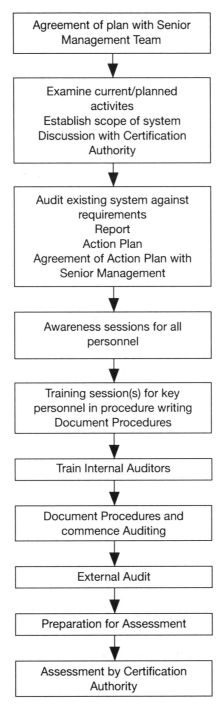

Figure 9.4 Outline of recommended approach to implementation of BS 5750/ISO 9000

this way will errors be identified and corrected and suggested improvements incorporated.

A major requirement of BS 5750/ISO 9000 is that the organisation must carry out its own internal audits of the Quality System and there is a need for auditors to be trained.

EXTERNAL ASSESSMENT AND REGISTRATION

As discussed earlier in this chapter, there are enormous internal benefits to be gained by documenting and implementing a Quality Assurance System. Such a system provides the organisation with a basis for improvement and a clarity of operating methods is achieved.

However, many organisations wish to obtain, and many customers are now insisting that their suppliers apply for, and achieve, formal certification for the documented Quality Assurance System. This has two major benefits for the organisation itself. First, external approval and certification provides public recognition that the system meets, as a minimum, the requirements of the standard. This can prove a valuable marketing tool. Second, the system is examined by competent professional auditors who are external to the organisation itself and therefore provide a pair of 'fresh eyes' to look over the system.

Quality Systems meeting the requirements of ISO 9000/BS 5750 can be officially approved by any of the thirty-five or so accredited certification bodies, who are approved by the National Accreditation Council for Certification Bodies (NACCB) which undertakes on behalf of the Secretary of State the impartial assessment of British Certification Bodies.

Accreditation was the Government's response to a demand for an independent testimony to the independence, competence and integrity of certification bodies, necessary if their certificates were to be respected as reliable evidence of good Quality Systems. The main requirements for accreditation are that the certification body should have a representative independent board, should assess quality systems to ISO 9000 or equivalent and should have staff competent for the work involved including Lead Assessors approved under the terms of the National Assessor Registration Scheme. There are also requirements for documentation and regular surveillance of certificated organisations.

Any organisation can apply to a certification body for certification to ISO 9000, but it should ensure that the certification bodies *scope* of assessment services covers the business activity concerned. Normally, following completion of a simple questionnaire and agreement of costs (which are borne by the organisation seeking approval), a copy of the documentation is reviewed by the certification body, who will notify the organisation of any deficiencies in the documentation and require measures to rectify them. Subsequently, they will then undertake a detailed, practical, audit of the operations of the organisation on site, to ensure that what has been written down is actually taking place. Following approval, and registration, the organisation will be subject to periodic surveillance audits, to ensure that the quality system is still being effectively implemented. A typical assessment process is shown in Figure 9.5.

BENEFITS AND INTEGRATION WITH OTHER ACTIVITIES

For most organisations there are two main reasons for interest in the Standard:

1 To meet customers increasing requirements for certification to the Standard and to demonstrate to clients that the organisation has adequate discipline and control to conduct and overview the work.
2 To improve, to regularise and to assure the quality of internal work and its conduct, so as to assure ultimate customer satisfaction. To facilitate the growth of the organisation by the reduction of ad hoc trouble-shooting, crisis management, uncontrolled changes of brief and the introduction of greater clarity of purpose.

The best practice advantages are of benefit to any organisation even if there is not a current need for a formal application for certification.

Compliance with, and certification to, the Standard can have many benefits for the organisation, including consistency of instructions, improved communication and facilitation of training. However, it is extremely important to recognise that while documentation of key procedures provides a basis for further improvement, it will not, of itself, effect that improvement. Organisations may be misled into believing that certification is the end point of the improvement process, whereas in reality it is only the beginning. It is crucial to recognise that we have, in fact, merely written down how we do things today, and not how they would ideally be performed. Furthermore, it must be remembered that two key aims of ISO 9000 are to provide an assurance of the

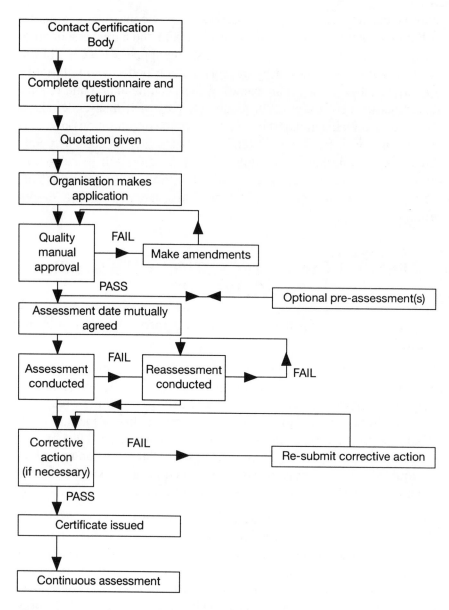

Figure 9.5 A typical process for assessment to ISO 9000

consistency of operations for the customer, and to demonstrate that the organisation has the *capability* to deliver the product or service.

Customers, particularly big customers, are increasingly requiring their suppliers to achieve ISO 9000 registration if they are to continue doing business with them. This is causing increasing concerns, particularly amongst small businesses, where if not done carefully, the cost of implementation and registration may impose further strains on already limited resources.

In all cases, therefore, it is essential that the purpose of ISO 9000 is clearly understood, and that the potential benefits of implementation and ongoing compliance are realised in full. For this reason, it is crucial that compliance with ISO 9000 is seen as the start of a continuing process of improvement.

Achieving certification can be considered analogous to passing the driving test. The minimum requirements have been met, and this is a cause for celebration. However, achieving ISO 9000 registration does not mean we are necessarily a World Class organisation any more than passing the driving test means we are necessarily excellent drivers.

We are all too aware that the Highway Code is not infallible, but is a good, basic working system. It is not a static document but has been developed and changed over the years as circumstances and conditions have changed. It does not guarantee good drivers and unfortunately does not ensure an accident free road system. However, without it we would have even more chaos! It does not give us perfection, but it is better than total chaos. We should look at ISO 9000 in much the same light.

Unfortunately, compliance with the Standard will not guarantee that disasters do not happen, but will reduce their likelihood. As someone stated to us 'It doesn't stop me losing money – it just helps me lose it more systematically.'

10

KEY GUIDANCE

Introduction

The following chapter does not attempt to put forward a prescriptive guide, for the introduction or implementation of quality within public sector organisations. What it does do, however, is set down some essential points that should be taken on board by those organisations wishing to make a start.

PLAN

Do not rush in. It is essential to plan the whole programme before commencing awareness training or issuing a mission statement. Where possible obtain suitably qualified help, but avoid 'ready-made' solutions. TQM needs to be built to the requirements of the particular organisation within which it is being implemented.

Three fundamental questions that any organisation must ask itself before embarking on a quality improvement initiative are;

1 **Where are we?**
2 **Where do we want to be? AND**
3 **How do we get from where we are to where we want to be?**

INTERNAL AND EXTERNAL ASSESSMENT OF THE ORGANISATION

To establish the answer to the first question, 'where are we?' an internal assessment must be made of the organisation. An appropriate method of achieving this is by undertaking two separate surveys – one that is directed at internal customers, the employees of the particular organisation, and the other that is directed at external customers; those individuals that use/receive the service that is delivered to them by the internal customer.

When drafting the questionnaires it should be remembered that the underlying purpose of the surveys is to identify gaps in practices, poor communications, inadequate management, how people work around problems and how these problems could be avoided. Questions asked should therefore be set around these concerns.

Specifically with regard to internal questionnaires try and incorporate some of the following:

- questions relating to opinions of the job they do;
- suggestions as to how it could be done better;
- what they believe is essential to carry out their job;
- what they believe is wrong with their job;
- whether there are any personnel within the organisation that have been involved in a quality initiative prior to joining; and
- whether they know of any established quality initiatives within the organisation and how successful/unsuccessful they believe these have been.

Do try and include the last two points since the answers to these questions will enable future quality plans to incorporate and build upon past individual and organisational achievements. This will ensure best use of resources is made which will save both time and money.

Specifically with regard to external questionnaires try and incorporate some of the following points:

- what they think of the quality of service provided to them;
- what they would improve, what they would keep the same;
- any special requirements;
- any specific and recurrent problems; and
- what they think of *how* the service is delivered to them.

Remember to make both the internal and external questionnaires anonymous. Anonymous questionnaires are a means through which more open responses are achieved, and fear of recriminations are removed. Also try and co-ordinate independent random interviews with a proportion of employees from different parts and levels of the organisation.

ANALYSIS AND USE OF DATA

Once information has been collected from the two surveys you should be able to assess:

1 where you are, and
2 where you want to be.

The answer to the third question, 'How do we get from where we are to where we want to be?,' is dealt with below.

QUALITY STEERING GROUP

Only when the data collection stage is complete can top management plan implementation. A good way forward is for a small Quality Steering Group, preferably chaired by a senior manager, to be established to manage the path to TQM. It should decide resources, monitor, facilitate and remove barriers to progress. Use of a steering group also creates and develops team and individual responsibility.

Basic awareness training is now necessary and senior management needs to commit itself *long-term* by issuing a mission statement to tell the employees, customers, suppliers and possible other stakeholders the path forward. Experience suggests that a 'cascade' model of training rather than a 'wall-to-wall' training is to be preferred for TQM awareness.

COMMUNICATION

It is crucial to inform the whole of the organisation of plans for the introduction and implementation of a quality programme. Ensure that everyone understands they have a part to play within the programme, and that they are aware of what their role is. This way the principles of ownership and responsibility are taken on board by everyone in the organisation. In the words of one of the quality gurus, Edwards Deming;

> *'Everyone doing their best is not the answer, it is first necessary for people to know what to do.'*

QUALITY SHOULD BE PART OF THE EVERYDAY WORK

It is important for the organisation to incorporate quality improvement into its normal management processes as soon as feasible, rather than keeping quality improvement separate from the real work.

Frequently, organisations make the mistake of believing that quality is not really part of the main work. Quality should be seen from the very beginning as part of the main work, if not the main part of the work. To be effective it must become part of the organisational strategy, the aim should be to see quality as an ongoing process and be integrated fully into the overall organisational strategy.

TOTAL QUALITY IS NOT A QUICK-FIX TO LONG-TERM PROBLEMS

Frequently organisations make the mistake of looking for quick-fix solutions to what are essentially long-term problems. Quality is not a short-term strategy; to be effective it requires time, planning, and continual measuring and monitoring. The most successful organisations are those that recognise that quality is a neverending journey. It is an ongoing process and should be regularly reviewed.

COMMITMENT FROM THE TOP

One of the most desirable factors for stimulating and encouraging a quality initiative within any organisation is top, senior level commitment and responsibility. Once a decision has been taken to embark upon a quality initiative it is essential that commitment from the top may be relied upon. The sort of commitment that is being referred to here is commitment that may be engendered from the beginning in terms of training and education as to what quality is, and how it can be utilised for the good of the organisation throughout, and how to implement those changes within the organisation.

The need for change within an organisation is usually identified by senior management. However, once identification has been made and a positive approach to implementation of a new initiative has taken place it will not be effective unless the whole of the workforce identifies a positive commitment from the top of the organisation. As previously stated senior management should be active members of the Quality Steering Group; this ensures their responsibility for the project. A quality initiative must be planned and as with other major programmes of change, there must be organisational policy in relation to it. This ensures continuity and clarity for both internal and external customer.

Activity must be steered and reviewed if the organisation is to receive benefits from the initiative. The only way that this may be accomplished is if management take responsibility for the initiative. It follows from this that the right things are done at the right time and in the best interests of the organisation. Top management must therefore be responsible for continuity, commitment, policy objectives and the direction that the quality initiative takes.

As with any new organisational strategy there must be an underlying belief in the need for the change. If there is a positive belief in the need for change from within an organisation, then something of real value will eventually be accomplished. It is essential therefore for management to generate an ongoing, continuous enthusiasm for changes within the organisation and for the initiatives that are responsible for bringing about those changes.

THE IMPORTANCE OF THE CUSTOMER

Never underestimate the value or importance of both the internal and external customer. It is vitally important to the success of any organisation to understand customer requirements, to clearly define those requirements and to find a means of measuring them. Key measures should be put in place to monitor both current performance and future improvements.

FINAL COMMENTS

TQM is a strategic approach aimed at producing the best product or service currently available through innovation and continual improvement. It is recognising that each person within the organisation is – or should be – the expert within their particular role or function, and it is that person who has, very often, first-hand knowledge of their part of the process and therefore ideas on how to improve it. All you need to do is construct a plan, identify problems and opportunities for improvement and systematically address these in priority order, reprioritising as the need arises.

Facilitators
- Full time
- Direct reporting to Senior Manager
- Trained
- Mentors/trainers
- Eyes and ears
- Do not solve problems
- Obstacle removers

Steering Committee
- Senior/decision makers/resources
- Strong
- Regular/frequently
- Monitoring/measuring/reviewing
- Approving/recognising
- Steering

Teams
- Clear terms of reference
- Approved projects/implement
- Trained
- Clear reporting line for team upwards
- Supported

Figure 10.1 Organisational requirements for TQM

A list of organisational requirements, Figure 10.1 and training requirements, Figure 10.2 can be used to aid the successful implementation of
Total Quality Management.

Awareness Training
- Cascade
- Deploy policy

TQM Role Training
- Programme manager
- Steering committee
- Facilitators
- Team leaders

Tools Training
- Team members
- Managers

Common Dangers
- Too complex tools
- Lack of cohesion
- Cultural barriers
- Lack of focus

Common Mistakes
- Lack of customer focused measurement
- Part time facilitators/no direct reporting
- Inadequate 'how to' training
- Tools-only training with no support
- No monitoring/lack of support to teams
- Competing unco-ordinated programme

Figure 10.2 Training requirements for TQM

11

HOW TO GET STARTED

ASSESSING YOUR STARTING POINT AND BUILDING AN ACTION PLAN

Having read this book, it is time to start! You will, we hope, by now realise the importance of carefully implementing quality in the public sector. This section, and the checklist and details included here, will facilitate the introduction of Quality Management and consideration of quality of service within your own organisation.

Use this section as a focusing tool individually, compare results with colleagues, or send them in for us to analyse.

1   STAKEHOLDERS

List your organisation's stakeholder's, their requirements of the organisation and their definition of and attitude to quality.

	Stakeholder	Requirements	Definition of Quality	Attitude to Quality
1				
2				
3				
4				
5				
6				
7				
8				

2   MISSION AND CRITICAL SUCCESS FACTORS

Mission/Vision Statement:

_____

_____

Has this been derived from a senior management
workshop?

| YES | NO |

Has it been examined for completeness?

| YES | NO |

Has it been communicated to all staff?

| YES | NO |

Have Critical Success Factors been identified?

| YES | NO |

Are these derived directly from the mission statement?

| YES | NO |

Critical Success Factors

Complete the following table, specifying your organisation's Critical
Success Factors and their implementation:

Critical Success Factor (CSF)	Measurable?	Is a target set?	Is it realistic?	Who is responsible for achieving it?
1.				
2.				
3.				
4.				
5.				
6.				
7.				

3   TARGETS

Renew and amend your organisation's Critical Success Factors. For each of your organisation's Critical Success Factors specify targets to be reached after 6, 12, 24, 36 and 60 months or other appropriate periods.

Critical Success Factor	6 months?	12 months?	24 months?	36 months?	60 months?
1.					
2.					
3.					
4.					
5.					
6.					
7.					

How do you select targets?..

Are they achievable? ....How do you know? ....

Is there a better way?..

4   CURRENT PERFORMANCE AND IMPROVEMENT ACTIVITY

Critical Success Factor	Current Level/ Performance	Improvement Action Plan	Who is responsible?
1.			
2.			
3.			
4.			
5.			
6.			
7.			

5   PROCESSES

Have you defined your core organisational process?

YES	NO

Are all stages listed, together with inputs, outputs, process owners and measurement points for each?

YES	NO

What do you measure for each process?

Core Process	Stages	Measurement Points	Process Owner
1.			
2.			
3.			
4.			
5.			
6.			
7.			

6   COST OF QUALITY

What is your Cost of Quality as a percentage of turnover? ....

How do you know? ....

How do you measure it? ....

What is excluded? ....

What is included? ....

How is it changing over time? ....

Please specify your major Quality Cost headings and how much they represent two years ago, today and in 12 months' time.

	COST £					
Major Quality Cost headings	24 months ago	12 months ago	6 months ago	Now	Prediction	
					6 months time	12 months time
1						
2						
3						
4						
5						
6						
7						
TOTAL						

7   USE OF MEASUREMENT AND MONITORING TOOLS

TOOLS	Areas being used	Areas could be applied to	Why is it not being applied?	How should we approach implementation?
Seven Tools of Quality Control				
1. Pareto Charts				
2. Cause & Effect Diagrams				
3. Stratification				
4. Check Sheets				
5. Histograms				
6. Scatter Diagrams				
7. Control charts				
8. Run Charts				
9. SPC (Statistical Process Control)				
10. Taguchi Methodology				
11. QFD (Quality Function Deployment)				
12. Process Deployment Flow Charts				
13. Cost of Quality				
14. Critical Success Factors				
15. Benchmarking				
16.				
17.				
18.				
19.				

For further details of tools and techniques of Quality see **Quality: Measuring and Monitoring;** Tony Bendell, John Kelly, Ted Merry and Fraser Sims; Sunday Times Business Skills Series/Century Business 1993.

8   APPROACH TO MEASURING AND MONITORING QUALITY

Use

Do all staff use measurement and monitoring techniques?

YES	NO

Who uses them? ....

For what processes/activities? ....

Specialists

What specialist groups undertaking quality mesurement and monitoring exist?

....

....

How integrated are these groups into the organisation? ....

....

Are there any communication problems? ....

....

Training

What training in quality measurement and monitoring techniques is carried out?

....

....

....

Who receives training? ....

How is training carried out? ....

....

What is the focus of training? ....

....

Coherence

How is quality measurement and monitoring used? ....

....

Is it a coherent programme or isolated uses? | Coherent | Isolated |

Specify any difficulties experienced with quality measurement

....

....

Measurement

Is measurement of outputs, inputs or
the process (any 2 or all)? | Outputs | Inputs | Process |

To what is output measurement applied? ....

....

....

To what is input measurement applied? ....

....

....

To what is process measurement applied? ....

....

....

Where could further process measurement be introduced? ....

....

....

Feedback

Is measurement used for feedback and change? | YES | NO |

If yes, where?

....

....

....

Where not? ....

....

....

Where could feedback be introduced? ....

....

Timescale

Is measurement current or historic?

Current	Historic

Examples

....

....

....

Is measurement directly related to customer requirements or to internal requirements?

Current	Internal

Where could further relationships to customer requirements be introduced?

....

....

Stakeholders

What measurement/monitoring exists related to other Stakeholders in your organisation (ie not customers)?

....

....

....

Specify your Stakeholders and the Critical Success Factors that relate to them:

Stakeholder	CSF	Is it Measurable?	Is it a Target Set?
1.			
2.			
3.			
4.			
5.			
6.			
7.			
8.			

9   VOICE OF THE CUSTOMER

Does your organisation listen to the 'Voice of the Customer?'

YES	NO

How is it obtained? ....

....

....

How should it be obtained?..

....

....

Construct a 'House of Quality' for one of your organisation's products or services:

Step 2
Enter here your operating arrangements to help achieve customer wants

Step 4
Here benchmark your performance on each customer requirement against that of your customers on 1–5 scale (5 is the best)

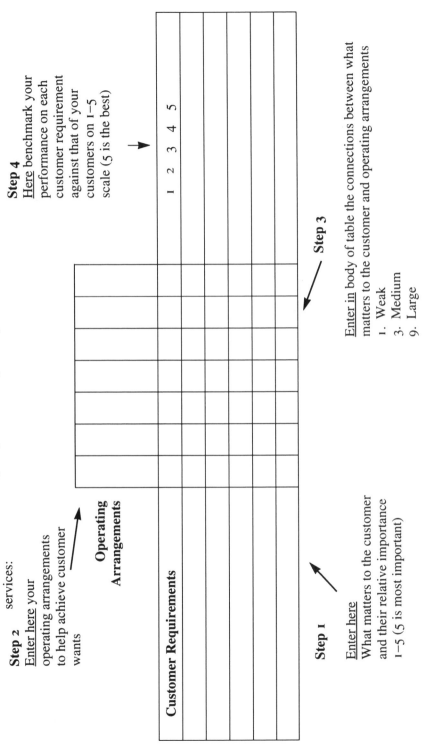

Operating Arrangements

Customer Requirements

1 2 3 4 5

Step 3
Enter in body of table the connections between what matters to the customer and operating arrangements
1. Weak
3. Medium
9. Large

Step 1

Enter here
What matters to the customer and their relative importance 1–5 (5 is most important)

10   PERSONAL QUALITY

HOW DO YOU MEASURE YOURSELF?

....

....

....

DO YOU SET YOURSELF TARGETS?

....

....

....

Select one of your core activities, define the stages of the activity and inputs and outputs and draw/chart it below:–

What are *you* going to do to improve?

....

....

....

By when?

....

....

11   BENCHMARKING

What processes for making comparisons with other organisations do you have in place?

....

....

....

How do you obtain relevant data?

....

....

....

....

Specify below possible measurements within your organisation that could be the basis for benchmarking:

Measure	Current Performance	Physical Limit (If Applicable)	Other Organisations Performance A B C			World's Best Practice	Target/ Date	How to Close the Gap

For further details of benchmarking, see *'Benchmarking for Competitive Advantage'*; Tony Bendell, Louise Boulter and John Kelly, Financial Times/Pitman 1993

12   WHAT NEEDS TO BE DONE?

Action	Purpose	Who should be responsible?	Date to be Complete

13   WHAT SHOULD BE DONE WHEN?

Month Date / Activity	1	2	3	4	5	6	7	8	9	10	11	12	13	14	15	16	17	18	19	20	21

12

AFTERTHOUGHTS

ACCELERATING REFORM

The preparation of this book has, of necessity, taken much time. The accelerating momentum of change means that almost as soon as we had written a description of an attribute of the public sector world, the wheel turned, the counter clicked and the world changed.

We knew that when we started, but we failed to appreciate quite the speed! However, while the world may have moved on a little by the time you read the book from our last pre-print review, the key description of change, the new thinking and focus, the meaning of quality and its relevance and application in the public sector are all still relevant. By its nature, some of the details and contents of the book will need regular updating and this we and the publishers will keep in mind.

WHITEHALL REFORM

Already on the table we have the Government four-year plan to cut 50,000 civil service jobs making the Whitehall structure 'more taut and flatter' than it is now. On Wednesday, 13 July, 1994, the government pushed its campaign for what some commentators called an improved public service to the heart of Whitehall by publishing plans for the most comprehensive restructuring of the British civil service in decades.

In the long awaited White Paper, the Government outlined a set of reforms which will dramatically reduce the size of the civil service and expose Whitehall to management practices that are increasingly commonplace in the private sector.

The reforms should give individual Whitehall departments more autonomy over the selection of senior staff and the determination of running costs. It is also proposed that more senior civil service posts should be open to candidates from the private sector and that the salaries of senior officials should be partly linked to their performance.

In addition, departments will also be obliged to introduce a fundamental reform of accounting practice; monitoring capital expenditure more comprehensively.

At the centre of the proposals is the creation of a senior civil service, which will be composed on the top 3,500 officials. It is proposed that such senior civil servants should receive explicit written employment contracts for the first time, and that salaries should be partly based on performance. Fixed term contracts could also be exceptionally used.

Open competition for posts should also become a more normal part of the process of selecting people for senior appointments.

The planned switch from cash based to 'accruals' accounting, in line with practices in the private sector, will impose for the first time on the civil service the need to account for capital expenditure and to develop a series of more accurate management indicators.

DOWNSIZING MOD

Another major impact on the ethos of the public sector is the inevitable downsizing of the Ministry of Defence. On 14 July, 1994, Mr Malcolm Rifkind announced that 18,000 ministerial defence jobs are to be cut, but he softened the blow by announcing orders for new weapons worth about £5bn.

The heaviest job losses will be in the Royal Air Force which will lose 7,500 personnel, while another 7,100 civilian jobs are to go. His announcement marked the conclusion of an eight-month study designed to cut £750m from the annual defence budget from 1997 onwards. To partly offset the job losses, Mr Rifkind announced firm orders for £2.4bn of weaponry and invited tenders for additional hardware worth a similar amount.

The cuts are at the top level in the forces with some 20 million military and civil service posts of the rank of major general or above being abolished. At the Ministry of Defence Headquarters in London, a further 1,500 jobs are to go and two buildings are to close.

Some 500 jobs will also go at the defence procurement executive in Bristol, where logistic support is being rationalised with the closure of 17 stores and the loss of 1,500 jobs. Several small RAF stations, including RAF Pitreavie in Fife, Scampton in Lincolnshire and Finningley in Yorkshire are also to close.

A major aspect of the change is a move towards tri-service operations despite senior officer opposition. A joint service rapid deployment force, including paratroopers, marines and RAF aircraft, is to be formed. Also, several new institutions to be used by all three services will replace single-service facilities.

SELLING THE BUILDINGS

Nor is the very fabric of the civil service, the prestigious Whitehall buildings themselves, safe. Press coverage during July, 1994, drew attention to supposed 'low-key' plans for a huge sale of Whitehall assets being drawn up quietly by the Chancellor, Kenneth Clarke. It was alleged that he hoped that the scale of the disposal of surplus land, property and equipment would make a significant impact on curbing the public sector borrowing, easing the way for tax cuts.

The proposals were contained in the Treasury Green Paper, *Better Accounting for the Taxpayer's Money*, issued with the White Paper on the future of the civil service.

The Treasury said it 'should give rise to additional benefits for the management of the economy as a whole by offering the possibility of reduced borrowing through identifying, and then disposing of, under-utilised fixed assets, and through the better management of working capital.'

The plans for downsizing MoD fit with this approach until an announced further cut of a quarter in the central core of London Head-quarters staff, with these working from two buildings instead of four. The armed forces' recruiting work of many of the country's 200 careers information offices will now be diverted to Job Centres; there will be a single helicopter flying training school for all three services, and the number of service hospitals will be reduced from three to one.

According to the *Observer*, 17 July, 1994, a senior Whitehall source said *it was possible that a similar pattern of cuts could be introduced across all government departments*. The first task would be identifying departments' assets; Ministers would then have to ask what purpose they served, and whether the cash tied up in them could be better used elsewhere.

EVEN THE TREASURY IS NOT SAFE!

According to *The Financial Times*, 18 July, 1994, what began in early 1992 with an internal enquiry into the style, workload and external image of the Treasury has burgeoned into a drive for management reform and a crusade to change the culture of Whitehall's 'pivotal' ministry in readiness for the 21st century.

Reform is part externally generated since the Treasury, which oversees the government's economic and budgetary policy, is having to adapt to decentralisation and delegation among its 'client' ministries in Whitehall. Even before the White Paper for restructuring the civil service, the creation of more autonomous bodies such as Next Step agencies, and the questioning of traditional civil service activities were forcing the Treasury to change its ways.

'Sagging morale' may also be connected with past policy failures and accusations of not understanding the needs of business. Perhaps not surprisingly, an attitude survey of its 1,400 staff, early in 1994, revealed deep unhappiness. Senior officials complained of long hours spent on unnecessary work, whilst staff lower down feared for their jobs in the event of contracting out activities to the private sector and market testing.

With the launch of the fundamental review of the Treasury's spending and running costs announced in the November 1993 Budget, the scene was set for a large-scale, internal shake up.

The present review is examining the sort of jobs the Treasury is doing and should do. Because of the breadth and depth of the department's self examination, the Treasury has adopted a gradual approach to change. But change is under way, nonetheless, in the form of management delayering and pushing down responsibility to lower levels. In late 1992, the Treasury effectively took out a layer of top management immediately below permanent secretary level. Its top officials are now known as directors and they have greater responsibility for their budgets than before and their duties are more clearly defined in their job titles.

Change is also underway in terms of relations with the Treasury's 'customers' elsewhere – from conflict to partnership. For the public sector to achieve Quality, the internal customer–supplier relationships must be right. The evolutionary revolution is underway!

Index